STOCK MARKET PROFITS

By

R.W. SCHABACKER, M.A.
*former Financial Editor of Forbes Magazine
and author of
"Stock Market Theory and Practice,"
"Technical Analysis and Market Profits," etc.*

Marketplace Books
Columbia, Maryland 21045

This publication is designed to provide accurate and authoritative information in regard to the subject matter covered. It is sold with the understanding that neither the author nor the publisher is engaged in rendering legal, accounting, or other professional service. If legal advice or other expert assistance is required, the services of a competent professional person should be sought.

This book, along with other books, is available at discounts that make it realistic to provide it as a gift to your customers, clients, and staff. For more information on these long lasting, cost effective premiums, please call us at (800) 272-2855 or you may email us at sales@traderslibrary.com.

From a Declaration of Principles jointly adopted by a Committee of the American Bar Association and a Committee of Publishers.

ISBN 1-59280-243-5

Printed in the United States of America.

CONTENTS

PAGE

Chapter I. — Introduction 1

The Profit Motive in Market Operation — Usual Reasons
for Failure — Incomplete Preparation the Major Handi-
cap — Trying to Get Something for Nothing — The
Wrong Approach to the Market — Who is to Blame? —
Unjust Attitude Responsible for Criticism by " Reform-
ers " — The Proper Attitude toward Market Operation
— Proper Attitude Fully Justifies the Market — The Re-
sponsibilities of Capital " Stewardship " — The Simple
Approach to Market Success — Simplest Rules Most
Often Overlooked — The Simple Rule of Humility —
Wall Street Looks Too Easy — The Simple Rule of Con-
servatism — Diversification of Risk — The Simple Rule
of Avoiding Over-Enthusiasm — The Simple Rule of
Avoiding Hasty Decisions — The Simple Rule on Consideration of Market Tips — The Logical Cultivation of
Independent Thought — The Advantages in Thinking for
Oneself — Ride the Economic Tides, Don't Fight Them
— Some Simple Rules for Avoiding Heavy Loss — Handling Incorrect Commitments the Real Test — Necessity
for Limiting Losses — How Insignificant Losses Grow
into Crippling Ones — Mental Loss Limitation Preceding the Commitment — Plan for All Eventualities in Advance — Consider the Worst, Not the Best, that May
Happen — Forward Planning Leads to Proper Conservatism — The Importance of Loss Protection — A Review
of the Simple, but Important, Rules.

Chapter II. — Cycle of Business and Securities . . 27

The Negative Approach — Importance in Long-Term
Success — The Positive Approach of Profit — Studying
the Background of our " Business " — " Buying Low and
Selling High " — The Cyclical Theory — Logical Basis for
Security and Business Cycles — Practical Proof in His-

xiii

tory — Cyclical Extremes Result from Human Tendencies — The Psychological Extremes of Hope and Fear — Effect of a " Planned Economy " on Cycles — Legislation Cannot Change Human Nature — Smaller Swings Natural after " New Era " Collapse — Profits Easier in Normal Cycle of Limited Amplitude — Component Stages of a Complete Cycle — Planning Investment Policy on the Cyclical Basis — Orienting the Stages of Business and Security Cycles — Another Theory of Successive Market Stages — The " Psychological Cycle " — Learning to Sense the Cyclical Transition.

Chapter III. — Long-Swing Investment 42

Three Main Types of Market Movement — Playing for the Major Moves — Inactivity of the Long-Swing Investor — Back to the Basic Problem of Profit — Difficulties of the Long-Term, Cyclical Method — Advantages of the Method — Accurate Gauging of the 1932 Bottom — Basis of " Extremes " in Cyclical Analysis — Value of the Composite Judgment — Some Automatic Theories of the Business Cycle — Difficulties in the Automatic Formula Field — Formulae Often Late or Vacillating — Which Leads the Cyclical Turn, Business or Securities? — The Answer Based on Logic — Comparison of the Two Factors — Sensitivity of the Market Indexes — Psychological Comparison of Business and Securities — The Answer Based on Fact — A Study in Comparative History — The Normal Cycles up to 1925 — Conclusion Based on Logic and History — Attacking the Practical Problem — Following the Cycles in Actual Operation — Consistent Profit from Cyclical Analysis — The Long-Term Investment Principle — Cyclical Extremes in Allied Factors — The Cyclical Interest-Rate Formulae — The Price-Earnings Ratio Formula — The Formulae on Brokers' Loans — Minor Formulae Helpful but Not Always Positive — Formulae for Volume of Trading — The Composite Picture — Some Formulae Based on Popular Psychology — When to Buy and Sell — The Summary of Extremes in Cyclical Theory — Conflicting Indications vs. Unanimous Ones — Applying Past Theory to Future

Practice — Two Important Rules for Long-Term Success
— The Necessity for Patience — How Cycles Tend to
Disparity — What of the Next Future Cycle? — Will the
1929 Peak be Reached? — Summary of the Long-Swing
Investment Approach.

Chapter IV. — Short-Swing Trading   72

From Long-Term to Shorter-Term Consideration — Advantages in Both Types — Chart Examples of the Inter-
mediate Move — Intermediate Swings in Major Moves
— Total Travel vs. Net Travel — Greater Profit Oppor-
tunity in Short-Swing Operation — Greater Risk and
Necessity for Close Attention — Superior Qualities of In-
termediate Technique — Average Investor Should Know
Both Types — Dangers of Confusing Short-Term and
Long-Term Trades — Type of Trade and Aim Should Be
Decided in Advance — Original Policy Should Be Fol-
lowed Through — Short-Term Trading More Natural —
Practical Difficulties in Pure Long-Swing Investment —
The Psychological Hazards — Dangers Diminished if
Investor Understands Both Types — Short-Term Trad-
ing Multiplies Profit — Advantages in Capital Rotation
— Summary of Short-Swing Advantages — Approaching
Short-Term Practice — Difference in Basic Technique of
Intermediate Trading — Variable Movement vs. Formula
Movement — Cyclical Stages Applied to Shorter-Term
Moves — Studying a Practical Chart History — Inter-
mediate vs. Major Move — How Cyclical Theory Aids
Short-Swing Analysis — Signals for Short-Swing Rever-
sal — Watching the Moves Develop on a Practical Chart
— Three Intermediate Swings in One Major Cycle — Dif-
ficulties in Practical Operation — Applying the General
Rules to Practical Trading — The Gospel of Compromise
— Tendencies More Practical than Dogmatic Extremes
— Summarizing the Short-Swing Approach.

Chapter V. — The Fundamental Factors   99

Long-Swing vs. Short-Swing Operations — Fundamental
vs. Technical Approach — Technical Factors are Closer

to the Market — Fundamentals Act More Slowly — Easier and Clearer in Forecasts — Fundamentals Usually Superior for Long-Term Operation — Also Valuable in Short-Term Technique — Applying Fundamentals to Short-Term Analysis — Two Aspects of Fundamental Approach — Conventional Aspect Well Known to Average Investor — Conventional Fundamentals have Lost Chief Value — Disadvantages of Old Approach — Conventional Fundamentals Often Misleading — New Attitude Toward Fundamentals is Necessary — Element of Time in Fundamental Technique — Anticipating Fundamental Factors — The New Approach to Fundamental Forecasting — Back to Simple Common Sense — Practical Application of the New Fundamental Approach — Anticipating New Factors Instead of Analyzing Old Ones — The Case of Prohibition Repeal — Applying the New Approach to Motor Stocks — Analyzing Development of a Profitable Situation — Common Sense vs. the Old Fundamental Approach — Selecting Individual Stocks on the New Basis — Applying Fundamental Logic to Other Fields — Profit in Individual Situations — Correlating Our Progress.

Chapter VI. — The Technical Factors 124

Slow-Acting vs. Quick-Acting Factors — Technical Factors vs. Fundamentals — How Technical Position Crosses Fundamentals — The Manipulative Angle — The Logic of Illogical Market Action — The Basis for Technical Studies — All Other Factors Reflected in Technical Analysis — Professional Activities Revealed — The Direct Answer to Market Profits — How Fundamentals are Automatically Weighed — Technical Basis is Not Infallible — But It is Highly Important — No Technical Details in this Study — General Consideration of Technical Approach Sufficient — The Logic of Technical Science — Subjective vs. Objective Logic — Technical Basis Depends upon Main Trends — The Dow Theory — Simple Logic of the Dow Theory — Practical Illustrations of Dow Theory Logic — Simplicity is an Asset — Dow Theory Logically Applied to Long-Term Trends

— Shorter-Swing Applications — A Practical Example —
The Chart on Western Union — Valuation of Dow
Theory Principles — " Pattern Theory " or Line Method
— Some Major Patterns — Conventional Analysis of
Western Union Chart — Practical Application of Trend
Lines — Flattening Trend Reversal — Logic of Conven-
tional Analysis — The Pattern Technique — Practical
Analysis of Pattern Formations — Volume of Trading in
Technical Analysis.

Chapter VII. — The Proper Use of Stock Charts 149

Vertical-Line Charts vs. Other Forms — The Point and
Figure Chart — Chart Examples of the Unit System —
Plotting the Intra-Day Moves — A Technical Chart Lib-
erty — Ignoring Fractional Moves — The Geometric
Form — Advantages of Geometric and Figure Charts —
Disadvantages of Geometric and Figure Charts — One-
Point vs. Multiple-Point Charts — Time and Expense in
Figure-Chart Approach — Comparing Various Types in
Practice — Reviewing the Practical Charts — Back to
the Basic Logic of Technical Analysis — Objective Logic
on the Major Swings — How Market Reverses its Own
Technical Forecast — Cutting Losses Short — An Ex-
ample in Long-Term Analysis — The Daily Average
Chart — Pattern Formations Applied to Major Move-
ments — Distinguishing between a Reaction and a Re-
versal — Applying Trend Lines to the Average Chart
— Long-Term Success vs. Perfection — Technical Record
in History of Major Trends — Summary of Technical
Advantages — The Defects in Technical Approach —
Weaknesses are Largely Personal — Chief Danger is
Over-Confidence — Simple and Basic Rules Overcome
the Dangers — The " Chart-Bug " — Beware of Dog-
matic Faiths — Exploitation of Technical Science —
Dangers of Too-General Familiarity by Public — Such
Dangers not Serious for Technical Theory — Most Prob-
able Future Danger is " Whip-Sawing " — Dangers of
Government Regulation — Effects on Technical Value
Practically Negligible — Even Restricted Operations
Need Technical Basis — Concluding Summary for the
Technical Approach.

PAGE

Chapter VIII. — Market Psychology 177

From Technical to More Simple Consideration — Psychology Seldom Applied to Market Operation — The Author's Simple Definition — Logic of Psychology as Applied to Market Forecasting — Detecting Changes in the " Public Mind " — Why Pure " Public Psychology " Doesn't Work — The Factor of " Crossing " Operations — The Theory of Crossing Activity — One Man Gains, Another Loses — Buyers vs. Sellers — A Practical Example — Crossing Necessary for Market Profit — Gains and Losses Cancel Out — The Professionals Must Make a Living — Who Pays the Professionals? — Professionals vs. the Public — The " Business " of Making Profits — The " Insiders " Reap Consistent Profit — How to Join the Successful Group — The Problem Summarized — The Simple Solution — Why We Must Understand Professional Operations — Two Types of Professional Crossing — An Example of Public Psychology — Psychology Naturally Generated — Psychology Artificially Generated — Psychology Directly Connected with Crossing Operations — Government Regulation No Obstacle — A Practical Example Suggestive of Inside Crossing — Public Psychology in Paramount — Theory vs. Proof — Attitude More Important than Precept — The Practical Application — Why the Market Seldom Does the Obvious — " What Would the Insiders Be Doing Now? " — Why Prices Move Counter to Reason — Crossing the Technical Indications — Crossing the Fundamental Indications — Some Specific Examples — The Summer Declines of 1934 — Back to Common-Sense Thinking — Following Logical Lines of Market Reasoning — How Psychology Ties in with Basic Rules — Results of the Proper Attitude.

Chapter IX. — Common Sense and Foresight in Trading 209

Continuing the Logical Approach — More on Conservatism — Back to the Protective Technique — Plunger vs. Conservative — Advantages in the Conservative Attitude — The Basic Theory Involved — How it Works in Prac-

tice — "One out of a Thousand" — Plunging Success
Rests on Luck — The Cardinal Theory of Compromise
— How to Correct Market Timidity — How to Treat In-
decision — How to Avoid Worry — Importance of the
Stop-Loss Principle — Mental vs. Actual Stop Order —
Automatic Limitation of Loss — In Harmony with Basic
Rules — The Dangers of "Holding On" — How Small
Losses Grow — Stop Principle in Short Trading — Dis-
advantages of the Stop Principle — Proper Uses of the
Stop — Examples in Actual Trading — Operating on the
Master Index — The Positive Uses of Stop Protection —
The Coupled Formula — Use in Successful, as Well as
Unsuccessful, Trades — The Basis in Logic and Common
Sense — Increasing the Chances for Profit — A Practical
Illustration — A Speculative Campaign in American Can
— Risking Small Losses for Large Profits — Practical
Success of the Coupled Method — Summary of Stop Ad-
vantages — Some Corollary Rules — Play Fair with the
Theory — Another Important Principle of Success —
The Market Confirms Previous Analysis — Meeting the
Dangers in Such a Situation — The Proper Course to
Follow — Restraining the Tendency to Plunge — Buy on
Weakness, Not on Strength — Don't Let a Fast Market
Hurry Personal Analysis — The Proper Time for Regu-
lar Analysis — Cancel the "Date" or Cancel the Order
— Don't be Afraid to Change Your Mind — A Cancelled
Order May Mean Profit.

Chapter X. — Diversification of Risk 244

Reasons for Lack of Diversification — Usual Human
Weaknesses Involved — Over-Enthusiasm on Profit Pos-
sibilities — The Average Trader is Not Immune — Logic
of Diversification — The Element of Misfortune — The
Element of Good Fortune — Diversification vs. Concen-
tration of Risk — Diversification in Depression Markets
— A Practical Example in History — Minimum Limits of
Operation — Larger Commissions Money Well Spent —
Diversification in Groups as Well as Individual Issues
— The Degree of Risk in Selected Groups — Variable of
Theoretical Safety — Compromise Principle in Diversi-

fication — Gradual vs. Headlong Shifting of Risk — Importance of the " Tendency " — Formula for Diversification — Classes of Investment — Classes of Investor — Policy of Risk Constantly Changing — Dangers in Over-Reaching the Class Boundary — Listed vs. Unlisted Securities — Advantages in an Active Market — Limits of Investment in Unlisted Issues — " Keeping Control " of the Personal Policy — " Averaging " Operations and Diversification — Misleading Attractions of Averaging — Arguments Against Averaging Down — Logic vs. False Logic — How it Works — Averaging Down to Catastrophe — Practical Example of Averaging Misfortune — The Psychological Temptations — Too Big a Loss to Sell? — Deeper and Deeper — $16,000 vs. $43 — Great Losses from Little Ones — Right and Wrong Way to Average Down — Averaging on the General Market — Averaging Combined with Diversification — Trading on Margin — The Element of Market Analysis — The Element of Risk — Dangers in Marginal Trading — The Temptation to Over-Trade — Use of the Stop Principle in Marginal Trading — Making Margin Trading Safe — The Impropriety of the Margin Call — Defense is the Best Attack.

Chapter XI. — Market Counsel — Good and Bad . 281

The Independent Approach — Does not Mean Being a Hermit — Contacting the " Outside World " — The " Service Line " — Classifications in Advisory Services — Discretionary Accounts — Tricks of the Trade — Supervisory Accounts — Investment Trusts — Dangers in the Market Advisory Principle — Advantages of the Service Subscription — Crossing Operations and the Advisory Service — A Rule and Its Exception — Degree of Accuracy in the Service Line — Responsibility Remains with the Individual — Selecting the Proper Service — Advertising Ethics — Misleading Promotion Claims — From Good Counsel to Bad — From Conscientious to Fraudulent Services — The " Sell and Switch " Racket — The Sucker List — Gaining the Investor's Confidence — Fraudulent Advice Follows Good Advice — Selling

Worthless Stock — Fraudulent Approaches Constantly
Changing — General Characteristics Easy to Detect —
How to Spot Fake Stock Rackets — Some Simple Rules
of Protection — Summary on the Market Counsel Field.

Chapter XII. — Conclusion 304

Summary and Review — The Basic Aims — Maximum
of Gain — Minimum of Physical Labor — " Hobby " of
Market Operation vs. " Business " — Hobby Can be a
Thorough One — Summary of Fundamentals — Summary of Technical Factors — Summary of General Considerations — Co-ordinating the Rules and Theories —
The Goal of " Subconscious Assimilation " — Tendency
vs. Dogmatism — Composite Analysis as Second-Nature
— Full Market Policies Seldom Advisable — Gradual Ac-
cumulation — A Practical Illustration — Scale Accumu-
lation Campaign — Results of a Compromise Policy —
The Advantages Over a " Plunging " Policy — Playing
for the Final Turn — Catching the Bottom in 1932 —
Feeling the Market — Paper Trading — Approaching the
Conclusion — Stock Rules Applied to Other Markets —
Trading in Commodities — Growing Possibilities in
Commodity Operation — Results of Securities Exchange
Act of 1934 — Effects on Future Trading — Old Rules
Still Apply — Technical Analysis Remains Basic — Leg-
islation vs. Human Nature — Valedictory.

Appendix 329

Quantitative Comparison of Business and Stock Index
Movements. Monthly, 1915–24.

Index 333

ILLUSTRATIONS

PAGE

I. Dow-Jones Industrial Average. Showing monthly high and low ranges from 1897, on ratio Scale . . . . *Frontispiece*

II. Business and Market Cycles. A detailed comparison from 1915 through 1924 55

III. Daily Chart on Atchison. Showing several complete, intermediate cycles in price movement, with daily volume in thousands of shares 91

IV. Daily Chart on National Distillers Products. Showing period of slow accumulation prior to Prohibition repeal boom 115

V. Daily Vertical-Line Chart on Western Union. Showing the gradual upward turn in the Spring of 1933, and the major upward move which followed . . 141

VI. Geometric and Figure Charts on Western Union. Showing three-point technique in both styles, with data taken from the conventional line chart in Plate V 153

VII. Times Daily Average of 50 Stocks in 1931. Showing details of the intermediate recovery and later resumption of the bear market 163

VIII. Times Daily Average of 50 Stocks since July, 1932. Showing the final turn of the long bear market and subsequent movements 193

IX. Daily Chart on American Can. Illustrating detailed trading movements from the close of 1933 through the Spring of 1934 231

X. Tabular representation of a sample diversification formula in four broad investment classes . . . 257

XI. Monthly Chart on Paramount Publix. Showing the almost steady depreciation in price, and illustrating the dangers of " averaging down " 269

CHAPTER I

INTRODUCTION

The Profit Motive in Market Operation

Among the galaxy of individuals interested in the stock market with whom it has been the writer's sometimes dubious privilege to come in contact, there have been literally thousands of different types, ranging from stupid to brilliant, from greedy to conservative, from rich to poor and from dismal failure to brilliant success.

In fact, no two individuals bring to their market operations identical attitudes or attributes. They are all different; yet they are all identical in one respect — they want to make a profit from their operations. The profit motive is the universal aim in all market activity, yet by what devious and warped methods most individuals go about their operations is known only to the stock market analyst, or " adviser," in all the pathos of its ineffectiveness.

Usual Reasons for Failure

And the greatest tragedy of all, from the author's standpoint at least, is the realization that by far the greater portion of those who come to the market-place with hard-earned savings, high hopes and enthusiastic ambitions — only to leave it with disappointment and loss — could be saved from their misfortune by the simple medium of a few logical rules of policy, by a small amount of consideration and common sense.

The author would not arouse the misapprehension that it is sublimely easy to make consistent profits in the stock market. He is quite willing, however, to go on record with the assurance that there are certain general rules, certain definite policies and methods of approach which, if properly ingrained and properly carried through, can increase the average chances for profit and decrease the risk of loss by an amount that is out of all proportion to the time and effort involved in studying such rules and making them an integral part of one's personal market policy.

Incomplete Preparation the Major Handicap

Nor is such a statement an exaggerated one. The average individual who comes into the market is so utterly lacking in the fundamental groundwork for practical success that it is almost a foregone conclusion that his operations will prove a disappointment unless he stops to digest the fundamentals of his new enterprise and to observe the basic theories of safe operation before he wades in with his sublime, but misplaced, self-confidence.

There has always been something of wonder for the author in the characteristic independence and sureness with which most people approach Wall Street. It is perhaps a quirk of human nature or pride that leads even the amateur novice to enter the market all unprepared and yet sublimely (or tragically) confident of early success and rapid gain.

For some reason or other, a man who has made his fortune in one particular line of endeavor through long experience, hard work, expert study and knowledge, will literally throw the bulk of that hard-earned fortune into the stock market and expect to double it, without a semblance of experience, work or study such as he had to give his own personal business in order to make a profit.

Even if one's market operations are a side-line, a hobby, it still seems logical to expect the individual to study at least some of the rules of the game before he stakes a fair share of his fortune on the play.

Trying to Get Something for Nothing

For there is perhaps no truer observation applying to the stock market than the old adage suggesting that an individual gets out of any activity only what he puts into it. There are two characteristic attitudes toward the general field of market operation, and they illustrate the proper and the false approach.

The first attitude is that of the man who looks upon the stock market as an easy medium for quick and spectacular profit. He sees a single stock double in price over a few short months. He hears fantastic rumors of the "killing" that old man So-and-So made last year, and decides that he too can follow this apparently public road to fine houses, expensive cars and the other trappings of sturdy prosperity. And so he enters the market to "clean up" for himself, but without asking the logical question of what he will do to justify such a profit.

He does not stop to consider the difference between his own ability, his own study, background and approach, and that of Mr. So-and-So. His first mistake is in jumping to the conclusion that his more prosperous neighbor makes profits all the time and runs no risks. His second mistake is his failure to estimate the long study, the careful analysis, the systematic planning which account for Mr. So-and-So's success. His final mistake is the result of the others: his

completely false and illogical attitude toward market profits
as something that anyone can get by the simple process of
opening a brokerage account and beginning to buy and sell
stocks.

The Wrong Approach to the Market

We may feel sorry for the tragic losses and the disillusion-
ment which will soon fall to the lot of this first individual,
but we may also observe that the stock market is not so de-
void of justice and logic as many people think and would
have us believe. Why should the stock market pay back so
much more to this individual in profit than he has put into
it in study, in energy, in thought and in careful analysis?

The answer is that the stock market will do nothing of the
sort. It may tantalize him for a while with false success, but
eventually it will exact its toll for this improper attitude and
approach. Our friend will eventually lose even his present
capital, his estate, his fortune.

His experience will make him bitter, if it does not actually
warp his entire life. He will blame the stock market. He
will blame his "adviser," whether he actually followed him
or not. He will inveigh bitterly against bankers, against Congress, against "unscrupulous" promoters and stock brokers.

Who is to Blame?

He will blame everyone except himself. And yet, if he
were only wise enough to realize it, only he himself is truly
to blame. He entered the market with the wrong attitude.
He expected stock market operation to yield him a perfectly
exorbitant and unjustified profit, without adequate balance
of effort or application on his part. The fact that the stock
market refused to give him "something for nothing" is a

reflection on his own gullibility and false logic, rather than the basis for indictment of the market itself.

One of the most tragic characteristics of our past "new era" psychology is nothing more nor less than this false approach to market operation. Due largely perhaps to the rapid inflation of security values during the 1927–29 boom, the general public began to embrace the false premise that anyone could get rich in the market, that whereas other lines of business and serious activity required hard work, careful planning, serious thought and application, here was one field where no such effort was necessary for quick riches and easy wealth.

Small wonder that a great proportion of thinking citizens have inveighed against security speculation on such a basis. If their fundamental premise were correct, they would be entirely justified in proclaiming the unmorality and social demoralization in any institution which offered huge profit without the investment of a compensatory amount of capital, risk, brains and hard work.

Unjust Attitude Responsible for Criticism by " Reformers "

The fact that their attitude toward market operation is entirely unfair and unwarranted is due simply to the falsity of their basic premise. The stock market does *not* offer any such easy rewards. And it is not the unmorality of the market or the huge losses which these "false investors" have had to take which form the true basis for public criticism. It is simply this improper attitude, on the part of the public and the unwary operator alike. They have tried to make of the market something which it is not, and which they should not logically expect it to be. And then, when they discover, to their own loss, that the market is not this easy and simple means for quick riches, they proceed to criticize the market instead of altering their own fundamental ideas of it.

What then is the proper attitude and approach to market success? We have said that there are two attitudes — one proper, the other false. We have just examined the false approach. The proper attitude toward all security operation is simply a willingness to treat it as we do any other serious business. It is the personal understanding of our original hypothesis, that no man ever gets more out of any human activity than he puts into it.

The Proper Attitude toward Market Operation

Such a proper attitude is simply the willingness and the sincere resolution to understand the market before one begins to operate in it, to give time, study, thought and planning to this business, just as one would expect to do in any other type of business, and thus to make eventual and consistent profit a logical reward rather than an unmoral gift of luck, or easy income.

If we put away this illogical and false attitude of "something for nothing," and accept the proper attitude of paying for our success in security operation as we do in other lines of endeavor, then we shall not only provide the practical basis for profit instead of loss, but we shall justify such profit, instead of making our gains of dubious character, at least, if not actually illegitimate. By merely changing our attitude and our approach to security operation we shall make of the stock market a respectable thing of standing, of legitimacy, of economic service and just reward, instead of a thing of degenerate gambling, of vice, chance and illegitimate machination.

Proper Attitude Fully Justifies the Market

And we shall do even more than that. We shall not only justify the stock market and our own stock market operation, but we shall raise them to their more proper pedestal of service, usefulness and practical obligation. For, when we free security operation from this false stigma of luck, of gambling, of easy wealth, we leave it in its proper light of service for all men.

For business, industry and the millions of workers dependent upon industry, the security markets and operation in them provide the practical necessities of capital for inauguration of enterprise, for operation and for expansion.

And for the individual, whether business man, clerk, doctor, lawyer or retired scholar, the security market offers the just-as-useful medium for the serviceable and profitable employment of surplus funds. When properly approached and properly used, therefore, security markets and their active operation lose the too-common stigma of unsocial speculation and assume their rightful heritage of service and usefulness for the national good and for individual duty, welfare and stewardship.

The Responsibilities of Capital " Stewardship "

Nor is this aspect of one's personal stewardship a minor one. The author has no intention of moralizing unduly or of becoming overly spiritual in his justification of security operation, but the biblical parable of the talents of silver is not out of place. The citizens of a healthy nation must of necessity both gain and cultivate the surplus values in their personal estate. And a healthy nation remains so only when the bulk of its citizens are willing and able to put those surplus funds into active service rather than burying them in the ground for dubious safe-keeping.

Thus, on the additional principle of personal stewardship, the adoption of a proper, logical and enlightened attitude toward security operation makes it a respectable duty rather than a reprehensible vice or a questionable hobby. And, what is much more important for our future consideration in this current volume, the adoption of this proper approach toward market operation is the primary corner-stone of success as contrasted with failure — of consistent profit instead of disappointing loss.

The Simple Approach to Market Success

Having established the legitimate basis for sincere study of the essentials for market success, however, the reader may be relieved, at the very beginning, of any apprehension that such detailed study will carry him into paths too intricate, too tedious, too scholarly for average understanding. We shall attempt a thorough consideration of the basic and necessary principles for market profit, and there are plenty of such principles to be studied, but we shall concentrate not so much on intricate technicalities as on a purely logical and simple approach.

There are plenty of other volumes, including some by this author, which carry the market student into the " higher mathematics " of market technique. Such more intricate approach has its definite place and value in the science of security market forecasting and operation and is unquestionably important for even the average student.

But there is also another approach to market success. It is based upon much less intricate theories but it appears practically as important for consistent success and profit. That is the approach based upon the simple principles of logic and straightforward thinking. Such basis is much more easily understood, but it can be exceedingly valuable in guiding one's personal investment policies away from loss and into profit.

And it shall be the primary aim of our current volume to consider the catalog of these basic and important guides to success, through the mere application of logic, reasoning, careful thought and plain common sense to our practical market operation.

Simplest Rules Most Often Overlooked

As an earnest of such aim, we may begin our practical exposition with a few general rules for successful profit which are so simple that they are often overlooked. In fact, they are so simple that they may continue to be overlooked and taken for granted, unless special stress be placed upon them.

The author is constrained to say, therefore, that they are included here not simply to fill space, not to cover ground already covered in market fundamentals which the reader has probably digested in other volumes, nor yet to begin our education with simple rules and truisms. They are included here because the writer is convinced that they are generally overlooked, and because he is just as convinced that they form the basic corner-stone of successful market operation.

If he had had less experience with practical market methods and individuals, the author might possibly ignore principles which have been so widely preached in the past. But through personal contact with thousands of investors, successful and unsuccessful, it has been established again and again that most losses result fundamentally from failure to observe even the simplest of such rules. There is perhaps not a single case which has passed before the author's experience where tragic failure and loss could not be traced, at least in some measure, to the individual's neglect of the fundamental rules for safe and profitable investment.

The Simple Rule of Humility

And perhaps the most general, as well as the most apparent, of the rules that are usually overlooked is the cardinal one of a humble approach to personal market trading. Like most of the other basic rules for profit, this one is so simple that it needs little explanation, elaboration or argument. That is its very danger. The average operator is too likely to say, " Oh, of course, I know that. I'm humble. Now let's get on to something new and practical." Let all such be warned at this very point and moment that this rule is the most practical, the most profitable, one for him to learn and to observe in every transaction.

We have already alluded to the queer aspect of human nature which makes men think they can be successful in the stock market without material energy, preparation or study, when they have had to spend a lifetime of experience to make profit from their own personal line of business.

Assuredly, Wall Street looks easy, especially after the first few simple and lucky successes. It is an old story to have a young college student or graduate come to the author and say, " The market always moves up or down. Well, I'm going to wait until it goes down for a while. Then I'm going to buy a good stock and just wait for it to go up. Then I'll sell out and take my profit."

Or he will say, " I've never been in the stock market before, but I don't see why I can't make good money out of it.

For instance, I've been watching Cast Iron Toothpick for two weeks now. First it goes up to 20, then it goes back down to 15, then it goes back up to 20 again. Well, why can't I buy it when it's down to 15 and then simply hold it until it gets back up to 20, then sell and take my five-point gain, and keep on repeating that? It wouldn't take long to make a nice profit that way."

Wall Street Looks Too Easy

There is little that one can say to such enthusiasts except that " It won't work. You've got the wrong slant. You'll end up with a big loss and sleepless nights instead of a nice profit. Keep away! " And the sad part of it is that such individuals seldom take the advice. But eventually it proves sound advice, nevertheless. And the best that one can hope for them is that they will awake to the necessity for study, for work, for the humble attitude, before their capital is entirely gone.

Such examples, of course, are extreme ones. The reader may still say that he is not in that class, but let him ask himself if he could not have saved many losses in the past if he had not been so " cocksure " of his position. The stock market does not give something for nothing. It offers its chief rewards, both financial and psychic, to those who approach it with humility, with a desire for knowledge and with the will to work and study.

The Simple Rule of Conservatism

The corollaries of this first basic rule for market success are, of course, manifold. One of the most important is the rule against over-trading. The author would place much higher stakes on the eventual success of the investor who can afford more but who trades in only a few shares of his favorite stock to start with, than on the individual who is so confident of his own decision that he stakes the greater share of his capital and trades in large lots of his new-found favorite.

No matter how great the experience, no matter how certain the outcome may seem, conservatism in trading is one of the essentials for long life with one's friends and family, as well as for consistent profit in market operations. There can be, of course, an extreme of conservatism, which amounts to timidity and static, but the author would prefer the overly-conservative trader to the over-confident one, every time.

Conservatism and defense against the temptation to over-trade are, as a matter of fact, good signs of the experienced operator or analyst. The longer an individual has been in the market the more often has he seen the best-laid plans go astray, the surest bet lose, and the more likely he is, therefore, to consider the possibility of repetition in his current trade and thus to keep his risk within sensible bounds.

Diversification of Risk

Another corollary of the rule against over-confidence is the one for diversification of risk, which we shall examine more closely in a later chapter.[1] This rule is especially valuable in mapping out the longer-swing investment policy, but it is also valuable in any and all trading. Other things being equal, the trader who is going to be unsuccessful will probably be less so if he is operating in small blocks of a

[1] See Chapter X, p. 244.

large number of stocks. And the man who is going to be successful has a much better chance for greater success and greater profit if his operations are diversified than if they are confined to large blocks of only a few issues.

If the general situation has been properly analyzed, then a greater number of individual issues will carry out such analysis than will contradict it. There will almost always be some which do not fall into line, but through diversification in many different issues, and through the resulting law of averages, the investor will increase his probability for total profit in direct ratio with his measure of diversification.

One of the constant shocks for the market analyst is the number of individuals who present for examination a portfolio of hundreds of shares in only a few issues, when they should have divided their meager capital in odd lots among a great many issues. Under almost any set of general conditions, we should much prefer to own, or operate in, ten-share lots of ten different issues, than twenty-share lots of only five issues.[1]

The Simple Rule of Avoiding Over-Enthusiasm

Another simple but important rule, which is also indirectly related to a properly humble attitude, is the rule against over-enthusiasm in market operation. Calm, sane and unruffled judgment is necessary in most any business but it is especially important in market trading; likewise, it seems extremely difficult for the average trader to achieve while he is considering a future trade.

This is probably another result of the difficult psychological mixture that results when human nature is combined with the stock market. The two mingling factors are

[1] See Chapter X, p. 251.

a wholly natural eagerness for profit on the one hand, and the possibility for such profit on the other. The result is very apt to be over-confidence, over-trading, over-enthusiasm and a general crumbling of normal sanity, healthy caution and common sense.

Under such conditions it is a simple step from scholarly consideration of whether a certain procedure will bring profit, to an amateurish certainty that the procedure can result in nothing else but profit. The favorable factors are stressed, the questionable ones glossed over, and wishthinking takes the place of conservative rationalization. Needless to say, the results are almost always regrettable.

Even more regrettable, however, is the tendency to repeat such error. After each loss is analyzed the investor will say to himself, "Well, I've learned my lesson. I'll never do that again." If he has learned the lesson involved in the rule against over-enthusiasm, he has probably received his money's worth, but only too often the lesson is forgotten after a few weeks or months, and the same sort of psychological mistake is repeated.

The Simple Rule of Avoiding Hasty Decisions

Similar to over-enthusiasm is haste. In fact, it seems to emanate from over-enthusiasm and this same insanity that results from mingling the desire for profit with the apparent possibility for profit. When the trader becomes over-enthusiastic and over-confident, the certainty of profit which he conjures up in his own mind sweeps him along into precipitate and poorly-considered action. There sits the profit, smiling up from the chart, the balance sheet, the morning paper or the page of figures. "Why hesitate? Why run the risk of letting the profit escape? Grab it quickly. Write out the order right now or 'phone it in right now. Maybe the stock is already up a few points. Better make it 100 shares instead of only 20," and so on, *ad destructum*.

While all such evils of judgment accompany hasty decision, it happens more often that the mere condition of haste, in itself, brings on the evils of judgment. Remember that it is difficult enough to gain profit from stock market operation even under the soundest, normal conditions of personal analysis. When the element of haste, or anything else that interferes with sound judgment, is injected into the picture it usually becomes a fade-out.

Remember, also, that one does not have to trade this very minute, that any profit dependent upon hasty action is not worth the risk, that the market will probably hold opportunities for profit tomorrow as well as today, and that it is better judgment to forego completely the chance for a quick profit than to run the almost certain risk of substantial loss and ultimate regret which comes from acting upon impetuous inspiration and hastily-mustered theories and decisions.

The Simple Rule on Consideration of Market Tips

Another simple and general rule for market success is, " Don't take tips." By this the author does not mean shutting one's mind off from all intercourse with persons whose judgment can properly be respected, but rather the cultivation of a healthy suspicion regarding popular tips, rumors and gossip. This is especially true of board-room gossip, of course, but it applies also to any information which appears to have been circulated at all widely, whether by word of mouth, in the public press, brokerage house letters or even by the professional market advisory services.[1]

[1] See Chapter XI, p. 289.

A good rule is never to trust any such advice or information if it is heard from two or three different sources. Aside from the purely manufactured type of tipping information, there are plenty of really sound conclusions or facts which may come to one's notice. They may always be listened to, and perhaps may be useful in guiding one's personal attention and logical thought, but if they gain more than private circulation, then the chances are that they would prove misleading for practical action, no matter how soundly they were originally based.

The Logical Cultivation of Independent Thought

The natural, and proper, accompaniment for a healthy suspicion of all tips is the cultivation of independent thinking for oneself. This is another corner-stone of successful market operation and needs no current argument. Our entire volume will be one long attempt to guide the investor into the proper channels for purely logical deduction, for personal analysis and for independence from extraneous tips and advice, through recourse to one's own native powers of thought.

Such personal deduction also includes the admonition that basic fundamentals and long-term trends should not be forgotten in arriving at independent decisions on future policy. The author has no grudge against bankers, advisory services and market analysts in general, but rather considers them a great aid to the thoughtful investor. He simply realizes that they are by no means infallible and that, at times, the judgment of the intelligent individual may be right when the more professional authorities are wrong.

The author takes considerable pride in his own warnings of over-inflated stock prices in 1928 and 1929, yet he still receives letters fairly regularly from all kinds of individuals telling him how " I knew prices were too high before the crash in 1929 but my banker or my broker wouldn't let me sell. He said stocks were high but that they were going much higher, so I held on."

The Advantages in Thinking for Oneself

Making due allowance for the almost universal desire of the investor to shift his own blame on the shoulders of an adviser, it is still true that an individual judgment of such sort in 1929 was worth a hundred improper advices from professionals.

And, in the last analysis, the investor has only himself to blame, for he saw the handwriting on the wall but failed to have the courage of his convictions. Or, if he did not see the handwriting on the wall, then he is still to blame, because the letters stood out very clearly for anyone who was capable of doing his own thinking and had cultivated the habit of independent decision.

Even though professional advisers often go wrong in their deductions, the man who has formed this valuable habit of doing his own thinking, of standing on his own feet, or using his own head, is not the one who blames all of his troubles, his disappointments and his losses on others. As noted previously, it is a seemingly human and normal trait to take personal credit for one's successful operation, but to shift the blame for loss on someone else.

It is just as common to attempt to excuse a loss on fundamental conditions, and it is just as illogical and useless. Instead of blaming themselves for not seeing the necessity of future declines in 1929, literally thousands of investors in recent years have placed the blame on Congress, on the

Administration, on the bankers, on huge corporations, boards of directors, on consumers, and even on the World War.

Ride the Economic Tides — Don't Fight Them

Because they did not do their own thinking while yet there was time, these unsuccessful operators attempt to blame their losses on mere pawns in the great tapestry of economic change. They investigate the stock market to see why stocks came down. They urge the Government to lay out huge sums of largesse to portions of the population to try to put prices back to the unconscionable levels of inflation. Instead of analyzing the logical sequences of irresistible movements of economic law and profiting by them, they ignore the law and then try to keep it from working.

Such sequences, such logical movements, such universal waves of popular action and reaction are the stuff out of which cyclical movements and economic swings are made. Their destructive effects may be minimized but they cannot be utterly stemmed or even materially deflected from their primal course. Instead of first ignoring them and then fighting them, the successful investor, who does his own logical reasoning, will join hands with them, will take the proper action which such great forces suggest for the future, and will thus ride along with the unalterable waves of human and economic change to profit, instead of trying feebly to buck them when it is too late.

Thus we have examined some of the more general, simple but profitable rules which the successful market operator must cultivate until they become a living, subconscious portion of his being, before he can go on to the less simple, and perhaps more technical rules of profitable operation.

Some Simple Rules for Avoiding Heavy Loss

Before we leave our introductory survey, however, we must inculcate one more basic rule for success, which differs somewhat from the others in that it applies more to practical market operation than to the personality of the trader. That is the cardinal rule of limiting loss.

Most of our other rules, previously examined, and most of the material to follow, will be devoted to aiding the investor in making proper decisions for himself, decisions which will be correct much more often than they are incorrect, which will lead to action that is successful in the light of future events and will, therefore, bring profit to the investor. But no trader can ever expect to be correct in every one of his market transactions. No individual, however well he may be grounded, no matter how much experience he has had in practical market operation, can expect to be infallible.

There will always be some mistakes, some unwise judgments, some erroneous moves, some losses. The extent to which such losses materialize, to which they are allowed to become serious, will almost invariably determine whether the individual is to be successful in his long-range investing activities or whether such accumulated losses are finally to wreck him on the shoals of mental despair and financial tragedy.

Handling Incorrect Commitments the Real Test

It is easy enough to manage those commitments which progress smoothly and successfully to one's anticipated goal. The true test of market success comes when the future movement is not in line with anticipated developments, when the trader is just plain wrong in his calculations, and when his investment begins to show a loss instead of a profit. If such situations are not properly handled, if one or two losing positions are allowed to get out of control, then they can wipe out a score of successful profits and leave the individual with huge loss on balance.

It is just as important — nay, even more important — to know when to desert a bad bargain, take one's loss and count it a day, as it is to know when to close out a successful transaction which has brought profit.

There are various rules for the limitation of loss, most of them largely automatic, and chief of which is the stop-loss principle, which we shall examine later in greater detail.[1] There are also various theoretical formulae for limiting loss, such as never allowing a stock to decline more than 5, 10, or 20 per cent below the original purchase price.

Necessity for Limiting Losses

The author is not so much interested in the mechanical details of such limitation as he is in impressing upon the investor the prime necessity for some sort of mental limitation on the amount of loss he is willing to take on any given transaction. The staggering catastrophes which ruin investors, mentally, morally and financially, are not contingent upon the difference between a 5 per cent loss limit and a 20 per cent limit. They result from not having established any limit at all on the possible loss.

Any experienced market operator can tell you that his greatest losses have been taken in those, probably rare, instances when he substituted stubbornness for loss limitation,

[1] See Chapter IX, p. 218.

when he bought more of a stock which was going down, instead of selling some of it to lighten his risk, when he allowed pride of personal opinion to replace conservative faith in the cold judgment of the market-place.

A glance at Plate I, the Frontispiece of this volume, showing the Dow-Jones industrial average recorded monthly from 1897 to recent date, should serve to offer practical proof of the advantages in loss limitation. Let the reader take a pencil, and take a mental position in the market at most any point he chooses, but opposite from the true future movement of the market. Let him calculate his eventual loss on most of such mental transactions, if he had failed to limit such loss, if he had continued to "buck the trend" and hope for a reversal in his favor on which to get out even.

How Insignificant Losses Grow into Crippling Ones

Or, let him glance back over his record from 1929 through the long bear market which followed, and recall specific examples of incorrect long positions which might have been taken in the early Autumn of that year. Then let him consider how rapidly the road would have stretched away to ruin without the use of some mental limitation on the amount of loss he would accept, some mental point at which he would have called a halt to further devastation and sold out, taking his final beating while he still had the strength to stand it.

It may be hoped, of course, that such considerations are entirely hypothetical with the reader, but if he can recall specific illustrations where his losses not only might have been large, but actually *were* large, then let him resolve at this point on the future use of at least some sort of mental loss limitation in all of his market trades.

While the establishment of such limitation of loss is much better after a security has begun to decline than never at all, it is a hundredfold more valuable if it is established entirely in advance of the original commitment. Its chief service in such case is to provide mental ease and peace of mind through the whole period of the transaction, to guarantee a definite plan of campaign, a certain aim, in advance of its beginning, and often to reduce eventual loss by cutting down the size of the commitment originally planned.

Mental Loss Limitation Preceding the Commitment

The first two advantages need no explanation or argument. If a stock is purchased at 100, with the mental proviso that if it should decline under 90 it will immediately be sold out, or the original commitment at least materially reduced, the stress of worry is immediately and automatically cancelled to all practical intents and purposes. It is cancelled because such a decision for limitation of loss relieves the individual of any future necessity for making a decision under the mental strain of accumulated misfortune.

It is assumed, of course, that the trader is financially able to stand the ten-point loss if it has to be taken. That being the case, he need no longer worry about how large a loss he may have to take. He already knows. If the stock advances, as he expects it to do, he can take his profit whenever he desires, and preferably at a point which has also been mentally established at the time of purchase.

But if the stock declines, he simply lets it decline, hoping that it will reverse before it touches his selling point. But he is not particularly disturbed, simply because he is not forced to make any further decision in the matter. He has already made his decision, when he bought the stock. If it drops to 90 he sells out, takes his loss like a man, and is glad he didn't have more of it. There will be occasions when he could have gotten out at a better price later on. Such experiences are exasperating, but they should be taken philosophically. The risk in banking on such a recovery is far too great to make it advisable.

Plan for All Eventualities in Advance

The entire efficacy of this rule for establishing limitation of loss before actually making a commitment revolves about the general advantage in having a definite plan in view for every transaction. The importance of building such a campaign, or policy, in advance of each trade cannot be overemphasized. Too many individuals buy first and plan their campaign afterward.

It is much easier to buy than to sell. It is easy to calculate the profit on a stock if it should go up, but it seems difficult for the average trader to concentrate his attention on the possibility that, once he has purchased the stock, it may go down instead of up. What is he to do then? If he waits until he *has* a loss before making that decision, his judgment is almost certain to be warped and beclouded by such loss. And the longer he waits and the greater the loss becomes, just so much greater become his mental confusion and his inability to take proper action.

All that such mental preparedness, in advance of the contingency, means is that the investor has his entire campaign completely mapped out in his own mind before he takes the initial step. His plans may, of course, be influenced after the trade is entered, by rapidity of profit, but not by rapidity of loss.

Consider the Worst, Not the Best, That May Happen

So important does the author consider such advance planning that he is definitely in favor of completely reversing one's hopes and expectations for an individual security before trading in it. The investor contemplates buying 1,000 shares of Consolidated Elephant Ration at 100. He has analyzed the situation carefully. Everything looks bullish and he confidently looks forward to an advance to around 130 inside of a reasonable period of time.

Very well, then. It is easy enough to plan one's campaign if Consolidated Elephant Ration goes up to 130 after purchase at 100. But let the trader look at the opposite extreme of possibility *before* he buys his 100 shares. Suppose the stock does not go to 130. Suppose, instead, that it goes down from 100 to 30 over the next year.

Ah, but that is impossible. Look at the balance sheet. Look at the earnings. Look at the technical position. The reply should be, " Ah, but it is *not* impossible. Such things *have* happened in the past under similar circumstances, and they *may* happen again. They *might* happen right now to Consolidated Elephant Ration." To say that a decline is impossible is merely to fool oneself. It is possible, even though improbable. The point is, what will the investor do if the stock *does* go down instead of up, after he has bought it.

Forward Planning Leads to Proper Conservatism

The author probably need not pursue this example further. The reader should be able to see for himself how valuable such an attitude of humility and conservatism would be, in avoiding large losses, in restraining the trader from too large a risk, and in elimination of the worry that goes with the necessity for making important decisions while a stock is piling up increasing loss day by day.

The result of such consideration might be to cut down the original commitment from 100 shares to only 50, and so reduce a risk that would be too great if the stock did actually decline to 30. Or, it might be simply to set a mental loss limitation at 90 for the entire 100 shares, with a profit objective at perhaps 115 or 120. Such decision made and a definite campaign planned in advance, the investor could buy Consolidated Elephant Ration with a clear conscience and, what is much more important, he could thereafter sit back and wait, without undue mental strain, until such time as the stock went to either 115 or to 90.

The Importance of Loss Protection

If his original analysis were correct, he would take his 15-point profit. But if his calculations were not correct, and the stock did go down to a possible bottom of 30 over the next year or so, our investor would have taken a 10-point loss instead of a 70-point loss. He would have protected his capital, avoided a long tie-up in a discouraging situation, and would also have avoided loss of appetite and many sleepless nights.

We shall examine the details of this particular formula for objective campaign in a later chapter,[1] but it may be hoped that we have here established the logical advantages, not only for mental limitation of possible loss, but also for the necessity of having a definite plan mapped out in advance of every operation.

[1] See Chapter IX, p. 227.

A Review of the Simple but Important Rules

Thus, in concluding our introduction to some of the more general but valuable rules for successful market operation, we may note once more the utter simplicity of such rules. They are not highly technical. They are not difficult to explain or to justify. But somehow or other, they are exceedingly difficult to ingrain in the subconscious nature of the average investor.

Don't be over-confident. Don't be over-enthusiastic. Don't over-trade. Don't put all of your eggs in one basket. Don't accept tips blindly. Don't ignore fundamentals. Do your own thinking. Have a definite plan of campaign mapped out before you start. Consider the possibility of being wrong instead of right, before you enter your trade. Limit your losses and live happily, even though you're in the stock market.

Simple, logical rules they are, every one of them. But far too often ignored, taken for granted or overlooked, perhaps because of their very simplicity. Yet they lie at the very foundation of stock market success and profit. All that we learn hereafter, all of our future experience, will tie in with these basic rules and will testify to their fundamental value.

CHAPTER II

CYCLE OF BUSINESS AND SECURITIES

The Negative Approach

In the preceding introductory chapter we noted some of the very general but very important rules of conservatism and common sense which should be ingrained in the market operator's subconscious make-up as a prerequisite for consistent profit and success.

Those rules were simple and quite broad in their scope and application. The analytical reader has perhaps already noted that most of them were almost negative in their precautionary aspects. Many were rules which tend to safeguard the investor in case his market judgment should prove to be incorrect. They applied chiefly to the limitation of loss rather than to the more positive aspect of making a profit.

Importance in Long-Term Success

The author is quite conscious of this almost negative approach to his subject, but the arrangement of the material is quite intentional. Not only are the introductory rules quite general and easily understood but long experience has shown that the safeguards against loss may easily be even more important than the rules for profit, so far as consistent success is concerned in long-term market operation.

No matter how complete, how detailed or practical our future study may be with regard to making sound decisions and profitable commitments, there is no rule which is infallible, and no individual who can expect to be correct every single time in his market judgment.

The better part of valor, therefore, is to disillusion oneself at the very beginning, admit the probability that there will be incorrect forecasts and unprofitable commitments. If this volume has any merit, the wrong decisions should be far in the minority, but it is such infrequent mistakes which most often demoralize the trader and which turn consistent profit into rapid loss.

The Positive Approach of Profit

It may be hoped, therefore, that we have already learned considerable of the " protective " technique. Thus fortified, we may go on to a more positive consideration of how properly to reduce the emergencies and increase the chances for successful commitment.

In attacking this more positive approach, we shall build our groundwork more soundly, and hasten proper understanding of market movements, if we prepare ourselves with fair thoroughness in the history and background of our subject. No physician would consider undertaking practical treatment of his patient without first examining him and his record. No merchant would plunge headlong into a new line of business without first making himself familiar with the principles of supply and demand, with prices, past performance and many other necessary details of his new venture. The individual who is desirous of active and successful operation in the security market has no more right to expect profitable results without applying himself to the past history of his subject than has the business man or the physician.

Studying the Background of Our "Business"

In the first place, then, with what are we dealing in market operation? The fundamental idea of securities as pieces of property has been developed sufficiently in other volumes and by other writers to need no detailed consideration here. Suffice it to say that, whenever an individual buys a security, and more particularly a common stock, he immediately becomes a part-owner of the business represented by that security. Just as in any other business, therefore, he becomes interested in profit. In a general, but not less fundamental, way, his own profit or loss in such security will depend upon the profit or loss of his business or company.

Corporations earn their profit from business operation. And the man who buys securities and thus becomes part-owner of a corporation must, therefore, interest himself in the prospects of profit or loss from that particular business.

From a fundamental and long-term standpoint, then, a study of successful investing in the stock market is confined not merely to stock market records but also to the history, record and consideration of business.

Perhaps the most simple rule for success in the stock market is to "buy low and sell high." It is so simple and so naïve a rule that it is generally considered to be merely a good joke, but the fact remains that it can be made the basis for practical success in longer-term investment policies.

"Buying Low and Selling High"

The quite obvious retort, of course, is that such a rule simply begs the question — that the real difficulty is to *know* when stocks are low and when they are high. A study of business cycles would not be of any tremendous aid for the short-term trader who relates the qualities of "high or low" purely to a weekly basis, and to a range of 10 or 15 points. But for the longer-term operator, who is willing to relate the question of "high or low" to a yearly basis and to a range of 50 to several hundred points, the study of business cycles can be not only a useful aid in the consideration of longer-term investing, but can go far toward a very practical application of the simple rule to "buy low and sell high."

This is true because of the very definition of a cycle, which is a fairly regular sequence of up and down moves. If we can find that business has some semblance of a long-term cycle, then it is only logical to anticipate that security prices will follow a similar cycle, in a broad and general way, due to our previously noted relationship between business profits and security profits.

Such a relation does actually exist between business and security prices. And such cycles do also exist in both business and security prices. In the succeeding pages of this chapter, therefore, we may find some fundamental aids to profitable market operation in a study of these cyclical movements.

The Cyclical Theory

The author does not claim, or believe, that there is any well-defined pattern of time or extent in cycles of business and securities. He believes firmly, with special regard to the stock market, that "history never repeats itself." But he does claim, and he does believe, that both business and security movements have a definite cyclical action, and that business and market history do repeat themselves, not exactly, but with sufficient approximation to make their study profitable.

For the fundamental logic of such approximate cycles in business and securities, we need go no further than a consideration of human nature. By far the great majority of human beings react to special stimuli in fairly characteristic and unanimous manner. The most important of these reactions, related to cycles, is the human tendency to go to extremes. The average individual is so swayed by his general hopes and fears that when either of these two qualities is engendered in the human breast it tends to be cumulative, to feed on itself, to grow and to assume greater and greater motive power until its own momentum carries it far beyond the bounds justified by logic or actual events and circumstances.

Logical Basis for Security and Business Cycles

Since security prices depend in large measure upon the profits of business, and since business profit depends largely upon human purchases and desires, and since these in turn depend upon human nature, we arrive quickly and directly at the logical relationship between the extremes of human nature and the extremes of business and the security markets.

Such logic is perhaps the most fundamental aspect of the connection, but if further and practical proof of this cyclical pattern is desired the reader need simply turn to Plate II, on page 55 of our next chapter, and see for himself how the entire period from 1915 to 1924 was made up of recurring upward and downward cycles, in stock prices as well as in business. Or, if he wishes even longer-term confirmation, let him turn back to Plate I, the Frontispiece, and observe the recurring bull and bear market waves in stock movements.

As will be noted later,[1] there is no universal opinion as to whether the business cycle directs the security cycle or vice versa. The most important point for current observation is simply that for a period of 35 years the Dow-Jones average of industrial stock prices displays alternate cyclical waves of bull and bear markets.

Practical Proof in History

Further observation of Plate I will suggest, of course, that there is no dependably exact interval of time, or extent of movement. But at any point on such a chart, it should have been possible for the investor to decide for himself whether prices were high, low or uncertain.

If he had purchased stocks when he could conscientiously say, from careful study of the past record, that they were low, and had sold stocks when they seemed high, he ought to have made substantial profit over the entire 35 years, even though he would have made numerous errors, and would have been out of the market entirely from perhaps 1923 until 1931. For conservatism we may use these two dates, although the experienced investor might well have delayed his major liquidation until early in 1925, and his reaccumulation until the early part of 1932.

Naturally, the author does not advise such a single rule of investment. We are merely establishing the logic of our current study, even though there are probably plenty of living investors who have wished, in recent years, that they had operated solely on such a theory and had, in fact, been " out of the market " from 1923 until 1931.

[1] See Chapter III, p. 50.

Cyclical Extremes Result from Human Tendencies

Even if we had not already established the direct relationship between business, profits and security prices, the security cycle could easily be tied directly to the tendency of human nature to go to extremes in hope and fear, in enthusiasm and despair. The great bulk of individuals think more or less alike, their ideas being influenced by the same type of stimuli, through conversation, easy communication and travel, radio, newspapers, etc.

The views of these great, modern molders of public opinion are, in themselves, partly responsible for cyclical movements because they also tend to add momentum to previous judgments. Very often, they remain bearish and pessimistic for a year or so after conditions have turned toward improvement, and they are just as likely to remain bullish and optimistic for a year or more after conditions have turned downward.

The Psychological Extremes of Hope and Fear

Public opinion, thus bolstered by the general temper of news, either innocent or purposely misleading, almost always carries its hopes and fears to an extreme. At the top of a long industrial expansion, when business should be retrenching, it goes ahead recklessly and confidently, thus insuring that the eventual reaction, when it finally does come, will be just as extreme as the previous advance.

Likewise, at the top of a long bull market, when the public should be selling stocks, it goes on buying them eagerly and thoughtlessly, still imbued with the success of previous easy profits and advancing prices, thus also assuring that the security decline, when it does finally arrive, will once more go back down into the extreme depths of the cycle.

And, conversely, fear and hopelessness also feed on themselves, so that business and security investors remain timid and pessimistic long after the time when conditions have fundamentally turned to improvement.

Effect of a " Planned Economy " on Cycles

For the last few pages many readers probably have been raising their hands feverishly to suggest that such theories as we have been discussing are a thing of the past, that with a " planned economy " the cycle of business and security markets will flatten out and profit opportunities thus be discounted.   The author admits quite freely that a real planned economy can smooth out the extremes of cyclical movement to some extent, but he is dogmatic in his opinion that no amount of effort at Government regulation and systematic planning can do much more than remove some of the more extreme swings, and he would hesitate to offer a definite guarantee that it can accomplish even this.

The reader need not infer that we are out of sympathy with various steps and plans toward smoothing out the cyclical pattern.   The end which is sought is a laudable one, and many of the means are also laudable, but there is no percentage in blinding ourselves to fundamental analysis, simply in an effort to be patriotic or optimistic.

The author is most sympathetic and co-operative in the general effort of civilization to eradicate war, but it is no contradiction of that spirit to face the facts of life and human nature squarely enough to weigh candidly the practical chances of world peace.   Likewise, the feeling that a planned economy will not be able to eradicate the cycles of business and security prices is no earnest of a personal lack of sympathy for the final aims.

Legislation Cannot Change Human Nature

In order to eradicate war, it would first be necessary to change human nature, and that is a much more difficult and lengthy feat than trying to set up laws and international agreements prohibiting war. In order to eradicate natural cycles, it would first be necessary, also, to change human nature. And here again we have a much more difficult and lengthy process than the mere laying down of law or regulation by Governmental agencies.

So long as people are swayed by public opinion, by popular thought, by hope and fear, by desire for material and rapid gain, by mass propaganda instead of by their own careful thought and personal analysis, so long will the cyclical pattern be with us. And it is the author's opinion that human nature will not be changed very much or very rapidly by planned economy, by Government regulation, by legal restriction, a " commodity dollar," or what not.[1]

Smaller Swings Natural after " New Era " Collapse

Indications are that future swings, at least in the security markets, will not be so wide and spectacular in the next decade as they were in the last. Efforts toward Government regulation and " planned economy " may get the credit, but it is the author's opinion that the credit will belong to human nature once more.

In all past history, nations have experienced tremendous eras of security speculation only about once in a generation

[1] See Chapter XII, p. 325.

or more, just as has also happened in the historical record of world wars. After each holocaust there is a public reaction, and the danger of repetition does not become serious again until a new generation grows up which has not had the bitter experience of its forebears.

Profits Easier in Normal Cycle of Limited Amplitude

A glance at the Frontispiece should serve to convince the reader, however, that such radical departures from the normal cycle as we had during the " New Era " days of 1928 and 1929 are far from profitable vehicles for the long-swing, common-sense investor who plans his policies on a logical basis. There were plenty of profits in that tremendous boom but it was much more difficult to make and hold such profits wisely than in a more normal cycle. And eventually, of course, the ensuing losses theoretically wiped out the profits.

Therefore, rather than despairing of future gain on a basis of the more moderate price swings which appear probable for the coming decade, the sensible investor should actually welcome a return to more normal and more logical future swings.

Plenty of fortunes were made in the cyclical movements preceding the out-of-line movement which started in 1925. And there will be plenty of profit opportunities in a mere return to the cyclical patterns which preceded the rampage of later years. While the swings may flatten out comparatively, we simply anticipate that they will go back to the more normal patterns prevailing in the first part of the century. And we certainly do not feel that they will disappear from the picture under a governmental, or planned, economy.

Component Stages of a Complete Cycle

Having spent considerable time in establishing our logical basis for, and proof of, the existence of a profitable and regular cycle in business and securities, we may go on to the relatively better-understood and more simple examination of the characteristics of such cyclical patterns.

In the business cycle, we have four typical stages — depression, recovery, prosperity and deflation, following each other in that order. In the security cycle there are also four main stages, consisting of accumulation, mark-up, distribution and mark-down. These are somewhat technical terms and the author is not particular about their habitual nomenclature, so long as the movements themselves are understood. They might just as well be called, more simply, the succeeding stages of bottom, advance, top and decline, or low, bull market, high and bear market.

Broad Boundaries between Stages

Regardless of their nomenclature, they are all rather general so far as their practical application to the security market is concerned, for we have already noted [1] that, while we recognize the definite existence of the cyclical pattern, we also recognize that no pattern is *exactly* the same. There is no specific rule as to how far or how long its various stages will run.

The reader need not become discouraged on this account, however. If there *were* such specific rules, then profitable investing would indeed be a simple matter and everyone should be wealthy in a very short time.

[1] See p. 30.

Planning Investment Policy on the Cyclical Basis

The advantage in studying the cyclical theory is that it brings a semblance of scientific planning into the long-swing investment program, and it furnishes a point of departure for profitable operation, even if it does not guarantee such profits infallibly.

Study and experience can, as a matter of fact, bring considerable assurance in definite forecasting of the time and extent for these stages of the cycle, not so much in long-range prophecy as in a proper *feeling* of the time when one of the stages passes over into the next succeeding one. For the average investor, however, the greatest single advantage of the cyclical theory is that it gives him assured grounds for anticipating what the *next* wide, profitable, long-swing movement is going to be, as soon as he has properly labelled the current one.

The very principle of the cycle suggests the orderly succession of the different stages which we have outlined. In the security market, for instance, the order of staging is accumulation, mark-up, distribution and mark-down. After the final stage of mark-down has taken place, the investor goes back to the beginning of the series again, his next anticipation being accumulation, and the whole cycle starts over again.

Orienting the Stages of Business and Security Cycles

There is no use glossing over the fact that one of the practical difficulties lies in proper determination of what stage of the cycle is currently in vogue. That, indeed, is the corner-stone of the entire theory for practical forecasting and profit, and we shall study, in the following chapter, some of the more useful methods for determination of this important point.[1]

But, granted that the investor has definite proof or conviction that the market is in a stage of accumulation, for instance, the next step is easy. Mark-up always follows. When the mark-up stage is coming to an end, the next one to look for is distribution, then mark-down, etc. A stage of accumulation, for instance, would never lead directly into distribution in the normal cycle. The mark-up stage would always intervene.

The practical profit from the stages of the normal cycle develops, therefore, from the fact that the stages always succeed themselves in the same order.

Incidentally, of course, there is a general, but by no means exact, connection in time and extent between the four stages of the business cycle and the four stages of the security cycle. Accumulation generally takes place during business depression. The next stage is business recovery and security mark-up, then business prosperity along with security distribution, and finally, the last stage of business deflation accompanied by security mark-down.

Another Theory of Successive Market Stages

It may also be useful to note briefly the additional theory that there are six stages of public, or psychological, impetus in the security market cycle. Somewhere near the end of business depression and security accumulation, and near the beginning of business recovery and security mark-up, comes the first of these six successive stages, which may be described as recovery from fear and forced selling. Business,

---

[1] See Chapter III, p. 42.

and especially security prices, are almost always driven to unreasonably low levels by panic conditions, when equities are offered for whatever they will bring, and are thus depressed to levels under the prices even logically justified by the depression.

When this stage of panic ends, prices recover, often quite swiftly, not yet on true fundamental improvement, but simply on a basis of the return to rational thought instead of unreasoned panic. After this first stage of recovery from fear and forced selling comes the second stage, when security prices respond to actual improvement in business and to higher earnings. This advance is usually slower and less regular than the first.

The "Psychological Cycle"

The third stage of public market impetus is the stage of over-enthusiasm, when security prices go higher than they should, on hopes of continued future improvement, on speculative enthusiasm and recklessness. The fourth stage is the simple reaction from over-enthusiasm, a return to more normal public thinking and to prices more nearly justified by conditions, good as they are.

The fifth stage of this special psychological cycle, is the response of security prices to declining business and to reduced profits. Then comes the sixth, and final, stage from which we started our cycle — the period when fear replaces reason, when panic reigns and when forced selling drives prices down once more to levels far below those justified even by current low business activity.

We need not enlarge upon this cycle of public psychology, since it should be almost self-explanatory. It should prove especially useful for the more advanced type of market student, but the average reader should first master the four primary stages in the business and security cycle, for it might easily be confusing to attempt to superimpose these six cycles of psychology on top of the four cycles of primary market movement.

Learning to Sense the Cyclical Transition

There is no real inconsistency in the simultaneous consideration of the two varied cycles, however, for the reader must realize that there is no definite or clear-cut dividing line between any of the various stages which we have been discussing. We can never say, with definite assurance, that yesterday we were still in the stage of business depression and security accumulation, but that today we have crossed the line into business recovery and security mark-up.

Such stages merge into each other gradually, often almost imperceptibly. Next to developing the faculty of discerning which cyclical stage we are in at any given time, our next most valuable achievement, for the cyclical theory, will be to get the " feel " of those transitional periods when one stage of the cycle is gradually but surely giving way to the succeeding one.

In the following chapter, we may perhaps approach some useful theories in developing this knack, and in applying the stages of our cyclical pattern to practical trading or investing for the long-swing. In the final analysis such analytical ability comes largely from study and experience, but there are plenty of rules which may assist us, may make our progress more rapid and our analysis more successful.

CHAPTER III

LONG–SWING INVESTMENT

Three Main Types of Market Movement

In the last chapter we devoted our study chiefly to the cyclical theory in itself. We established the basis, both in logic and in fact, for the recurring up and down swings in the indexes of general business and security markets. In the present chapter we shall attempt to convert the theory of this cyclical pattern into something more useful and directly practical for market profit.

A glance at almost any detailed stock chart will make it clear that security movements may roughly be divided into three types, the very short day-to-day movements, the intermediate fluctuations of anywhere from a couple of weeks to several months, and, finally, the longer and more important trends which occupy years in their development. Our theory of cycles is applicable chiefly to this third type of movement, the long-swing or long-term trends, commonly characterized as bull and bear markets.

Playing for the Major Moves

Buying and selling stocks in accordance with this long-swing pattern is perhaps the surest and safest method of market profit, but we shall also see that it is not necessarily the easiest or the best method. It certainly is not the fastest. It is a slow and tedious method, chiefly because it is based upon the theory of extremes in popular sentiment, in business and security prices, and because such extremes are reached only over long periods of time.

The very basis for our theory of extremes implies slow action, because it takes a year or more of rising prices and improving conditions to get the public into the psychological state for careless thinking and radical chance-taking. Likewise, it takes considerably more than a year of declining security markets and falling business to get human nature into that psychological state of panic and hopelessness which carries prices down to the lower extremes.

Inactivity of the Long-Swing Investor

The reader may note for himself about how often we have reached such extremes of popular hope or fear by studying once more the Dow-Jones market average since 1897, as shown in Plate I. As we have noted previously in our study of cycles,[1] there is no hard and fast rule of time or extent in such a theory, but the record of the past 35 years would give weight to the inference that the security markets touch the peaks of enthusiasm once in about every three to five years and that they touch the depths of panic just about as often.

The investor who was able to operate on such cyclical patterns with a fair degree of accuracy during the present century would thus have accumulated a long line of securities only about every three to five years, and would have sold out at only about the same time-interval. If we strike an average of four-year peaks and bottoms, therefore, the true long-swing investor would have entered the market actively only about once in every two years over the past third of a century. And an even slower type of cyclical

[1] See Chapter II, p. 32.

pattern, and therefore a slower rate of activity, also holds if we go back even to the Civil War, or for a period of 70 years.[1]

Back to the Basic Problem of Profit

It may thus be seen why the theory of cyclical action must be left largely for the true long-swing investor, the man who is content to buy stocks, put them away and *almost* forget about them for several years. He may not be our ideal, or average, market operator, but his investment policies are useful, important and well worthy of consideration for the individual interested in taking slow but consistent profit from security operations. As a matter of fact, this cyclical theory is the most valuable basis of operation for the individual who does not care to trade actively, who is not interested in the greater profits of shorter swings, and who is fully content with the conservative policy of being a " long-term investor."

But, having granted our current interest in this method of buying and selling securities for the long pull, our practical problem comes into clearer focus. It is still the old question of buying low and selling high, of knowing when to buy and when to sell.

Difficulties of the Long-Term, Cyclical Method

The reader has perhaps already questioned our entire hypothesis by finding many points on the long-term chart of security prices where the current situation might easily have been open to question, where prices were already as high as the previous long-term peak but where the current

[1] See " Stock Market Theory and Practice," p. 675.

bull market was by no means ended. The author has no alibis for such occasions, at least with direct regard to our current theory. In almost all such cases, the long-swing investor could have saved himself from premature action by making use of some of the other rules which we shall study in this volume, especially the shorter-swing application of technical analysis.[1]

Confining ourselves merely to the " theory and materials at hand," however, we must admit that there must of necessity be times when the long-swing investor, acting solely on the cyclical theory, will sell out too soon or buy too soon. But one of his comforts will be that he has almost certainly taken substantial profits on his campaign, and need not therefore be " piggish " about the matter. He may also rest assured that it is much better to take a correct action too soon than too late, but he must also guard against reversing his judgment and position simply because the market goes on further after he has deemed it time for a turn.

Advantages of the Method

We have already referred [2] to the situation of an investor operating on the cyclical theory in the bull market which culminated in 1929. The individual formulating his policies along the lines of this theory would have been well accumulated with stocks in 1921. He would have sold them out anywhere from 1923 to 1925, but he would have sold them gradually, if he had followed the rule of conservatism which we noted in our opening chapter,[3] to say nothing of the rule of compromise which we shall study later.[4]

[1] See Chapter VI, p. 124.   [2] See Chapter II, p. 32.
[3] See Chapter I, p. 12.
[4] See Chapter IV, p. 96, and Chapter IX, p. 215.

He would then have been "out of the market" from 1925 through 1931. He might have kicked himself around the block once every week through those intervening years, at least until the close of 1929, but he should by no means have let the continued bull movement fool him into going back in again at the higher levels. He would have missed the biggest bull market in American history, but he would also have missed the biggest bear market in history.

Accurate Gauging of the 1932 Bottom

He would have missed the chance for several hundred per cent profit on his 1921 purchases, but he would have taken a profit of well over 50 per cent in 1923 to 1925. Furthermore, he would have been taking a sure profit, whereas if he had held on he would never have known where or when to sell. From 1925 on, there were no longer any previous yard-sticks to go by, so far as the cyclical theory was concerned, and he might easily have held on until his profit was much less, in the subsequent bear market, than the profit he took, honestly, conservatively and logically, in 1925.

And, finally, it may be noted that if he had followed the cyclical theory with sincere exactitude, he would not only have taken his substantial profits in 1925 but he would not have re-entered the market to purchase securities again until early in 1932. There are very few other theories which hit the time and level for long-swing reaccumulation any better than that.

Basis of "Extremes" in Cyclical Analysis

Such examples as we have noted thus far, however, have been based almost purely on the extreme ranges of the security price movement. When the workings of our cyclical theory are confined to the pattern of extreme fluctuations in a predetermined range, there is no great difficulty in judging which of the four market stages we are in. When prices get up into the extremely high ranges of previous bull markets and churn about, the stage is well defined as distribution in prosperity, and we may sell long-term stock holdings with confidence. When prices drop to the bottom levels of our historical range in business depression, then the stage of long-swing accumulation is marked and we may buy securities with equal confidence.

And when we are thus able to recognize the two extreme stages of our cycle, then the other two intermediate stages need not bother us overly much. Having sold long-term securities near the top of our cyclical range, during the stage of distribution, we may simply sit back and wait patiently for the next succeeding stage of mark-down to bring prices back into the lower ranges once more, when we shall again begin to buy during the following stage of accumulation.

Then we again wait patiently for the final stage, that of the mark-up, leading once more into the selling zone of distribution, to complete our cycle. Patience is perhaps the greatest virtue in such a long-swing campaign, and it is absolutely essential for consistent success.

Value of the Composite Judgment

While close observation of the price movement is one of the most important and dependable tools for practical application of the cyclical theory in long-swing investment, it is by no means the only one. If he has not already done so, the reader should learn, before he concludes this volume, the importance of depending not merely upon one single factor, theory or element, for his market conclusions, but letting them rest rather on the composite evidence furnished by a great many theories pointing to the same analysis.

In formulating long-range policies based on the theory of cycles, for instance, we find plenty of specific assistance from other factors beside the extremes of price movement. They may not always point unanimously in the same direction, but they usually do, and there is almost always a majority decision that calls, with unmistakable balance, the proper conclusion at important turning points.

Some Automatic Theories of the Business Cycle

The number of such aids in determining cyclical zones of accumulation and distribution is almost legion. Some of them are reliable, others not so conclusive, but most of them are worthy of composite consideration. There is, for instance, the rather old and somewhat outmoded rule of "blast furnaces." Stocks were considered a long-term purchase when the rate of blast furnace activity dropped below 60 per cent of capacity, and were considered a sale whenever blast furnace activity advanced above that figure.

Almost identical are the more modern rules on steel production, scrap-iron prices, activity, the rate of steel operations, and so on. Most of them suggest selling securities when such data reach the higher cyclical ranges and buying them when they drop to the lower fringe of historical precedent.

Difficulties in the Automatic Formula Field

For general business activity, there is the rule to begin buying securities when general business declines to 10 per cent or more below normal, and to sell when the index advances to 10 per cent or more above normal. Fundamentally, such a rule as this is quite logical under the cyclical investment theory and, as a matter of fact, it appears, from past history, that its use should have proven profitable over the long swing. If the reader cares to follow such a theory back for 50 years or so, he may refer to the chart on business and stock indexes since 1877, published in a previous volume by the author.[1]

The practical difficulty with all such automatic rules based upon various business indexes is that they go through periods of considerable indecision themselves, crossing and recrossing the critical action line perhaps several times in as many months. If the long-swing investor trusts such rules and indexes implicitly he might easily be badly " whipsawed," to the destruction of his own faith in the theory, and to the enrichment of his commission broker.

Formulae Often Late or Vacillating

Perhaps even more serious, however, is the potential objection that security prices quite often move so rapidly and so far ahead of business that it is too late to buy or sell for the long pull by the time the relatively slow monthly figures on such business indexes are compiled and published. On a purely long-swing investment basis, it is difficult, of course, to conceive that such a lag would make investment action too late, when we are playing for moves of a year or more, but detailed examination of practical records offers unmistakable evidence that such can easily be the case. In various instances the investor could have lost by far the greater share of his cyclical profit by waiting for such lagging busi-

[1] See " Stock Market Theory and Practice," Plate 72, p. 463.

ness figures, even though the interval was only a few months. The rapid market advances in 1932 and 1933 are fair and recent examples of this disadvantage.

Which Leads the Cyclical Turn — Business or Securities?

Such a consideration brings us also to the question of the time relation between the turns in business and securities. We have seen in the preceding chapter[1] that there exists a definite relationship between the successive stages of the business and the security cycles. But which turns first? Does business lead security prices upward out of depression, or does the stock market lead business?

This is generally considered a moot question and it will probably continue to be debatable and debated, but the author's personal observation and study have led him to the definite conclusion that security prices more often lead business than vice versa.

The Answer Based on Logic

Here again we can first call upon logical deduction for our theories and then see whether the conclusions are supported by practical evidence. In the first place, we must remember that we are comparing two sharply divergent types of index. The business index is a rather general affair, consisting of anything from two or three important lines of production to a complicated series of several hundred varying lines, all, in turn, indexes in themselves.

There is thus almost certain to be a lag between the exact moment when the bulk of the fundamental business figures turns up until the " average " is painstakingly gathered from

[1] See Chapter II, p. 30.

many different sources and tossed out to the waiting world. Furthermore, all of the component parts usually included in a business index do not necessarily turn up at the same time. Some may lag several months and thus retard the sensitivity of the entire average.

Comparison of the Two Factors

Over against this bulky and slow-moving business average we are presuming to place what may be considered perhaps the most sensitive, the most rapidly reacting, index that we have — the stock market. Consider for a moment merely the comparison between the time it takes for general knowledge to develop that the public is buying more shoes or leather goods and the time it takes for purchases of stock to be made public.

The public demand for shoes may go up slowly; the retail shoe dealer hesitates to replenish his stock; finally, he mails in his order to the wholesaler, who mails in his order to the district distributor, who mails his report to the factory, which slowly increases its production. Then the "business index" begins to advance for the shoe and leather industry.

But what if the public, the insiders, banks, business men turn bullish? They begin to buy stocks today. Prices advance. How long before that stimulus becomes public? Not several months from now; not next week or even tomorrow; the evening papers tell the story, and the stock ticker has told it even sooner.

Sensitivity of the Market Indexes

Thus, it stands to reason that the stock market is a much more sensitive index of changing general sentiment than are business data. The latter are not only slower to react, but the reaction, even when it comes, is much slower in getting into public channels and practical usefulness.

Consider again that, when orders do begin to come into industrial booking offices, they may not become public for weeks or for months. They may not show in larger production figures for many moons. They may not affect the ordinary business index at all for quite a while. Yet almost the first individual who feels that quickening impulse in general business is the corporation executive. He receives his daily and hourly reports on the pulse of his business, and he is not tardy in realizing that a change in popular sentiment has taken place.

Shall we expect him to wait until the "business index" turns up before placing his orders for long-swing security buying? Far from it. He buys today, before others realize the good news and put prices up further. His early buying, and that of the other "corporation insiders," brings a rise in the market well ahead of any advance in the slow-moving indexes of business.

Nor is it necessary to suggest that the individuals who have first access to such information are usually the fairly large-scale operators, who can. afford to buy in thousand-share lots, and whose buying can hardly be hidden from the sensitive indexes of current security prices.

Psychological Comparison of Business and Securities

Or consider, finally, the psychological effect which the trend of security prices has upon popular feeling and upon consumer resistance. In the last analysis, business influences security prices, because the market seldom is able to run counter to business trends for very long. But in the shorter-interval movements, and in the countless small waves that often go to make up a real storm, the trend of security prices can influence business in tremendous degree. It is almost an axiom that the general public is in better buying spirit, more courageous, more enthusiastic and more ambitious, when security prices are rising than when they are falling. The business rise in late Summer of 1932, for instance, was almost certainly abetted by the advance in security prices, rather than the security advance being preceded by actual business improvement.

Thus, on several varying scores, we may adduce fairly substantial evidence, not only that security prices are likely to lead business in a basic turn more often than vice versa, but that when a turn actually occurs it is almost certain to become publicly apparent in the security market before it shows up in the commonly-used business indexes.

The Answer Based on Fact

When we apply such logical theories to the practical test of history we again find that they work out with sufficient regularity to form a dependable rule. For a current example, we have chosen the most recent series of years which offered several complete cycles of business and security movements, previous to the stock market inflation which carried security levels to heights out of all proportion to fundamental values as well as to business, an abnormality which we shall discuss more fully at the close of the present chapter.[1]

For our current study let us glance at Plate II, on page 55, showing the chart on business and stock prices from 1915 through 1924.[2] The stock market index is based on

[1] See p. 69.

[2] See Appendix, p. 329, for numerical comparison tables.

monthly closing prices for the New York Times average of 50 industrial and railroad stock issues, while the business index is based upon Col. Leonard P. Ayres' monthly compilation for his long-range study of business activity. The scales of the two indexes have been superimposed to begin at approximately the same point and the time scale is, of course, identical for both series.

A Study in Comparative History

Note how characteristically the stock index lags slightly behind business improvement at the start of the recovery cycle after the New York Stock Exchange reopened for trading, in 1915, and then how it tends to run ahead of business toward the end of the upward cycle. But note also that the flattening out of the stock index at the close of 1915, around Point B, precedes the same formation in business, which really did not develop until in 1916.

Both indexes reached their peak at Point C, in October of 1916, but stocks declined immediately thereafter, while business held up for at least another month. As a matter of fact, the downward cycle in stocks ran well ahead of that in business through the entire depression cycle of 1917.

Note also that stocks made their extreme lows in November of 1917, while business reached only an intermediate low in January of 1918, around Point E. At Point F appears a period of slight confusion but great interest. Stocks had been advancing through most of 1918 but here is one intermediate example of how the market must eventually bow at times to the final and powerful word of business, when that word becomes too strong and insistent.

Business started a marked, even though intermediate, decline in August of 1918, and the security market was forced,

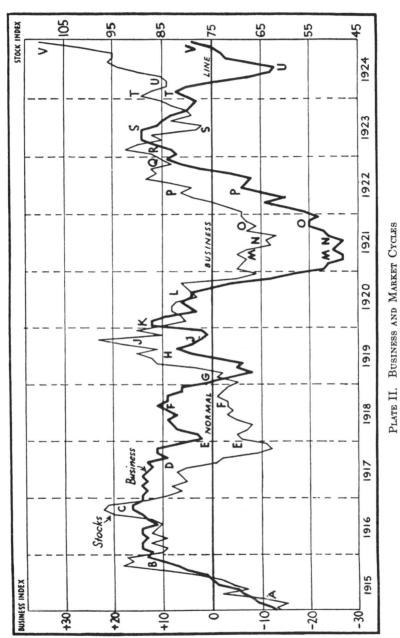

PLATE II. BUSINESS AND MARKET CYCLES

A detailed comparison from 1915 through 1924.

rather grudgingly, to follow, though in much smaller measure, with a decline from October of 1918 to January of 1919.

The Normal Cycles up to 1925

But the market was right nevertheless in its longer-range vision, and it started rapidly upward at Point G, not being followed by the business index until April of 1919, even though the occasion was the huge post-war expansion period. Again the market outran business but it also led the intermediate reaction at Point H.   And the market reached its extreme peak of the upward cycle, at Point J, at least four months before the business index passed its own individual peak and started down into the depression of 1921.   At Point L, business caught up, however, and dropped abruptly off well ahead of the stock market.

There is fair evidence for either index as the leader on the bottom turn of 1921, for business actually started up a month ahead of stocks, at Point N.   However, the author still considers that the stock index did a good job in that period, for it began to flatten out far ahead of business.   It certainly led it in the Spring rally of 1921 and again established its lead at Point O.   It again led business at Points P, Q and R, turning down at the latter point about four months ahead of the business index.   As a matter of fact, the stock market was practically through with its reaction, at Point S, before business had actually begun to decline.

Thereafter, the stock index displayed much greater strength than business, giving a foretaste of what was to come in the run-away markets of later years.   Even at the end of our chart, however, the market again led business at Points T and U.   It was well on its way in the new bull market of 1924 before the business compilation had even touched bottom and started up.

Let it be remembered also, in all such comparisons, that while the stock index was available immediately, the business index figure might not be published for a month or more after the period in question.

Conclusion Based on Logic and History

Thus, it may be hoped that we have established our previous statement that business indexes are usually behind the market and are therefore of secondary value in automatic formulae for long-swing investment on the cyclical theory. They are of unquestioned aid and should be used to influence the investor's composite judgment, but they need not be relied upon too dogmatically.

We have dwelt at some length on our exposition of the business-market relation, however, not merely to show the practical relationship between the two cyclical patterns but also to familiarize the reader with the practical application of such patterns. Let us go back, for instance, to a detailed study of the investor's long-swing problem as evidenced by this practical chart on page 55.

Attacking the Practical Problem

A glance at the "master-chart" in Plate I will quickly convince us that the cyclical investor would have loaded up fairly well with securities as soon as the stock exchange reopened for business after the World War closing in 1914. The first high point in stocks, at around Point B, on Plate II, would represent his fair objective for profit-taking, especially after business began to flatten out in prosperity.

He could justifiably have ignored completely the small and temporary new high levels of both business and stocks around Point C, and he would have taken a long-term profit of 50 per cent in only about a year. On such a basis, the long-pull investor could *afford* to wait even several years for another such " killing," staying out of the market patiently until cyclical conditions, or extremes, again became propitious for definite judgment and accumulation.

Following the Cycles in Actual Operation

He had not long to wait, however, for in only about two years stock prices were back at their historical low levels. In this case, however, during 1918, the issue was beclouded by the fact that business held relatively good. Stocks had apparently gone through their mark-down stage and into accumulation, whereas business had hardly lapsed into serious decline. Our friend, the "compromise" rule,[1] would have been the proper solution to this problem at the very worst. And at the best there were plenty of indications for cyclical advance in both indexes following Point E.

The intermediate decline in business, at Point G, might easily have given concern but it did not last long enough to be harmful since market action was so impressively strong that any partial sales for the long pull should have been replaced as soon as business turned up in the Spring of 1919.

Consistent Profit from Cyclical Analysis

The distribution phase around Point J was much easier to recognize, with business fairly prosperous and security prices up to their previous historical extremes. The long-swing investor would have sold his holdings at an average

---

[1] See Chapter X, p. 254.

of perhaps around 90, and would again have accepted close to 50 per cent profit in less than two years.

In 1921 it was the turn of business to go further toward the extreme pattern than did stocks, but there was again unmistakable evidence of the depression stage in business and the accumulation stage in securities. As previously noted,[1] the long-swing purchases of 1921 would have been sold out, on the cyclical theory, in 1923 or 1924, perhaps at an average level of 85, and thus with another profit of around 30 per cent or more in a couple of years.

Thus we have seen a practical example of how the long-swing investor may attune himself to the recurring cycles of business and security prices, to reap slow but fairly sure and fairly substantial profit without dependence upon the intermediate waves of shorter-term analysis and consideration.

The Long-Term Investment Principle

Our recent study has also brought practical proof that, while there is a direct relation between the business and the security cycle, we may expect security moves to lead those in business more often than the business moves lead those in securities.

Our rule for buying stocks at extreme lows of the pattern in both of these cycles is still valuable. Likewise, such automatic formulae as are based upon the extremes of less direct business factors, like steel production, blast furnaces and other business indexes, also remain valuable, though secondary, and should be used more to influence our composite judgment than as separate and decisive signals in themselves.

[1] See Chapter II, p. 32.

Cyclical Extremes in Allied Factors

Having considered at some length the business indexes in relation to the cyclical theory for long-swing investment, we may go on to an examination of some other helpful, but by no means conclusive, formulae. One group of such rules concerns itself chiefly, for instance, with the money market and with interest rates.

There is the formula which suggests the long-term purchase of securities whenever the average rate for prime commercial paper or other first-rate loans has been under some certain set figure, say 4 per cent, for perhaps three to six months. The same rule would suggest the sale of long-term security holdings whenever such interest rates went above an average of perhaps 6 per cent for a similar period.

As usual, this rule is a valuable aid but is not infallible. If the reader is interested in further study of such a formula relationship, he may refer to various long-swing charts comparing market movements and average interest rates.[1]

The Cyclical Interest-Rate Formulae

A similar formula theory, which appears to have a somewhat better basis in logic, suggests the purchase of securities when high-grade bond yields advance above commercial interest rates, and indicates the sale of such securities whenever the bond yield average declines below the interest-rate figure. Still another such formula relates the yield on bonds to the yield on stock, and so on.

Perhaps even more logical are those additional formulae which take into consideration the relation of security prices

[1] See "Stock Market Theory and Practice," Plate 101, p. 675.

to the yield on those same securities, or to the rate of corporate earnings on such securities. In this classification, the most popular and most appropriate yardstick appears to be the price-earnings ratio, or the figure by which annual per-share earnings must be multiplied to get the price at which the stock is currently selling.

The Price-Earnings Ratio Formula

The logical price-earnings ratio is ten. A stock earning $2 per share per annum is justified in selling around 20. A stock earning $6 a year may sell at 60, and so on. The formula, if indeed there be one, is quite indefinite, but might be said to suggest the purchase of stocks when their general, or average, price-earnings ratio declines under 8, and to sell when it advances above 13 to 15.

Even such an indefinite formula is here noted more for completeness than for practical use. The logic of such a rule is apparent, but in practice it is very often misleading. In times of extreme depression the price-earnings ratio would suggest that many securities sell below zero, while in times of prosperity, per-share earnings may be increasing so rapidly that a high ratio is not dangerous.

The main difficulty is that such ratios must ordinarily be based upon previous earnings, whereas the actual price of the stock is discounting future earnings rather than past profits.

The Formulae on Brokers' Loans

The relation of security prices to brokers' loans is another basis for long-swing investment formula. An extremely simple type is based merely upon the total of brokers' loans,

taken either from the New York Stock Exchange compilation or from other series. When brokers' loan totals are at
low extremes the suggestion is that securities are in the accumulation stage. When the loan totals are near their high
extremes, then the distribution stage is indicated.

It seems more sensible, however, to consider brokers' loans
not by themselves, but in relation to the market value of the
listed stocks on which such loans are made. For many years
the New York Stock Exchange has compiled and published
each month its figures on total net borrowings on Stock Exchange collateral of member firms and also the total market
value of all listed shares. 'The ratio of member borrowings
to the value of all listed stocks makes an interesting series
which has ranged from a high of around 10 per cent in 1929
to a low of only about 1 per cent in 1932.

Minor Formulae Helpful but Not Always Positive

The series is usually termed the brokers' loan ratio, and
the formula would suggest the purchase of securities for
long-term holding when this ratio drops below a figure of
perhaps 4 per cent and their sale when it advances to perhaps
above 8 per cent. The reader is warned that there is nothing particularly dogmatic in the definite figures, or limits,
which are quoted in connection with the formulae here ad-
duced. They are offered more for illustration than for
precept.

Many of the limits which would have worked successfully
previous to 1924 would have brought loss during the following bull market, while many figures which seem logical,
based upon the experience of recent years, would not work
satisfactorily for the more normal cycles previous to 1924.
Once again, let the reader understand fully that we are work-

ing more toward developing a great many different aids for his composite judgment, rather than attempting to set up any one, definite, individual rule by which he must regulate his long-term investment.

Formulae for Volume of Trading

Pursuing this aim still further we find that the relative volume of stock trading furnishes the basis for still another long-swing investing formula. When the stage of mark-up has been under way for a normal space of time, when prices have advanced considerably, and when the upward movement begins to lose momentum while volume of trading soars to the high limits of extreme past ranges, then we have a definite suggestion that the cycle is passing over from the mark-up stage into that of distribution and that the long-swing investor had best begin to take his profits.

Conversely, when the declining stage of mark-down has been in progress for a normal interval, when prices are comparatively low once more, and when the bear market tends to lose headway and to round off its decline, while public interest languishes and volume of trading over a period of weeks or months drops to the low extremes of the cyclical pattern, then the suggestion is also strong that the markdown stage of the cycle is giving way to the accumulation stage and that we may again begin to purchase securities for the longer swing.

The Composite Picture

The reader may note that high volume or low volume of trading are not conclusive proof, in themselves, of such transition periods. When taken in connection with the rest of the picture, however, as suggested above, they do quite regularly offer valuable evidence and profitable suggestion for proper action on the cyclical basis of long-swing investment.[1]

We have thus noted some of the more important and more useful theories, many of them based upon almost automatic formulae, for aiding the investor in a decision as to when long-swing views on the cyclical movement of securities should be changed from bullish to bearish, and vice versa.

There remain a few additional theories which, while based more upon psychology than upon definite statistics, are considered none the less useful by the author. As a matter of fact, the ability to interpret properly such psychological situations is quite often more important than the easier judgments based upon actual figures, especially in those troublesome cycles which do not offer the usual signals of "going to statistical extremes" before executing a major reversal of the cyclical stage.

Some Formulae Based on Popular Psychology

The most important and most general of such psychological formulae is based directly upon public interest in the market and, in fact, the other rules are little more than individual methods for measuring this popular interest. We have just examined one of them, the volume of trading. Although many other factors enter into the picture, it may still be said that when trading is high, large and active the public is usually interested in the market, and that when volume is low it generally indicates public apathy.

The formula, of course, is that high public interest suggests the distributive stage of our cycle, while low interest

[1] See Plate I, Frontispiece.

suggests the accumulative stage. Buy stocks for the long pull when public interest is low and sell them when it is high, provided, of course, that the other factors bear out such indications.

When to Buy and Sell

We can even formulate the other minor, but helpful, rules directly on this basis. Buy securities when there is no bullish excitement in the news, when there is a dearth of " tips " on the constructive side, when no one reads the financial pages of the newspapers, when the public has become sick of watching prices, when the brokerage offices are practically deserted. Such conditions are most apt to be prevalent during a time of slow accumulation.

Conversely, the psychological time to sell long-swing holdings is when bullish news is featured in the press over a considerable period of time, when " bull tips " are circulating swiftly, when everyone (even the crowd in the subways) is reading the financial section of the newspapers, when you can get market advice from your barber or your elevator boy, when there is " standing room only " in the board-room of your broker's office. Conditions like these always strongly suggest that the long-term cycle is nearing the end of the distribution phase and is about ready to begin the next stage of mark-down and decline.

The Summary of Extremes in Cyclical Theory

Having thus completed our study of the more important signals which indicate the turning stage of the cycle from up to down or from down to up, the reader should be struck with one common element in such factors. They all take their direction, their importance and their usefulness, from our basic consideration of an "extreme" condition or situation.

When security prices, business, steel operations, bond yields, interest rates, earnings, volume of trading, public interest and the general speculative fever are at an extreme level, that is our most dependable signal of a turn from one stage of the long-term investment cycle into the next stage which we know must follow.

Conflicting Indications vs. Unanimous Ones

Laying down such theoretical principles is, of course, an easier task than bringing them all into focus on any given situation, especially the more difficult cases which are bound to occur in practical investment. Very rarely, in fact, shall we find every one of these factors showing the extreme indications at the same time. That would be too easy. Very rarely shall we find the composite picture so definite in its forecast that our judgment on a dogmatic and certain conclusion is fully justified.

So true is this statement that the author would immediately suspect his conclusions based upon such a unanimous situation, if it were actually offered. For any market indications that are too apparent, too easy, too nearly unanimous, are also likely to be too widely appraised and too popularly held, and therefore most likely to be wrong.

So, the rules which we have studied are not the easy tools to rapid profit which they might appear to be on first examination. Their proper application, in composite, must be the result of careful personal thought, analysis and experience. But for the investor who uses them as an aid to his own common sense and to his consideration of all the other available factors, they should prove of tremendous practical value in the proper formulation of long-swing investment policies, based on the theory of cyclical pattern and movement.

Applying Past Theory to Future Practice

Before we close our present chapter, however, it is only logical to give some thought to the question which has perhaps long since assailed the reader of these pages. This cyclical theory of extremes works out very well in retrospect, after we have before us the long-term record of past cycles and can see the regularity of their extreme swings. How would it have worked if we had tried to apply it back in 1900, for instance?

Furthermore, even our easy record of past cycles shows us that the extremes are not always the same. New cycles go farther than, or not so far as, previous ones. How does that affect our theory in practice? And finally, we have had to admit that the whole principle went awry from 1924 to late in 1931. What assurance have we, right now, that future cycles will go back to the previous pattern? Does the 1929 bull extreme set up a *new* pattern for our future highs?

Two Important Rules for Long-Term Success

Such questions are both natural and logical. Some of them are frankly troublesome. Some of them cannot be answered at this time with any dogmatic guarantee of certainty. But none of them, in the author's opinion, are so unsatisfactory as to detract serious value from our basic theory of cycles.

We have already answered, with practical illustrations, the first question. It is most certainly easier to trace the past record than to forecast the future. But two considerations are important. First, let long-swing investment action be slow, gradual and in line with the principle of compromise.[1] Begin to sell as soon as the composite indications grow definite, but sell gradually, and do not throw total investment holdings overboard at the first danger signals. A corollary of such principle, of course, is the author's long-held theory that long-swing investment selling should never be entirely concluded and likewise that long-swing investment accumulation should never be consummated to the full limit of 100 per cent of reserves.[2]

The Necessity for Patience

In the second place, once the investor has switched his position, even gradually, on a basis of true and rational indications from our cyclical theory of pattern extremes, he should not allow himself to be turned back on his program by further continuation of the previous cyclical stage which he has deserted.

Our chief example is the extreme duration of the mark-up stage in 1929. The investor who had sold out in 1924 and 1925 was acting on sound cyclical policy and he should have resisted the strong psychological pressure to "get back in again" at higher levels.

How Cycles Tend to Disparity

The answer to our second question is similar to the first. The extremes are most assuredly never exactly the same in

[1] See Chapter IV, p. 97.   [2] See Chapter XII, p. 314.

successive cycles. The two points made above take care of a goodly portion of this anticipated discrepancy. But there is also another important suggestion in this respect. And let us remember that we are now talking only about the extremes of actual security price movement. We are leaving entirely out of consideration the invaluable aid of our other rules, like business indexes, public interest and the rest.

Considering solely, for the moment, the extremes of security price movement, however, it is only fair and reasonable that we make allowance for gradual change in trend of our cyclical extremes or the historical cyclical path. If one or more cycles have fooled us to the extent that they have gone farther in one extreme direction than previous cycles, then we may make due allowance for that tendency in the next cycle. There is still no certainty, but there is at least the valid suggestion that, if recent cycles have tended to advance their extremes higher or lower than preceding cycles, then the future cycles will continue this tendency.

What of the Next Future Cycle?

Such consideration brings us directly to the problem of our final question: the extreme case of the 1929 bull market, which went three times as high as the extreme of any preceding bull cycle in our American pattern. What does that out-of-line movement mean for the future? There are various angles of approach for a sensible answer.

In the first place, our cycle theory is not destroyed by such action, because "it has happened before"—not in American history, but in British history, which naturally carries security price data back much farther than our own.[1]

[1] See "Stock Market Theory and Practice," p. 701.

Insofar as it is possible to trace cyclical history back over the centuries it appears that such out-of-line movements occur only once or twice in a century, and that after each upheaval the normal cyclical pattern is resumed for many years. The author does not presume to utter a dogmatic forecast for the future of our own security markets, but merely states an observation of what appears to have happened in the past.

Will the 1929 Peak be Reached?

On a basis of our previous consideration, however, we should have no objection to a hypothesis suggesting that the influence of the tremendous extreme in 1929 might result in a somewhat higher peak for our next bull cycle than might be anticipated by ignoring that out-of-line era from 1925 to 1931. Here again, however, we disclaim any effort at current forecast.

Perhaps the most significant point of all in recent market history is the promptness with which our American cycle returned to the *lower* level of its normal pattern, in 1932, after the exuberant rampage only a few years previous. It may be valuable to note that such tendency approximates the record of England and other nations whose longer security market records afford our chief measure of comparison.

Dependence upon such comparisons is perhaps discounted by recent American devices, notably currency devaluation, but more human considerations like " the burned child " motif can hardly be changed by Government edict.

Summary of the Long-Swing Investment Approach

Thus, in spite of a conservative view that history never repeats itself exactly, in spite of the fact that no individual theory or market aid may be depended upon infallibly and over-confidently, it may still be hoped that we have gained a fair idea of the practical value inherent in the principles of long-swing, cyclical investment.

As has previously been noted, our current discussion has been based upon the mere extremes of security price movement. We do not claim to have removed all long-term difficulties or complexities. But the reader should at least have a fair grasp of the logical basis for our cycle theory of business and securities. He should be able to judge for himself the practical value which such a theory, and all of its minor and helpful corollaries, can bring to his own program and future policy on a basis of conservative, patient investment for the longer term.

CHAPTER IV

SHORT–SWING TRADING

From Long-Term to Shorter-Term Consideration

We have previously noted [1] that security price movements divide themselves roughly into three main types, the major or long-swing movement, comprising the great cyclical trends of a year or more, the intermediate, or short-swing movement, consisting of much smaller waves of anywhere from six weeks to six months, and the minor, or day-to-day, fluctuations of perhaps only a few points in extent and only a few days or weeks in time.

At the beginning of our last chapter we also noted that our entire study of the cyclical theory must relate chiefly to the first of these three market movements, the major, or long-swing, trends. Thus, our study of the past two chapters has been given over largely to a consideration of the fundamental theories of investment policy for the long-swing investor, who is content to take a position in the market and hold it patiently for a year or more.

Advantages in Both Types

In all of our discussion we have tried to be perfectly fair to this long-swing cyclical theory. We have studied its unquestioned advantages, to the exclusion of other valuable theories, and we have, it is hoped, gained a helpful insight into the very worth while basis of such long-term study and operation.

---

[1] See Chapter III, p. 42.

In the present chapter, however, we may go on to a more direct consideration of other theories applied not so much to long-swing movements as to the shorter swings of the intermediate pattern. These are the two important types of market activity from the standpoint of the average individual. We may dismiss the third type, or the minor, day-to-day fluctuations, with the simple statement that it is too speculative, too misleading, too dangerous for any but the specialist, the professional, the experienced and agile speculator to play with.

There is perhaps no very decisive dividing line between our two remaining, and important, types of movement, the long-swing and the short-swing pattern. Having already become familiar with the long-swing, or major, type through our preceding study of cycles, it should be easier to understand its differentiation from the intermediate type. If we refer once more, for instance, to Plate II, on page 55, we can detect numerous examples of the intermediate movement as opposed to the major trend.

Chart Examples of the Intermediate Move

In the Spring of 1915 there was a short intermediate movement, lasting only about a month, but a better example is seen between Points B and C, when the market touched a high point at the close of 1915, dropped off for a loss of more than 10 per cent, and then proceeded, almost a year later, to go on up into new high ground, well above the previous top. Near the end of the same chart, from Points R to S on the stock index line, we have another good example of the intermediate move. Here the major upward cycle was interrupted by an intermediate decline of better than 15 per cent and one which lasted for nearly five months, only to be followed by resumption of the long-swing advance into new high ground.

In both of these examples we have short movements of less than a year, constituting temporary reversals of the major direction. They are samples of the intermediate type, but they are merely a part of the larger, stronger and more important trend of the major, or long-swing, movement, which was checked but not permanently turned by the smaller reversals.

It may be admitted that these are not ideal examples, although they have the advantage of appearing on a chart which we have already studied. Clearer specimens of the intermediate fluctuation in a major move may be noted at Points E–G, and O–P, in Plate III, on page 91, and also in Plate VIII, on page 193, to say nothing of the examples which the reader may find for himself on practically any market chart.

Since the intermediate movement must set itself apart, so to speak, from the major trend, it usually develops as a minor move counter to that major trend. Most short-swing patterns are thus marked by their tendency to run temporarily against the main, or major, direction.

Intermediate Swings in Major Moves

This fact is the true foundation for the profit advantages inherent in operation from the short-swing standpoint, and also for the greater speculative dangers which such operation implies. A major, long-swing, cyclical advance may start its mark-up movement at 50, advance to 65, react to 55, advance to 80, react to 60, advance to 95, react to 85 and then stage its final advance to an objective of 100, where the long-swing cycle reverses. The long-term investor would buy at 50 and hold to 100, taking a profit of 50 points, or 100 per cent, but ignoring all of the intermediate, or short-swing, moves which interrupted the major one.

But the intermediate trader, who caught the short-swing reversals, had the opportunity of buying at 50, selling at 65, buying at 55, selling at 80, buying at 60, selling at 95, buying at 85 and making his final sale at 100. His theoretical profit would be 90 points, or 180 per cent, even if he continued to use only his original capital and not his accumulating profits.

While the major movement was travelling the distance from 50 to 100, taking perhaps a year or two in the process, the intermediate movement was playing tag from hither to yon, travelling a total distance of 130 points, in the same time that the major movement was progressing from 50 to 100, or only 50 points. In the example mentioned, therefore, the net travel distance of the major movement was only 50 points, but the total travel of the intermediate movements amounted to 130 points or about $2\frac{1}{2}$ times the long-swing distance.

Total Travel vs. Net Travel

Another glance forward, to Plate VIII, on page 193, will show a practical example of the same phenomenon. By the Summer of 1934 the major, or long-swing, trend of stock prices had been upward for two full years, following the extreme low point just under 35 in July of 1932, yet the averages had risen a net distance of only about 50 points, to the early Summer levels of around 85.

Yet if we take notice of the intermediate moves, we can find not only plenty of them but we can find a rather large distance of total "travel" for the same averages during those same two years. Note the important intermediate movements, interrupting the major upward trend, from September of 1932 to March of 1933, and the shorter one from late March to early April of the same year. Allowing for only the fairly substantial intermediate swings, and ignoring the minor, day-to-day moves, the total travel of the averages in these two years work out to a total of not so far from 300 points, or about six times the net travel of the major trend.

Greater Profit Opportunity in Short-Swing Operation

It is not difficult, therefore, to envision the tremendously magnified profit opportunities offered by short-swing operation as against cyclical, or long-swing, policies. Even the most experienced operator would hardly expect to get a perfect record out of his short-swing operations, or to achieve 300 points of total profit out of 300 points of total travel distance in any such major cycle. But if he had developed keen judgment on the intermediate turns he might be well satisfied with 200 points of such profit. And he *should* be well satisfied, for that return would compare with a maximum, or perfect record, of only 50 points, which would be the greatest profit possible for the long-swing investor, even under conditions of perfect judgment.

So far as success is concerned, the odds between the two types of operation are about equal, if we assume an average individual with average intelligence and market qualification. If he elects to play for the long-swing movements he has less worry, fewer chances of making a mistake, smaller brokerage commissions, and a much smaller profit if he is 75 per cent accurate in his judgment.

If the same man elects to play for the short-swing, intermediate movements, he will probably have more worry,
more chances of making mistakes, and higher brokerage
commissions, but he will have a much larger profit if he is
also 75 per cent accurate in his judgment.

On such a basis the election might be boiled down to a
question of whether the individual has good market judgment, whether he is willing to pay closer attention to the
market and to study a little more extensively.

Greater Risk and Necessity for Close Attention

In any comparison between short-swing and long-swing
trading with respect to necessary time, study and risk, it
must be admitted that the long-swing policy demands less
of such elements. It is, therefore, the safest course for the
average individual who is just starting out in his market
activity. For many types of personality, it must always
remain the proper policy, for some investors are simply not
suited for the greater attention and ability required by intermediate trading. Experience and some self-analysis are
necessary to show whether the individual is suited by nature
and inclination for the more advanced, more active and more
interesting stage of intermediate trading, with the tremendously magnified profit which it can bring to one's market
operation.

It may merely be stated at this point in our consideration
that this advanced type of activity is absolutely practical
for the average individual who is willing to give it the moderate amount of additional time and study which it demands
for true success and profit. The rules are just about as
definite, clear and practical for short-swing trading as the
ones which we have already studied for long-swing invest-

ing. The principles for the intermediate type of trading will be discussed in our later studies.

Superior Qualities of Intermediate Technique

While the author is being perfectly fair to the longer-term angle of investment, therefore, in admitting its simpler demands, he must also go on record as holding to the opinion that the shorter-swing method of operation is the more proper one for all except those who are automatically ruled out through special circumstance of faulty understanding, personal inertia or incomplete ambition.

Such a statement does not condemn long-swing investment by any means, for the ideal state is a combination of the two methods. The author simply feels that the truly successful investor will be the one who does not confine his operations either entirely to long-swing investment or entirely to short-swing trading, but who combines the two in a healthy mixture to make up his permanent operating policy.

Average Investor Should Know Both Types

There is still another reason, however, why the successful operator should be familiar enough with short-swing investment to use its principles in at least a part of his investment policy. That is, because a complete understanding of both methods will serve to guarantee that he knows one method from the other, that he will not confuse the distinct principles of the two, and that he shall know to which category he is committing himself in respect to each and every market action he may take. There is perhaps no more common or fundamental defect in the average investor's long-range activity than this one of confusing the separate aims and plans of long-swing investing and short-term trading.

The author holds no brief for practical separation of the two methods. As just mentioned, a healthy market program will include them both. But it is of the utmost importance that the individual be fully aware of his aims and his policy with regard to each separate commitment which he makes. He should decide in advance whether he is buying this security for the long pull or only for the short swing. And, barring very powerful upsets which could not have been foreseen, he should stick to that attitude straight through the entire campaign in that particular security.

Dangers of Confusing Short-Term and Long-Term Trades

This is, in fact, one of the reasons why long-swing investment is not so easy as it appears on the surface. It is comparatively simple to buy a stock and tell oneself that it is purely a long-swing proposition. But it is often exceedingly difficult to stick to that original policy. The stock goes up, a reasonable profit accrues; why not take it? Business is still depressed, there are no signals that the mark-up stage of the cycle is completed, but here is a profit.

As soon as such ideas are given head-room, the investor has deserted his original policy and has turned a long-swing investment into a short-term speculation. Taking profits is not to be condemned, by any means. But practical experience shows that psychology usually misleads the man who takes a profit at the expense of his basic investment policy.

If the profit is taken and the original plan was justified, the stock will almost certainly continue on up. Then there begins a gnawing at the psychological offices for repurchase — at the higher price. Yes, the investor took a fair profit, but look where the stock is now — why, he could have taken a profit double or triple the one he actually accepted. He knew it was a good stock. "Well, let's go back into it again."

The result is that long-swing and short-swing policies are confused in the investor's campaign. And the chances are that he buys the stock back fairly close to the point where he would have been selling it and taking his justly large profit, if he had held it straight through on the original long-swing premise.

Type of Trade and Aim Should Be Decided in Advance

Or, suppose that the stock declines after having been purchased for long-swing investment. Under such circumstances it is often even more difficult to keep one's perspective, and the danger is great that the long-swing stock will be sold out, just as though it had been bought for short-term speculation, very near the bottom of its cycle and just before the mark-up stage started it on the proper road to substantial long-term advance.

If there is danger in confusing long-term policy with short-term, then there is double danger of confusing short-term speculation with long-swing investment. The individual buys a stock which his best judgment indicates should advance rapidly over the next month or two. He buys it not for long-swing investment but for short-term speculation. The stock doesn't advance. It declines. Instead of getting out, and cutting his loss short, the speculator now decides to become an investor. But in switching his fundamental campaign policy he runs a most certain risk of holding his stock down through a long and disappointing cycle of mark-down.

He was justified in his purchase from a short-term standpoint, even if the stock was an intrinsically weak one and even if the cycle was indicated as near its top. But he was by no means justified, especially under such dangerous circumstances, in turning what started out to be a speculative campaign into a long-swing investment policy.

Original Policy Should Be Followed Through

In the final analysis, therefore, the danger of confusing our two major types of market policy arises once more from human frailty, from human nature, from cupidity and from unnatural and unreasoned bases of extreme hope or extreme fear. Without regard to their well-springs, however, it is safe to say that one of our greatest and most fundamental stumbling blocks is this simple failure to realize the difference between long-term investment and short-term speculation and to respect those differences implicitly and consistently throughout every practical commitment.

The individual should therefore be well aware of the particular specifications required for each of these two policies, as regards market conditions, general background, specific characteristics of the security involved, the size of the commitment, the risk to be taken and, above all, the future campaign policy, the aims in view when the commitment is originally made.

For, needless to say, once the fundamental differences between the two policies are clarified, then the varying treatment on the above scores becomes easily apparent. The long-swing investment is timed with fundamental and cyclical forces and should carry due allowance for temporary loss and the exercise of considerable patience. The short-swing speculation, on the other hand, is timed with more temporary and quick-acting technical factors, may comparatively disregard cyclical trends, but should be closely protected by well-laid plans for quick retirement and limitation of loss if action is not almost immediately favorable.

Short-Term Trading More Natural

Having surveyed the dangers in long-swing policy through failure to follow such policy through, patiently, bravely and confidently, to the finish, we may see another reason why adequate familiarity with the shorter-term method of operation is advisable even for the average individual. It is more nearly in line with human nature, with a desire for fairly rapid action. It takes much more mental and psychological restraint to hold a stock patiently, through long periods of drastic decline or heavy loss, perhaps for a tedious period of years, than it does to operate on the shorter-swing principle of intermediate swings.

A backward thought at the position of the long-swing investor in 1928 and 1929, will show how difficult the self-restraint may be that is demanded for true investment discipline on the cyclical principle. Not a great many individuals who sold out their stocks in 1924, adhering to the proper dictates of cyclical policy, were able to go through the hectic days of the next few years with a healthy smile, or without "taking on some flyers" on the side.

Far from condemning such action, the author would heartily approve it — provided only that the individual realized that he was no longer following the cyclical theory of long-swing investment, but was compromising in shorter-term speculation.

Practical Difficulties in Pure Long-Swing Investment

Our answer is now perhaps more plain to the man who says, " Well, you admit that long-swing investment is safer, easier and clearer than short-swing operation, and that it does offer a substantial profit. Very well, I'm not piggish and I don't care to be very active in the market or to bury myself in it. Take away your short-swing speculative stuff — I'll stop here, and I'll stick to the simpler elements of long-pull investment."

The conservative answer is, " All right, mister, you can try it, but I warn you that you won't succeed — not because all those statements aren't true, but simply because you won't stick to your theory. You'll start out with the best of intentions, but you probably won't be able to buck human nature. And even if you do succeed in holding conscientiously to your long-swing basis all the way through, it will be so difficult that you won't have much fun doing it.   If you win through, you should come out all right in the end but you are likely to be in 'hot water' a good part of the time, and it's a big question whether the game would be worth the candle."

The Psychological Hazards

It is impossible for the author to explain with proper emphasis, or for the uninitiated investor to realize, the purely psychological forces which assail the operator who is working purely and solely on the long-swing investment basis, without at least some allowance for emotional outlet in " part-time " or part-capital operations from the shorter-term angle.   If he is 90 per cent accumulated on the long-swing basis and runs into even only a temporary, short-swing reaction in the early stages of a bull market, he is very likely to "play safe" by taking profits and selling out some of the long-swing portfolio, contrary though such action may be to the basic dictates of his investment policy.

But how much easier is his problem — how much more honest and consistent he may be — if he has only 50 per cent of his capital in long-pull investment holdings, and 40 per cent in short-term speculative securities. When doubts regarding the justification for his long-swing policy assail him during the temporary shake-out, or on the weak signals preceding such decline, he can simply sell out some of his short-term holdings and maintain his investment position intact. Thus, merely by a varying policy, he smooths the way for our cardinal rules of compromise, for playing safe, for easing the strain on human nature and for practical protection of accumulated paper profits, and all this without deserting any of the theories inherent in his long-term investment policy.

Dangers Diminished if Investor Understands Both Types

The best argument, therefore, for combining short-swing speculation with long-term investment on the cyclical basis is that the average operator will do so anyway. And he is far better off if he realizes what he is doing than if he fools himself and snarls his basic aims by deciding to "give in" and to compromise in the middle of his campaign.

We have thus noted the psychological arguments for including the principles of short-swing operation in any well-rounded investment policy. We have also previously observed the more practical factor of greatly magnified opportunities for profit, through catching the intermediate swings of total travel instead of being satisfied with the net travel of long-pull cyclical movement.

There are still other, though minor, advantages in the intermediate policy. Operations on the long-pull basis require substantial capital for anything more than slow and gradual profit appreciation. On a basis of the four-year cycle [1] the long-term investor can hardly expect a consistent profit of more than 50 per cent every four years, or not much over 10 per cent per annum. This could, of course, be increased by selling short during the distribution stages of the cycle, but short-selling, even if possible under Government regulation, is hardly consistent with the conservative principles of long-pull investing. Without such a "reverse play" of the cyclical pattern, even the 10 per cent profit noted above would be reduced to perhaps substantially less than that figure by the deduction of commissions, taxes and other carrying charges.

Short-Term Trading Multiplies Profit

On the other hand, short-term operations, based upon the intermediate moves within the total cycle, can multiply such profit by two to four times over, thus providing greater profit, more rapid profit and the building up of small original capital into fairly substantial sums over a far shorter period of time than would be probable under the long-swing policy alone.

Again, the principles of short-term speculation are more consistent with short-selling. If such legitimate operation is still so considered in future years, in spite of recent legislation against it, then the profits from short-swing trading may be even more greatly increased.

[1] See Chapter III, p. 43.

Advantages in Capital Rotation

Another advantage of the short-term intermediate policy as opposed to the long-term cyclical theory is the opportunity for rotation of security operation. When total market capital is tied up in a specific campaign under the cyclical theory, it is forced to remain there patiently until the campaign and cycle are completed, perhaps several years later. But it is no secret that individual securities and individual groups are rotated in activity, action and public interest many times during the tedious progress of a full general cycle.

Perhaps the motor stocks move up first. Then they rest or react while the steels are given a whirl, and so on. The long-swing investor must sit tight on his own intermittently-moving campaign issues, but the intermediate operator is free to move his capital and attention around from one group to another. He may "ride" the motors while they appear strong and take his quick, intermediate profits when they begin to show signs of exhaustion. He may then transfer his funds and interest from the motors into the steels and ride that group for a while until the signals suggest switching into some other section which has been lagging behind the market but currently gives promise of coming to life.

More dangerous, yes. More speculative, yes. But for the conscientious student who has mastered the rules, the rotation thus suggested may be seen to offer many times the profit, even with imperfect success, than is taken by the long-swing investor who must stick with his chosen portfolio through thick and thin, through rally and decline, until the end of his major cycle is attained.

Summary of Short-Swing Advantages

Thus we may sum up the advantages of the intermediate approach to market operation in such factors as greater diversification of risk, greater mobility of capital and action, greater consistency with human nature, greater interest and personal satisfaction and, finally, the most important factor of all, the much greater opportunity for large and rapid profit.

It may, therefore, be hoped that the reader has attained sufficient faith and enthusiasm to lead him on into a more practical study of the intermediate type of operation and a consideration of the rules, theories and principles which can consistently be applied for success in short-swing speculation, just as we have already given consideration to the fundamental rules for long-swing investment.[1]

Approaching Short-Term Practice

From a fundamental standpoint, our introductory considerations shall not differ so much from those already noted in respect to the long-term cyclical pattern. In both types of operation, the final aim is the achievement of profit, and this aim, in its simplest form, is the purchase of stocks at low levels and their sale at higher levels. Our aim, whether we are operating for the long swing or the short swing, is still to " buy low and sell high." And in short-swing operation, just as on the cyclical principle, the logical method for such purpose is a cultivation of the ability to foresee turning points in the trend of security price movement.

[1] See Chapter III, p. 42.

Difference in Basic Technique of Intermediate Trading

In our consideration of the cyclical pattern for long-swing investment, we noted that the best method for such detection was the patient waiting until prices and other cyclical factors reached the extreme ranges of their preceding historical pattern.[1] Assuming that such patterns repeat themselves in a general way, we should anticipate a major turn in the price movement whenever our indexes touched the previous extreme levels, either on the top side or the bottom side.

But the very definition of our intermediate swings, occurring inside the longer and larger cycles and usually as temporary reversals, precludes the use of this cyclical pattern as a reliable formula. We might almost say that the principles of long-swing investment apply to the cyclical pattern only insofar as the pattern tends to repeat itself, while the technique of intermediate trading applies itself to the internal irregularities of each cycle, to that portion which does *not* follow any general pattern and which constitutes rather the " *variable* " element in the recurring cycle.

Variable Movement vs. Formula Movement

On the theory of cyclical investment we say that security prices, being now around 50, may be expected to advance to around 100 some time over the next few years, but we are by no means justified in saying what path prices will pursue during that long-term advance. It is this variable quality of the intermediate swing which comprises the principle of short-term speculation.

[1] See Chapter III, p. 47.

While we cannot foretell the intermediate swings so directly from the cyclical pattern, or so far in advance, we shall find plenty of basis for logical judgment as to the intermediate turning points, in our subsequent study.

So far as the movements in themselves are concerned, then, the long-term cyclical moves and the short-term intermediate swings differ chiefly in their duration and their extent. So far as their practical uses are concerned, they differ chiefly in the methods of forecasting which are properly applied to them. In both cases, the turning points are the critical considerations for profit and successful market operation. In short-term trading, the turning points come much more frequently and are subject to varying forms of analysis.

Cyclical Stages Applied to Shorter-Term Moves

Although much smaller than the major, cyclical moves, the intermediate ones may be said to partake of the same general pattern. The intermediate swing, for instance, is usually subject to a breaking down into individual phases which suggest the stages of our major cycle. As a matter of fact, we may apply the four primary stages of the major cycle [1] equally well to our intermediate cyclical move. If we examine such short-term swings closely we can usually detect the four successive stages of accumulation, mark-up, distribution and mark-down.

Perhaps the quickest way of illustrating such analysis will be the study of a specific stock and its intermediate price movement, and we may note the chart on Atchison, Topeka & Santa Fe common stock, shown in Plate III, on page 91, from February of 1933 into the early part of 1934.

[1] See Chapter II, p. 37.

If this chart went back as far as 1929, we should see that the extreme high of the major cycle in Atchison was around 300 in that year, and that the extreme low was slightly under 20 in the early Summer of 1932. We may consider that the long-term cycle was reversed at about that time and that the chart here reproduced is a portion of the major advancing cycle which followed the downward cycle of 1929–32. We are currently interested chiefly, however, in the cyclical pattern which may be found in the intermediate advances and declines beginning early in 1933.

Studying a Practical Chart History

Previous to the beginning of our current chart, Atchison had staged an intermediate advancing phase from 18 to 65 in the Summer of 1932. Then there followed an intermediate declining phase which carried prices slowly and irregularly back down to the base of 35, which we note on our current chart at around Point C. Ever since the higher levels at around Point A, the experienced observer might have been noting the increasing resistance to further decline and might have been expecting the bottom formation which gradually rounds out from Points B to D. This first portion of our chart, therefore, represents the first phase, or the accumulation stage, of our intermediate cycle.

Following Point D, the mark-up stage begins and the ensuing advance is rapid, up to the intermediate top of about 47 near Point E. Here we have another phase of hesitation, irregularity, or "congestion." And the gradual accretion of weakness suggests that the preceding "work" has been the distribution stage of our midget cycle, and that this is currently giving way, in turn, to the final stage of

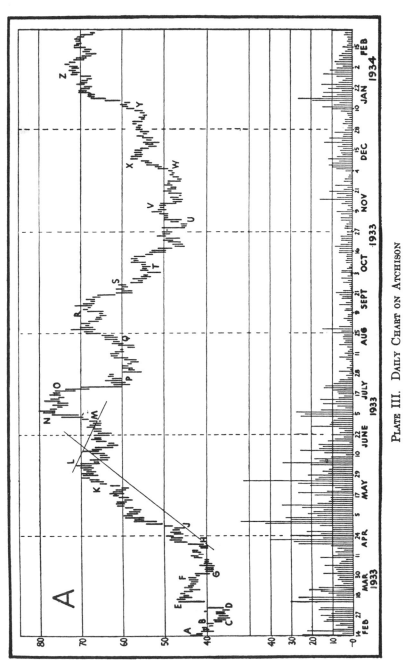

PLATE III. DAILY CHART ON ATCHISON

Showing several complete, intermediate cycles in price movement, with daily
volume in thousands of shares.

mark-down, which follows in the irregular reaction back to 39, at Point G.

Intermediate vs. Major Move

If we were looking at this chart action with eyes attuned only to the major, cyclical pattern, we should have to wait for further reaction to the old base around 35, or even the extreme bottom of 18, registered in July of 1932. We are careful, however, not to confuse our long-term cyclical pattern with the short-swing principle.

On the long-term investment cycle basis, the indications are strong that the July low in 1932 saw the extreme turn from the bear cycle into the new bull cycle. The current stage in the long-term investment cycle is, therefore, one of mark-up, and it would be illogical to anticipate that Atchison must retrace its course back to those extreme low levels before resuming its advance. This is true from the long-term angle, but it is much more logical, and much more useful, on a basis of our current consideration of the intermediate pattern.

How Cyclical Theory Aids Short-Swing Analysis

If the long-swing cycle is in the mark-up stage, then the intermediate reaction to around 39 at Point G is normal, but should end somewhere in that vicinity. We begin to note the familiar signals of increasing strength once more, notably just following Point G. Our proper guess is that we are embarking upon a new upward cycle of short-swing, intermediate movement, that the hesitation, or congestion area, around Points G to H may be considered accumulation, or the first stage of this new intermediate cycle, and that this phase is now giving way once more to the second phase of mark-up.

Our theories are practically confirmed following Point J, when the advance goes through into new high ground since the preceding March. If we should attempt to apply the same reasoning of pattern extremes in short-swing trading as we have used for cyclical investment, we should anticipate a top for this intermediate move at around 65, because that is where the preceding intermediate advance was stemmed in September of 1932.

By this time we know, however, that the long-term cyclical pattern of historical extremes does not apply to intermediate trends, and that, since the major cycle is upward, it would be logical rather to expect the present move to go above the top of the previous one.

Signals for Short-Swing Reversal

We have our difficulties, however, none the less, for from Points L to M the upward move turns over into what might easily be the distribution phase of the minor cycle. The author would not quarrel much with the short-term trader who accepted at least some profits shortly after Point L was reached. But by the time Point M was reached the stock was once more showing signs of strength.

The advance from M to N was sharp and rapid but the picture turned more definitely weak thereafter, especially in consideration of the high volume and activity, without material upward progress just after Point N. The picture was again unmistakably weak at Point O, and the intermediate trader should certainly have suspected the final stage of his upward cycle here and taken additional profits, even if he did not do so following Point L.

Watching the Moves Develop on a Practical Chart

Again, the mark-down stage of our minor cycle, from Points O to P, followed once more by accretion of new strength from Points P to Q, suggested strongly that we were going into our third minor cycle, from mark-down, through accumulation, and on into the mark-up stage following Point Q. Here again, however, the advance was short, weakness developed and intermediate trading commitments might logically have been sold out, gradually perhaps, anywhere around Point R. At Point S, and again at Point T, the mark-down phase was interrupted but the strength was hardly sufficient to inspire much confidence of a new upward cycle until Point V.

The experienced trader, and especially the technical student,[1] would not have been misled at this point, for the bottom formation was not sufficiently regular for trust until after the third bottom approach preceding Point W. Also, the long top formation, now open to analysis as one long period of distribution from Points K to R, suggested that this next bottom phase of accumulation should be longer than merely to Point V.

Three Intermediate Swings in One Major Cycle

Even without such aids of experience, however, the short-term trader would not have gone far wrong if he had purchased the stock between Points U and V, for the mark-up phase of our third cycle soon developed. It was strongly confirmed near Point X. The subsequent short reaction was more natural than significant of reversal, and the new

---

[1] See Chapter VI, p. 124.

mark-up stage continued fairly consistently through to Point Z, in February of 1934, where new suggestions began to appear that the upward cycle was passing over into a new downward phase of at least intermediate character.

The reader may calculate for himself the approximate total travel of Atchison, and the approximate net profit which he might have gleaned, even from only partially-efficient analysis and trading on the intermediate swings which we have noted in this chart. Let him then compare such total travel, or total profit, with the net travel, or long-swing movement, from 45 to around 70. It is fairly certain that the intermediate trader would have garnered a considerably larger profit than the 25 points which would have accrued to the long-term investor from the beginning to the end of our chart study.

Difficulties in Practical Operation

The reader need not believe for a moment that, in actual practice and even with the many other aids at his future disposal, he would have garnered all of the profit which "hindsight" can find in the succession of these minor cycles. In subsequent chapters we shall attempt to gain proficiency in the art of intermediate trading, through consideration of many aids in addition to those already noted. But even at that, the author would not imply that actual intermediate trading is as simple as it may appear from our preceding consideration of the short swings in Atchison.

There were difficult situations which we did not touch upon. There are bound to be surprises, false moves, false starts and the many confusing factors which always enter into practical market operation. The point is, however, that if we can tune our judgment to even only an approximation of proper analysis in short-swing trading, we should reap fitting and substantial profits, which can well repay the trader for a good deal of conscientious time and study.

Applying the General Rules to Practical Trading

Buying low and selling high is no clear-cut, easy task, but the individual with average intelligence and average ambition should be able to pick the cardinal turning points of intermediate swings with profitable accuracy, if he is willing to apply himself to learning the basic rules of common sense and the easier theories of technical practice.

The very fact that he will never be able to " hit the bull's-eye " on every important turn is an argument for the use of common-sense rules, some of which we have already noted,[1] rather than the basis for mistrust or despair.   One of the most important of such rules is the gospel of compromise.   The author would not have accomplished his entire buying and selling at any one single point, during the intermediate trading in Atchison, and he should certainly not expect the reader to do so.

The turns from one stage of the minor cycle into the next one of reversal are usually accomplished gradually and without any clear-cut dividing line between the successive steps. Just as this transition from one phase into another is a slow process, so should the trader's operation be one of slow, irregular, intermittent and scale trading.

The Gospel of Compromise

He need not try to catch every intermediate swing, or to catch any of them perfectly.   In the first place, he should not stake his entire capital on this form of trading, for we

[1] See Chapter I, p. 20.

have already seen that the ideal policy is a combination of this intermediate type with the long-swing cyclical type of operation.[1]

In the second place, he should not expect to be infallible in his short-swing trading. He need not recognize fully the signals of an intermediate top or sell out all of his intermediate commitments before the mark-down phase commences. But he should try to recognize all that he can, without going to extreme dogmatism at any one point. If he recognizes signals that *may* suggest a turn but do not guarantee one, he need not worry overly much. He will merely sell or buy a *part* of his total commitment.

If the suggestions of a turn grow more insistent, he will simply buy or sell more of his total line. If his analysis proves wrong, he can right his position again without much damage. If it proves right, then he will be on the proper side of the trend with the greater portion of his intermediate position anyway, and should profit on balance.

Tendencies More Practical than Dogmatic Extremes

If the trader knew himself to be infallible, then he could profit more rapidly by being dogmatic in his decisions, by switching his entire line completely at the critical points. But this volume is written for the investor who knows that he is not infallible. The others will not be in the market long anyway. And for the operator who knows his limitations and those of the entire human species, who realizes that no one can be 100 per cent correct in his market judgment, the author merely repeats that he would much rather be right on balance than attempt to make his victories perfect, scintillating and of exceptional profit.

[1] See Chapter IV, p. 78.

The former type of operator will be successful and will reap very satisfactory profit, on balance, while the latter will take two or three complete and beautiful "clean-outs" for every complete and beautiful "clean-up," and he will usually end up in heavy loss and failure.

Summarizing the Short-Swing Approach

Finally, it may be hoped that we have established logical and reasonable understanding of the two cardinal types of investment policy and operation — the long-swing investment principles, based upon patient tuning with the pattern of cyclical extremes, and the intermediate type of shorter-swing operation, based upon the secondary, but more profitable, fluctuations which take place inside the larger, major trends.

We should understand what both types are, what promises of profit they hold in practical trading and how they may be combined for ideal investment policy. And we should have a fair understanding of some of the principles which go to make up successful operation in each type of technique.

CHAPTER V

THE FUNDAMENTAL FACTORS

Long-Swing vs. Short-Swing Operations

Our chief study in preceding chapters has been an understanding of the two major types of market operation — long-swing and short-swing. We have investigated the cyclical theories with special reference to practical long-swing operations, together with some general rules for consistent success in both types of market activity.

In our preceding chapter we noted the comparative advantages of the shorter-term trading approach over long-swing investment policy, using specific market illustrations to assure our thorough understanding of the two distinct types of operation.

In our consideration of long-term investment,[1] we not only outlined the theoretical basis for this approach, but also observed some of the important factors for detecting major turning points, through use of the cyclical pattern of extremes, and thus embarked on a practical technique for long-swing profit.

Thus far, however, we have undertaken no such complete study of buying and selling as related to short-swing, or intermediate, trading. Our preceding chapter merely touched upon such factors indirectly through chart illustration, but our chief concern was an understanding of what the intermediate approach really is and how it differs from the long-term investment basis. Having thus become familiar with

[1] See Chapter III, p. 42.

the intermediate basis of trading, we may go on to a closer study of practical aids to market profit in this type of activity, just as we have already done for the longer-term method through our study of cyclical technique.

In this earlier consideration it was not particularly necessary to label our method of approach, because it was a fairly simple and general one. But as we go on to a closer study of practical technique in short-swing operation, it will be advisable for us to understand the difference between the two major methods of forecasting — the fundamental method and the technical method.

Fundamental vs. Technical Approach

In very brief outline, the fundamental approach to market analysis is based upon factors which are highly important in themselves, but which relate more to the aspect of "property ownership" and the quality of the property represented by our security holdings, similar to the considerations noted in our cyclical approach to long-swing investment policies.[1] Fundamental factors, therefore, include balance-sheet items, corporation management, prospects for the business, price-earnings ratios and, basically, anything which would normally and logically have a bearing upon the future state of the company's position and profit.

As such, the fundamental factors are slow-moving. They are so important that they practically rule the *eventual* trend of stock prices but, because they generally change slowly and act slowly, their effect upon prices is likely to be of a similar quality. In other words, fundamentals are more in consonance with long-term movements than with the intermediate swings.

[1] See Chapter II, p. 29.

Technical Factors are Closer to the Market

The technical approach to the market, on the other hand, is based upon factors which relate chiefly, or at least more directly, to the market itself, to the price movement which results from the constant interplay between those who want to buy, and who thus advance prices, and those who want to sell, and thus depress prices. The technical approach is a scientific effort at judgment and forecast through studied consideration of such opposing forces which, in the final analysis, are directly responsible for the rise or fall of security quotations in any open market.

In other words, the fundamental factors suggest what *ought* to happen in the market, while the technical factors suggest what actually *is* happening in the market. The fundamental fact that the earnings of a certain stock are advancing rapidly would suggest that the stock ought to go up. But if, in spite of this argument, the technical fact is that there is more of the stock for sale than to be purchased, then the technical factor naturally wins out, at least temporarily, over the fundamental factor. It is, therefore, the more important of the two angles for the trader who wants to know what the movement of that stock will be in the immediate future.

The technical student does not stop to reason out the basis for this possibly surprising technical fact. He is willing to admit the logic of the fundamental argument that there *should* be more buying power than selling pressure, since earnings are rising. But when the technical position shows him that such is not the case, and that there is, in fact, more selling pressure than buying power, he does not sit down to ponder upon the inconsistency of the fact. He simply accepts the judgment of the market-place, which is technical action, and he anticipates a decline in the stock instead of the advance which fundamentals would have suggested.

Fundamentals Act More Slowly

We have previously noted that fundamental considerations, like the increase of earnings, are likely to rule the eventual course of the stock's price, since if earnings do actually continue to advance it is likely that the selling pressure, currently greater than the buying demand, will soon lose its force and the buying will become stronger than the selling. When this happens, however, it will be reflected in technical action just as definitely as is the current balance of selling pressure. And, therefore, until it does happen, the technical student will continue to lay greater emphasis on the fact that the stock is actually weak than on the fact that it should be strong.

If we understand the basic difference between technical factors and fundamental factors, therefore, we shall have no difficulty in realizing that the technical factors operate more quickly, are more directly related to the immediately future movement of a stock, but that the fundamental factors, though they act more slowly, are often the more important since they may signal a future change in the technical balance well ahead of its actual development.

Easier and Clearer in Forecasts

Another decided advantage of the fundamental aspect is a purely practical one. The technical factors, while closer to the market and thus more valuable for immediate forecast when properly analyzed, are less tangible than the fundamentals. If we could always depend upon technical analysis being correct, we would probably be justified in paying very little attention to the fundamental analysis. But the fact of the matter is that fundamental considerations are usually clearer, easier to evaluate and more dependable than are the technical factors.

Even though they work more slowly, therefore, and are not so directly related to immediately future price movements, the fundamental considerations are often more important, simply because they are more easily analyzed and more definitely apparent.

Fundamentals Usually Superior for Long-Term Operation

Since such is the case, it follows easily that fundamental considerations are much more important and much more useful for the long-swing investor, while technical considerations are generally more useful for the short-swing trader.

Fundamentals work out more slowly but often more reliably. The long-swing investor is in no hurry and can afford to ignore the more rapidly effective, but shorter, dictates of technical consideration. The intermediate operator, on the other hand, is more interested in these shorter and intermediate swings, which often run temporarily counter to the fundamental, or cyclical impetus, and he will therefore pay a great deal more attention to the technical factors than will the long-swing investor.

Having established an understanding of the basic differences between fundamental and technical approach, we may resume consideration of the chief aims in our current chapter, which are to note some of the uses of fundamental consideration, with special regard to the intermediate trading swings.

It may perhaps appear inconsistent to take up such a study immediately after we have noted that fundamental considerations are more important for the long-swing investor than for the short-term trader. There are two useful points of explanation which appear definitely in order.

Also Valuable in Short-Term Technique

In the first place, let the reader recall that we can never afford to ignore one type of approach to profitable market operation simply because another approach may seem to offer superior advantage. The author has stressed in the past, and will continue to stress in the future, his basic premise that success in market operation does not come from any one, single rule or type of approach, but that it develops out of a composite judgment resulting from common-sense appraisal of any situation from the broader aspects of its every conceivable angle.

The investor who operates on a basis of fundamental considerations, to the exclusion of all technical factors, is discounting his chances for success just as surely as the man who operates only from the technical basis and without regard for fundamental considerations. This is just as true as is the fact that the individual who utilizes both long-swing and short-swing principles of investment is giving himself many times greater chances for success than the man who uses only one method to the exclusion of the other.

Even though the author holds to his previous theorem that technical action is more practically important for the intermediate investor than is the fundamental approach, it remains not only advisable but necessary that we study both of them so that we may weigh the advantages of each and combine them in our practical judgment for future profit.

Applying Fundamentals to Short-Term Analysis

The second, and minor, point of explanation follows directly from such consideration. In Chapter III [1] we spent considerable time on a study of the more general but technical principles of cyclical pattern for long-swing investment, including the consideration of price movement as related to the historical extremes of preceding cycles.

In the same chapter we also applied the more fundamental aspects of business, profits and general conditions to this same problem of long-swing investment on the cyclical formula. And in our immediately preceding chapter we have advanced into a new consideration of successful operation from the standpoint of short-swing, or intermediate, operation. We may now apply the somewhat varying theories of fundamental and technical approach to this new study of intermediate trading, just as we did to long-swing investment.

The remaining study of our present chapter, therefore, will be devoted to the fundamental factors as they affect intermediate trading, while in our succeeding chapter we shall take up the more technical factors as they, in turn, may prove useful for success in this same type of short-term operation.

Two Aspects of Fundamental Approach

Our final point of exhaustive explanation should introduce logically the chief emphasis which we shall place upon

[1] See p. 42.

this study of fundamental theory in short-swing investment. Because we should already be fairly familiar with the basic considerations of the fundamental approach, as it has been applied to long-swing investment, and also because it is not so useful in short-term trading as in cyclical investment, the author does not intend to enter upon any exhaustive explanation or review of the fundamental approach as it is conceived by the average operator. We shall substitute, rather, an examination of factors which, while they may properly be termed fundamental, are not usually applied on such a basis, or which are usually not applied at all in practical trading.

Conventional Aspect Well Known to Average Investor

Plenty of weighty volumes, by this writer[1] and by many others, have been written with exhaustive excursions into the field of fundamental factors as they are ordinarily conceived. Any full discussion of such elements as corporation set-up, balance-sheet analysis, earnings, etc., should, therefore, constitute a mere review for the present reader.

Even as a form of review they are probably unnecessary and they will be passed over in quick order. They are important, without doubt, in the proper composite evaluation of any situation. But we have already touched upon some of the most basic factors[2] in our study of cycles, and if the reader is desirous of more complete discussion he may refer to other volumes on the subject.[1]

As a matter of fact, there are also other reasons for slighting full consideration of the usual fundamental factors in this study, in addition to the ones just noted. Not only are

[1] See " Stock Market Theory and Practice," and its Bibliography.
[2] See Chapter III, p. 65.

such factors less important for the short-swing trader than for the long-swing investor but they have lost, in the past decade, considerable of their previous usefulness even for all classes of investors.

Conventional Fundamentals have Lost Chief Value

This is due not merely to the rapid development of technical science, and its patent advantages over fundamentals, but also to a growing conviction that fundamentals are not so practical in themselves as they used to be. The basic difficulty probably is that such fundamental considerations have been too widely publicized and may, therefore, be used to mislead the investor in modern trading.

In bygone days, and before the development of technical science, the powerful and professional element appears to have placed considerable reliance on fundamental statistics, but that was because not many people had access to such figures or had the proper knowledge or desire to study them.

Then came wide dissemination of the theoretical advantages inherent in a study of fundamental considerations, followed by eager public demand for the figures. And later, answering this demand, came more complete statistics, more rapid and widespread circulation of them, through the medium of swift communication, newspapers, statistical advisory services, radio, and what not.

Disadvantages of Old Approach

We shall see from later consideration [1] that even this mere fact of wide public dissemination of fundamental statistics might easily sound the death-knell of their practical value,

[1] See Chapter VIII, p. 203.

at least for the short-swing trader. They can now be used either without much meaning at all, or for the purpose of actually misleading the public. If we grant the author's frank and dogmatic hypothesis[1] that the group of so-called "insiders" or market professionals are out to cross, or fool, the average operator, then such persons have a strong ally in the realm of fundamentals. If they know that a goodly portion of the public will buy stocks on publication of a bullish earning statement, then they can make their profits either by advance information and putting the stock up before the earning statement becomes public, or by depressing the stock soon after the statement has appeared and after the public has bought on the basis of that statement.

Both of these methods are not only possible but quite probably used to "cross" the public's market operation. We have already seen[2] that the average fundamental items of business news are slow-moving in their collection and publication, and that the market has usually started up or down considerably before such fundamental stimuli are made public. In addition to this consideration we may also recall our other observation[3] in this same regard, that corporation officials are in possession of such fundamental data long before the public, and that they often constitute in themselves a powerful moving force in market trends.

Conventional Fundamentals Often Misleading

When we consider further the usually close connection, at least for the garnering of information, which exists between many market professionals and this class of corporation official, we need not marvel so much at the frequent

---

[1] See Chapter VIII, p. 177.   [3] See Chapter III, p. 52.
[2] See p. 100.

suggestions that the bullish earning statement, and many other fundamental considerations, have been fully discounted long before they come to the public press and the public eye.

The natural result of such a tendency is still another detraction from the worth of the average fundamental "statistic." The public has been taught to buy stocks on the news of bullish fundamental reports but, since the insiders have discounted them by buying in advance of publication, they sell out to the public when "the good news is out."

Small wonder then that the public is often "crossed" [1] on fundamental theories, especially when the professional "insider" may frequently go even a step further and deliberately sell the stock in question, thus depressing it temporarily after the public has bought on good news, in order to discourage such buyers into selling out again at lower levels. Small wonder that there are so many practical examples of our previous illustration [2] suggesting that fundamentals show what *ought* to happen, while technical factors show what *is* happening.

New Attitude Toward Fundamentals is Necessary

Happily, however, such considerations complete the important and necessary indictment of fundamental factors as a basis for short-term trading. We would not have the reader turn his back upon such fundamentals merely because of the disadvantages mentioned. In spite of their drawbacks they are definitely useful, and definitely worthy of consideration in arriving at our composite judgment even for the short swing. And we have already discovered, in

[1] See Chapter VIII, p. 181.   [2] See p. 101.

previous chapters, their unquestioned value for guidance in cyclical theories of long-term investment.[1]

As a matter of fact, although he has long pioneered the cause of technical science over fundamentals, the author feels that there is now at least the potential danger of going too far to that new extreme, and that many short-swing operators do not pay sufficient attention to the old fundamental factors. Having first run them down, therefore, in fair attention to their drawbacks, we may again set them up, though in a somewhat newer and more valuable angle than the old-time conventional type of consideration.

Earlier in our current chapter, we promised that we should skip over the fundamentals, as conceived and studied by the average market operator, and concentrate on a new approach to the old subject. Our "skipping" has perhaps been drawn out into a tedious walk, but it may be hoped that the author's philosophy has been meanwhile clarified and that the way has been better prepared for this new approach to the practical advantages in fundamental consideration for shorter-term operation.

Element of Time in Fundamental Technique

Our easiest point of departure is from the previous consideration that the conventional type of fundamental information, applying to current or future earnings and prices, is very often made public too late to be of real service to the short-term operator, and is thus frequently a snare and a delusion instead of a valuable aid.[2] We saw that such fundamental factors as dividends, balance-sheet items, state of current business, advance orders and all of the other fundamentals affecting earning power, have their value re-

---

[1] See Chapter II, p. 27.   [2] See p. 108.

duced for the average individual because they are known to the corporation officials and professional insiders before they are made public.[1]

The important point, then, is not so much that fundamentals are not exceedingly valuable for the short-term operator, in themselves, but that their "time of action" is wrong for the average operator. Such fundamentals work successfully and profitably for the insider, but that is because his advance information has enabled him to anticipate future news and future public demand.

Anticipating Fundamental Factors

All that the average operator needs to do, therefore, in order to turn fundamental considerations from a stumbling block to a definite profit aid, is to place himself in such a position that he can also anticipate the future development or publication of such fundamental factors. If he is able merely to anticipate the *publication* of such elements, he will be on a footing closely equal to the average corporation official and insider whom we have been considering. If, in addition, he is able to anticipate the future *development* of such factors, as well as their eventual publication, then he will have placed himself even a few steps ahead of the more conservative and less imaginative of the "insider" group.

The New Approach to Fundamental Forecasting

Granted that such is the case, how can the average operator anticipate not only the publication of fundamental factors but their actual future development? When the au-

[1] See Chapter III, p. 52.

thor makes answer that the individual can accomplish this merely through a liberal utilization of common sense, keeping up with the daily news, analyzing future trends, and through logical reasoning and deduction, the reader is likely to be greatly disappointed. We have been "building up," through previous gradual and logical approach, to a money-making climax for the use of fundamental factors in successful short-swing operation. Yet all that we now offer is the simple advice to use one's head and to try to *anticipate* higher earnings, increasing orders, and so on.

The author is conscious of the possibility of such reader disappointment. He admits the extreme simplicity of his theorem, but he is just as thoroughly convinced of its basic value in practical trading as he is that the average operator loses countless opportunities for profit simply because he considers such basic rules too simple and self-evident for serious evaluation and study.

Back to Simple Common Sense

This entire volume has been conceived as an approach to market profits for the layman, or the average market operator. The author has written perhaps more weighty volumes on involved and technical theories. But he should never have undertaken the present approach if he were not firmly convinced that the average individual could gain new profits in his practical market operation through the re-statement of old rules, basic formulae, simple logic and normal common sense — through a new and more serious approach to such simple, and therefore often overlooked, considerations.

It is easy enough for the reader to say that he has known, from his market youth, the advantages of anticipating increased business and improved earnings for a company or its stock. But let him ask himself how thoroughly, how sincerely, how consistently he has actually concentrated his practical study on such simple consideration, and how often in the past year's trading he has really acted on the dictates of such a study.

If the answer is "not at all," as it may easily be, then the author's answer is that he has missed many opportunities for real profit, simply because he has not brought his native ability and normal analysis to bear on such a simple basis of market reasoning and forecast.

Nor are such statements the result of idle theory or impractical logic. There are plenty of recent examples. And we may develop our arguments and our new approach to the rediscovery of "gold in the abandoned workings" of simple, old-fashioned logic, as we consider a few of such examples.

Practical Application of the New Fundamental Approach

Take first the case of liquor prohibition and the history of the repeal movement. For many years prior to 1931 the movement for repeal was gaining force. Public sentiment was turning slowly but surely from the "great experiment" to the victory of practical reason. In the early Summer of 1932 the Democratic National Convention incorporated into its presidential campaign platform a strong plank for prohibition repeal. True, the Democratic party had done much the same thing four years previous and had been defeated. But the situation was by no means the same.

The American people had gone through the greatest depression in their history. They wanted change, they wanted revenue that repeal would bring, they wanted sur-

cease from " bootlegging." In short, they had swung tremendously in favor of repeal during those intervening four
years. Even the Republicans sensed this drift, and the
results might eventually have been the same no matter
which party won the 1932 presidential election.

Here was one of the greatest " experiments " of modern
times giving suggestion of dying a painless death. It might
be a slow death but it was strongly promised. And the financial repercussions, the security market implications inherent
in the progress of repeal were so tremendous, so revolution-
ary, that the accomplished fact of prohibition repeal was
highly worth waiting for, merely so long as the tendency
in that direction was under way.

We need not go into details on the corporations and securities which would profit from such repeal. Many of
those whom subsequent history shows to have profited
greatly could not logically have been foretold. Our arguments and our practical considerations do not concern such
companies. But they do concern the brewing industry, the
hard-liquor industry, the distilling industry, alcohol business, the glass business and the rest whose profit was self-
evident. They do concern companies and stocks like American Commercial Alcohol, United States Industrial Alcohol,
Schenley Distillers, Hiram-Walker, and, most of all, National Distillers Products.

Anticipating New Factors Instead of Analyzing Old Ones

National Distillers was, in fact, the chief remaining corporation of the pre-prohibition days, still legitimately doing
business on a consistent scale. It had continued volume
operations, even at reduced scale, in the manufacture of
medicinal spirits under Government authority. It owned

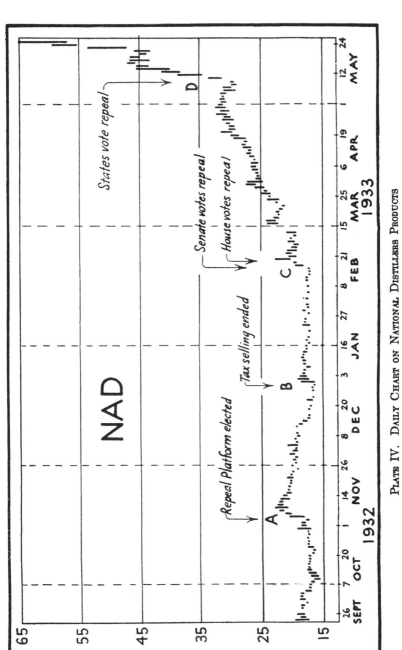

PLATE IV. DAILY CHART ON NATIONAL DISTILLERS PRODUCTS

Showing period of slow accumulation prior to Prohibition repeal boom.

the largest stocks of aged and bonded liquor legitimately available in this country. Yet throughout most of 1931, while public sentiment was growing constantly stronger for prohibition repeal, National Distillers common stock was available well under 25. And for several weeks preceding the Democratic National Convention of 1932 it was available below 15.

Even in the Autumn of 1932 the stock dragged around between 15 and 20. On November 8, 1932, President Franklin D. Roosevelt was elected on a strong repeal platform. What had previously been a good possibility was now become much more than a practical probability. Yet a glance at Plate IV, on page 115, showing the chart on National Distillers Products from the Fall of 1932 through the following Spring, shows an advance to only about 23, at Point A, on this significant news.

The author does not argue that the way for prohibition repeal was clear and easy. There were still many doubts, difficulties and uncertainties remaining in the picture. But he does maintain that mere common-sense consideration of the logical trend of future events should have led to moderate commitments in National Distillers on our basis of short-swing trading operation, during the months that followed.

The Case of Prohibition Repeal

At Point C, when Congress voted submission of repeal for state consideration, the logical suggestions took another upward bound, yet the stock did not advance far or fast. Not until Point D, when the first individual states began to vote strongly for the repeal amendment, did the true " markup " stage begin. Even then, with repeal a practical certainty, the stock was still available under 45 for several weeks, compared with a peak in July of 125.

The author does not argue that all of this spectacular advance was justified or normal. But he does argue that the short-term operator who had cultivated the proper utilization of thorough analysis and the logic of trends, would have made plenty of profit even if he had waited, conservatively, until the probability of repeal became a practical certainty at around Point D, and then sold out near the end of our currently presented chart, before pool manipulation became excessive.

Let the reader ask himself now whether such simple rules of logic, thought and common-sense reasoning as were indicated in this example are too simple and too apparent for his profitable consideration in practical short-term trading.

Applying the New Approach to Motor Stocks

Or we may take the example of the automobile industry, during the depression of 1930 and 1931, and on into the recovery period of 1932 to 1934. There was perhaps no special advantage in a 1929 realization that motor sales would be hurt exceedingly hard by the stock market panic of that year, because practically all groups and issues went down together.

There was genuine profit, however, from 1932 on, in a common-sense analysis of the trends which might logically be expected for the motor industry, and particularly for the low-priced manufacturers. Again the "depression" enters into the basic picture. The automobile had long since become a practical and established necessity for the average American family, but it was also a capital goods product, still partaking of the luxury classification in respect to the number of years that might elapse before replacement. The average family would ordinarily desire a new car about every three or four years, but automobiles were manufactured "good" enough so that they could be *made* to last at least twice that time if necessity so dictated.

Analyzing Development of a Profitable Situation

During the depression years of 1929 to 1932, and even through much of 1933, necessity *did* thus dictate in no unmistakable financial terms for most individual owners and families. The significant result was not so much the sharp decline in normal sales of new cars for the depression years as the common-sense and simple conclusions that the "short-term thinker" could so logically draw from this set of circumstances.

Fifteen minutes of simple reasoning was sufficient to suggest that the number of automobiles from six to eight years old and more, and therefore in dire need of early replacement, was growing rapidly, even while the motor business and general industry were in the throes of depression. For practical proof of such theories one needed merely to take an appraising notice of the old models which passed on the roads of 1932. Nor was it difficult, for the normal individual accustomed to using common sense as well as capital in his market operations, to reach the simple and logical conclusion that the first major capital purchase of the average American family, when the depression lifted, would be a new automobile.

New clothes, paying back rent, and other absolute necessities might come first for the hard-pressed, but such expenditures are in consumptive goods rather than in capital goods. They had held up fairly well through the depression, due to their classifications as prime necessities, their short life and the necessity for fairly regular replacement. No such security bargains were offered, therefore, in the consumptive goods field as appeared in the capital goods market. And it is doubtful if the latter classification held any more certain, more rapid or more profitable opportunity than the field of motor stocks.

Common Sense vs. the Old Fundamental Approach

In spite of the logical reasoning in this simple and almost certain conclusion, there were plenty of " skilled and experienced " operators who preferred to pore over tickers, balance sheets, earnings statements, bearish tips and brokerage letters. They passed up, perhaps as beneath their ability and advanced consideration, such profit opportunities as this situation offered, and as might have been analyzed by a few minutes of " simple " reasoning and common-sense deduction.

In the Spring of 1932 the author held many heated arguments with automobile writers and specialists, who were supposed to know their field, and who soundly berated his judgment because he was consistently recommending the motor stocks for early and profitable recovery. Their chief arguments were to the effect that motor prices had not come down sufficiently and that the public would not buy until prices had been drastically reduced. The author respected the technical judgment of such experts, but he questioned their common sense. They, like many average traders, were too busy concentrating on great and intricate problems of their field to see that the proper solution lay in the relatively simple and commonplace deductions inherent in plain logic.

Selecting Individual Stocks on the New Basis

A corollary of such reasoning, of course, included the suggestion that, when the nation began to come out of the depression and to replace worn-out automobiles, the major demand would be not for the higher-priced cars but for the extremely low-priced, but serviceable, ones.

When the author first began his insistent recommendation to buy automobile stocks, early in 1932, he concentrated on such low-priced leaders as General Motors and Chrysler. The former was selling around 10 and the latter at about 8. Even in the Fall of 1933, when the bevies of brand-new, and radically different-appearing, cars on the road offered practical proof that the theoretical reasoning was correct, and that the public was really buying new automobiles, General Motors dipped to below 30 and Chrysler to under 40.

By the early part of 1934 General Motors was above 40 and Chrysler had touched 60. Let the reader ask himself again at this juncture, whether our plea for the simple approach to anticipation of market fundamentals is still *too* simple for his thoughtful consideration.

Applying Fundamental Logic to Other Fields

There are plenty of additional examples in the history of recent stock market trading and profits. The New York City mayoralty elections in the Fall of 1933 resulted in a set-up which suggested a fairer facing of the traction situation. Yet it was not until many months after the election that Brooklyn-Manhattan Transit, Interborough and the other traction securities swung into their best advances.

Any individual who cared to spend a small amount of time on the subject could have noted that gold stocks are the outstanding group to benefit through a business depression, since their costs decline while the price of their product holds stationary.   Yet Alaska Juneau was still selling around 5 in the Autumn of 1930 and did not begin its spectacular advance until the Spring of 1931.

Likewise, when the United States deserted the official gold standard in April of 1933, there was only one logical deduction for the thoughtful operator, and that was depreciation of the American dollar and a consequent advance in the number of dollars payable for each ounce of gold. Yet the spectacular upward moves in the gold stocks did not come until June and July of that year.

Early in 1933, when Continental Can first began to publicize the sale of motor oil in individual tin cans, instead of in bulk, to insure a fresh and untampered product, the stock was selling in the 30's.   By the end of the same year, when the oil industry had responded, as any thinking operator could have foreseen, Continental sold above 80.   During the same period American Can rose from below 60 to over 100.

Profit in Individual Situations

When the writer began to hear people discussing the spectacular advance in Atlas Tack late in 1933, and to speculate on why Boston was telephoning insistently with advice to buy more of the stock, it was selling around 30.   When the obvious explanation was finally disclosed it had dropped to below 10.

When the brief announcement was made, in December of 1933, that Servel was building an addition to its plant at

Evansville, Ind., the stock was still selling below 4. In April of 1934, when a favorable earning report was published, and forward business was reported good, the stock was selling for more than double that figure.

In the Spring of 1933, when it first became apparent that the air-conditioning companies were finally prepared to "shoot" their product for the coming Summer, American Radiator was selling at about 5. At the height of the Summer selling season in the same year, the stock had advanced to 19.

Anyone who kept even moderately up with the times knew how rapidly and logically the "amateur movie" hobby was developing all through the depression of the early thirties, and common sense alone suggested the rapid impetus for Eastman Kodak. Yet the stock was available at 36 in 1932, and for a low of 46 in 1933. At a price of over 100, in the Summer of 1934, "the public" was still considering it a good purchase, for the earnings were only then becoming apparent, which common sense could have foreseen when the stock was selling 50 points lower.

And so we might go on, almost without end, citing specific examples of how anyone, with a reasonable amount of normal grey-matter and the will to use it, may realize short-term trading profits in substantial volume merely through the sincere application of logic and thoughtful reasoning power to the comparatively simple factors of fundamental analysis.

Correlating Our Progress

We have seen in previous chapters how the more conventional fundamentals of business and long-term trends can be applied to cyclical investment, and also how the more technical, or market, principles can also be applied to this type of investment through the pattern of price extremes.

In the current chapter we have tried to arrive at a new viewpoint through which the fundamentals may be more successfully applied to shorter-range, or intermediate, trading operations.

In the two following chapters we shall attempt a condensed appraisal of how the more technical factors of pure market movement may also assist us on our road toward consistently profitable operations on this same basis of the intermediate swings.

CHAPTER VI

THE TECHNICAL FACTORS

Slow-Acting vs. Quick-Acting Factors

In the preceding chapter we noted some of the differences between the fundamental and the technical approach to market consideration, as we attempted a specialized application of the fundamental factors to successful short-term, or intermediate, trading operations.

We saw that the fundamentals are basic factors, dealing with earnings, corporation balance sheets, dividends, etc., which are more reliable over long periods of market movement since they forecast the logical future trend. But we also saw that the technical factors are more likely to be valuable for trading forecasts in the *immediate* future, because they are drawn directly from price action and, therefore, show what is actually going on at the present moment, rather than what is likely to develop if fundamentals continue to point in a certain direction.

Technical Factors vs. Fundamentals

If we grant our previous hypothesis [1] that fundamentals suggest what the market ought to do over a period of time, while technical factors show what it is actually in process of doing, then we automatically imply that market movements are not always in direct accord with the fundamental indications.

[1] See Chapter V, p. 101.

Anyone but the veriest beginner will readily admit the truth of such a thesis. He can recall plenty of examples, without doubt, of a stock which he was led to purchase because of favorable earnings, or dividend yield, or book value, but which proceeded shortly to decline, in apparent denial of such fundamentally favorable suggestions.

How Technical Position Crosses Fundamentals

We have already seen [1] one important basis for such action in our discussion of the disadvantages in relying solely on published information of fundamental factors. Another reason, of course, may be incorrect emphasis by the individual, contrary to the more conclusive actions of other operators who place an opposing analysis on the same indications. Still another reason for the not uncommon " crossing " of fundamentals by market action is to be found in the speculative operation of the " inside " element. In view of the recent popular uprising against such tactics it is not necessary to call them " pool operations."

The Manipulative Angle

We need not give them any specific name at all, if we so desire. But it does seem advisable to keep in mind the possibility that even only loosely organized groups of traders, or even a single powerful operator, may quite conceivably buy or sell a stock in sufficient quantity to tend its price movement in a misleading direction, away from the logical trend suggested by fundamentals.

Nor need we enter here into any exhaustive discussion touching upon either the legitimacy of such " manipula-

[1] See Chapter V, p. 108.

tion," or its survival under the "new deal" meted out to security operation under Government legislation. Without recording any personal views on such questions, the author may simply repeat his previous statement [1] that it is much easier for law and Government to change the rules of a game than to change the human nature and the human traits and qualities of the individuals who play that game.

Plainly dishonest and openly unfair abuses will unquestionably tend to be corrected. But so long as our great security exchanges are allowed to perform their legitimate function as a market-place for free buying and selling of securities, there seems no reason to suspect that the so-called professionals or insiders will abandon their business of speculative trading.

The Logic of Illogical Market Action

On such a basis it is not difficult to see why market movements may, for considerable intervals, run counter to the dictates of what appear to be valid fundamental indications. If we simply grant the premise that there are shrewd individuals in security trading who profit from their large-scale operations, we must also grant that they must trade in opposition to the "public." If one group of operators makes a living out of trading, then some other group must provide those profits.[2]

No profit is made simply by buying or selling a stock. The profit comes from buying low first and selling higher later, or from selling high first and repurchasing later at a lower level. If the "inside element" buys when everyone else is buying, there will be no one left to sell to later on. The professional must, therefore, buy when the public is selling, and

---

[1] See Chapter II, p. 35.   [2] See Chapter VIII, p. 186.

sell when the public is buying, in order to realize his profit. A proper understanding of this simple piece of logic is at the bottom of trading success and the basis for the equally important consideration that the market does not always do what seems most logical or what the "public" expects it to do.[1]

The Basis for Technical Studies

Such consideration explains an important basis for the validity of technical factors. If security prices always moved directly in accord with earnings, dividends, news and the other fundamental indicators in the hands of the general public, or in their analysis of such factors, then there would be no overwhelming necessity or advantage in the study of technical indications.

But if we grant the hypothesis that prices often move counter to the fundamental suggestions, then we automatically establish the basis for advantage in a consideration of the technical factors which may suggest the immediately future trend of prices, and thus aid us in determining when the trend will be with fundamentals and when it will be contrary to them.

This is true by the very definition of technical considerations, for they are those factors which grow directly out of a study of actual price movements. Since the movement of prices is directly resultant from all the forces of buying and selling pressure, as they offset each other in the open market, the study of actual prices is our most direct approach to a proper weighing of all of the active elements and forces which exert themselves to make up security market movements.

[1] See Chapter VIII, p. 192.

All Other Factors Reflected in Technical Analysis

Earnings suggest that a certain stock should advance, for instance. But we have already seen [1] that it may not do so. Corporation officials, who knew of the increased earnings a month ago and bought the stock then, may now be selling it to take their profits, and thus may depress the stock instead of advancing it. "Professional insiders" may also have had advance news, or they may decide to discourage the public from its natural buying tendency by selling the stock in high volume, thus depressing its price temporarily. Such action is calculated to mislead the average individual into also selling, after which the insiders may buy the stock up again and proceed to advance it at a later date, on the same favorable earnings news.

Professional Activities Revealed

Technical action undertakes to answer all of such problems for the individual who properly studies and understands it. If the insiders are selling more stock than the public is buying, then the balance of power is on the side of decline. And technical factors, based upon price, based in turn upon the balance of buying or selling, will accurately indicate such a tendency. Nor can the insiders "fool the market" very successfully, when they again turn to the buying side. As soon as they begin to buy more stock than the public is selling, the price movement will begin to firm up, and the technical signals, based upon such price action, will again adequately suggest the turn in balance from selling pressure to buying support.

[1] See p. 125.

The Direct Answer to Market Profits

In practice, of course, technical action is not so simple or definite as its theory, but the basis remains logical and the connection direct. Since technical action is based upon price, and since price is the basic factor in our intermediate operation and profit, then technical action is, theoretically at least, our direct answer to such market profit.

It is the answer because our fundamental considerations of earnings, dividends, etc., are merely indirect signals preceding the more direct ones of sufficient buying to advance a stock in price. If we can find some other consideration which will measure more directly the balance of actual buying and selling in a stock, then we may forget all about fundamentals, because it is really not they which raise a stock's price but this more direct and resultant balance of buying power over selling pressure.

How Fundamentals are Automatically Weighed

At least from such a standpoint, fundamentals are of no practical use unless they lead to buying or selling. And since technical action, in itself, apprises us of buying and selling, we may simply drop the fundamentals from our current consideration. And this is, in effect, the proper procedure when we study the market from the standpoint of pure technical action.

In technical consideration, we concentrate on the price movement to the exclusion of all other factors. We do so justifiedly, at least in theory, because all of the other factors are automatically weighed and presented in their proper market perspective, through technical study of the price movement itself. Balance sheets, earnings, dividends, book values, general business, inside buying and selling, misleading professional manipulation — all of these are reflected in technical study of the price movement, and in their proper balance and importance, and thus need not be considered separately or in themselves.

In the final analysis, no market factor is important unless it is reflected in actual buying or selling of a stock. But every market factor which *is* important is even more directly and properly reflected in the balanced results of the buying and selling which it engenders. Technical market action, therefore, need not concern itself with the million individual arguments for buying and selling, simply because all of those million arguments are directly reflected by technical action itself, and in their proper composite balance and importance.

Technical Basis is Not Infallible

Such is the theory of technical study. The author has given the better part of his life to establishing this technical approach to market trading and profit, and yet he has never maintained that the successful investor should shut his eyes to the fundamental factors or to other considerations. We have merely stated the case for the technical approach. We have properly noted that pure technical study considers only market action and nothing else. But we may repeat that the broad and successful market operator will not be satisfied with dependence upon any single aspect, or "method," of trading but will glean his success from a common-sense weighing of the composite picture, containing all kinds of individual factors and considerations.

The author's previous writings speak for themselves as establishing his utter conviction on the value of technical study, but he is also quite willing to admit that technical action is not infallible and that it is properly used by the average operator as a corner-stone for market technique rather than as a sufficiency alone and in itself.

But It is Highly Important

In spite of this fact, the author may as well repeat what he has said in previous writings, that a familiarity with the rules of technical action is one of the most important channels of study for the modern market operator, be he long-swing investor or intermediate trader, and that no individual has completed his preparation for maximum market success until he has achieved a thorough ground-work in this field.

So sincere and so definite is this conviction that the author has devoted more time, space and effort in the technical field of market study than perhaps in any other. The subject, however, will not be covered in this volume to any great or thorough degree, for numerous reasons. In the first place, it is a subject which would require much more space than can practically be allotted to it in our current study. It makes at least one large-size volume in itself.

In the second place, we are currently attempting to provide a broad and general background for the average individual, and technical action is admittedly not the sole consideration. In the third place, the present work has been conceived as placing the emphasis upon less involved and more simple topics from which the average operator may draw the maximum of profit with the minimum of technical study and detailed labor.

No Technical Details in this Study

And, finally, in somewhat of a summary of all the other points just mentioned, the author has written so voluminously on the subject of technical action in previous and contemporary works that the reader may better be referred to such studies for thorough and complete exposition of the subject.

A few principles of technical analysis were outlined in his previous volume, "Stock Market Theory and Practice."[1] Perhaps largely because that volume was the first to submit any broad presentation of this new subject, popular demand for additional and detailed working material developed rapidly and insistently. The author's response has been the institution of a course on the subject, by mail, submitting new material and explaining the old in fuller detail. The course is called "Technical Analysis and Market Profits," and although its circulation has intentionally been restricted, for practical market reasons, it is available under certain conditions to the average individual interested in a complete and practical study of the field of modern technical science.[2]

General Consideration of Technical Approach Sufficient

We may consider the technical approach more important, then, than the fundamental, especially in connection with our study of intermediate trading practice. But we shall not devote much more attention to the subject, in the present volume, than we did to the fundamental aspect of our current problem in the preceding chapter. We shall merely sketch a general outline of the subject, leaving the more intricate details for "extra-curriculum study," if the reader is sufficiently interested to pursue it.

The entire science of technical action is comparatively so new that it is still little understood by the "public" and is still being gradually refined even by the so-called "authorities." Since the science deals primarily with price action and actual market trading, its fundamental basis is found in such study, carried on most satisfactorily, and almost entirely, through the medium of charts.

A chart is nothing more than a convenient vehicle for graphic illustration of technical market data, usually security prices and volume of security sales. The compactness and completeness of such easy representation provides the element for comprehensive and detailed study of past market action, with a view to better forecasting the probabilities of future action.

The Logic of Technical Science

Through the studious examination of market data, as represented in charts of varying type and design, a considerable catechism of technical theory has gradually built itself up. Most of these theories are based upon "trial and error," upon discovery of certain patterns, rules and theories which, having been found to forecast definite future trends over a term of past record, are assumed to be sufficiently well-based in experience to imply that they will continue to forecast similar trends in the future as in the past.

Another and perhaps even more significant and trustworthy approach is the consideration of logic. This method divides itself further into two sub-methods — subjective logic, and objective logic. Technical principles based upon subjective logic are theories which may be found to work out by the "trial and error" method of past experience, but which have the added prestige of being wholly logical from a theoretical standpoint.

It is entirely logical to anticipate, for instance, that a previously rising market price trend which begins to round off and gradually to turn downward, is registering a weakened technical position, because that is the normal expectancy in price movement if pressure of selling is gradually replacing the previously stronger demand of buying power. Such a rounding off is proved the signal of technical weakness from a standpoint of subjective logic as well as on a basis of practical experience in past historical record.

Subjective vs. Objective Logic

The objective logical approach is, however, in the author's opinion, even more important than the subjective, standing almost at the basis of all value in technical trading practice. This is the principle that the price movement progresses in certain trends which, while liable to interruption, are more likely to continue than to reverse over the bulk of any time interval. In other words, after the market has started in either direction, greater profit is likely to be realized by assuming that such direction will continue than by assuming that it will be immediately reversed. There are literally hundreds of different theories based upon technical action but the author cannot think of a single one which will not eventually dictate a bullish forecast if the market continues to advance long enough.

That does not mean that technical theory is so simple as to say that whenever prices start up they will continue up.

Many upward movements are ignored while technical action is working out a genuinely bearish signal. But the important point from our logical, objective approach, is that if those upward movements do not soon reverse — if they continue upward longer than provided by the particular bearish theory being postulated — then technical action automatically discards that bearish theory and substitutes, at some point in the extending price advance, the opposite theory of bullish forecast.

Technical Basis Depends upon Main Trends

In other words, the entire catalog of technical theories, be they reliable or fallacious, important or unimportant, makes basic provision for a quick switching from a bullish to a bearish forecast, and vice versa. The author is quite conscious that such a statement may make the technical approach sound a bit childish and simple. There is a great deal more to the science than such a logical consideration. But to the extent that this logic is true and basic for all technical theory, the author does not mind having it called simple and certain.

No one should mind what a theory is termed, so long as it is logical and practical. And this very aspect of all technical theory, simple, childish or what not, is still perhaps its greatest basic value for the trader. For, through this primary principle, it practically guarantees that the operator will be "riding with the trend" most of the time, that he will switch quickly if his original conclusion was wrong or against the trend, and that he will thus limit his losses and let his profits run. It is based on the simple theorem that profits are made by going along with the market movement and not by trying to oppose it.

The Dow Theory

There is perhaps no better example of this objective logic in any major theory of technical action than may be found in the so-called Dow theory. The major formulae of this theory were evolved by Charles H. Dow, one of the founders of Dow, Jones & Company and of the Wall Street Journal, early in the present century. But the real growth of the technical theory, while still called after its founder, has been slow and gradual, almost smacking of evolution, through the additional contributions, theories and studious interpretations of later disciples like William Peter Hamilton and Robert Rhea, the latter being perhaps the best-known contemporary interpreter. Mr. Rhea's capable volume, "The Dow Theory," has done much to bring this early branch of technical science back into public interest, and his treatment, together with that of other modern commentators, makes detailed description unnecessary in these pages.

As a matter of fact, the Dow theory is not only one of the most logical but also the earliest and simplest of technical theories. Stripped of its details, it suggests that the operator follow the main trend of stock prices by observing that such trend, once on its way, is likely to continue a considerable distance, punctuated by secondary corrections in the form of intermediate swings contrary to the major trend.

The Dow theory operator follows this major trend until such time as the secondary corrections may run contrary to the major trend long enough and far enough to break through the extremes of previous corrections, at which time he assumes that the major movement itself is changing and so switches his own position to coincide with this new trend.

Simple Logic of the Dow Theory

It thus follows, as does the night the day, that if the market goes far enough in any single direction, the Dow theory will soon signal that that is the correct direction for future movement. Another aspect of the theory requires that such penetration and signal given by one market average alone is not sufficient, but that it must first be confirmed by the other average. The two averages usually used are the industrial and railroad indexes and the ones generally followed, by the theory's chief sponsors, at least, are the Dow-Jones averages of these groups.

Here again, therefore, we have an additional aspect of the simple advantages in our technical approach on the basis of objective logic. If the industrial average gives a bullish signal it is a fairly certain indication that the market has been advancing for some time, which is, in itself, a logical basis for anticipating a rising major price trend. But if final confirmation of such change in the long-swing trend awaits similar action by the railroad average then there is even stronger logical basis for assuming that the major trend has in truth reversed from down to up.

Practical Illustrations of Dow Theory Logic

Illustrations of these two primary principles in the Dow theory may be noted by reference once again to Plate I, our Dow-Jones industrial average frontispiece. During the panic of 1929, reversal into a major bear market was signalled by the industrial average at the end of October when the intermediate decline broke below the support levels of the preceding intermediate decline which ended in May.

The Dow theory signals remained bearish for the long pull through the entire succeeding bear market. They did not, on strict interpretation of secondary movements, again turn bullish for the long term until May of 1933, when both averages had advanced far enough to exceed the previous highs of the first bull phase which ended in September of 1932.

In fairness to the Dow theory it must be noted that our considerations have been confined chiefly to only two of its principles. They seem to be the most important and most useful ones, but there are other details which might have suggested the above major turning points considerably in advance of the basic signals as strictly interpreted.

Simplicity is an Asset

In any case, our illustrations are not quoted to discredit this theory, but rather to show how and why it is an aid for the average market investor, through its fundamental approach to the problem of long-term price movement on a basis of objective logic.

As previously stated, the simplicity and logic of any rules for technical action are a recommendation rather than a detraction. In both 1929 and 1933, the primary major trends had gone a considerable distance in their new long-term directions before the Dow theory gave a confirmed and basic signal of the turn, but in both cases there were plenty of profits left. The long-term investor, or even the intermediate trader, who took cognizance of the bear market signals even as late as November of 1929, had no cause to regret the dictates of this theory over the next few years. Once again, that theory was correct because it depended so closely upon market action itself, and not on personal opinion.

Dow Theory Logically Applied to Long-Term Trends

A consideration of the Dow theory principles on the above basis is more advantageous, of course, for the long-swing investor, but it also offers valuable minor suggestions for the short-swing trader, also on a basis of the objective logic found in its suggestion that successively higher intermediate fluctuations are bullish while successively lower intermediate fluctuations are bearish.

Likewise, while the theory is perhaps more often applied to general market movements, through study of the averages, than to individual stocks, it is also valid and helpful in consideration of the latter. We may turn to Plate V, on page 141, to examine a practical illustration of the aid which this perfectly logical principle of fluctuating trend may offer. Our illustration shows the daily high and low price record of Western Union common stock through the first six months of 1933.

Shorter-Swing Applications

Previous to the beginning of our chart, Western Union had been declining gently since November of 1932. Each successive top had been lower than the last and each successive bottom had been lower than the preceding bottom, establishing the bearish forecast which had been not only logical but quite correct.

Points B, C and D are all lower than the previous support levels. But at Point E the price movement rises slightly above the top of the preceding rally highs, thus suggesting the further advance which followed the Bank Holiday closing of the Exchange.

A Practical Example

There ensued, from Points F to G, a short downward swing, going further than a normal intermediate correction, but still fairly maintaining a bullish suggestion, since it did not break below the previous bottom at Point D. At Point H, the new advancing phase carried through the top of a previous minor recovery but the true confirmation was offered at Point J, when the rising trend carried above the preceding tops at Point F. On strict interpretation of the Dow theory this signal would probably be considered an intermediate one, at best, but for our current purpose of technical aid in short-swing operation the suggestion was logical, useful and profitable.

On the same basis the forecast remained bullish throughout the remainder of our chart. The bottom at Point N held above that at Point L. The bottoms at Points P, Q and R were all successively higher and advancing.

The Chart on Western Union

The logic of this theory is thus clearly seen, for the succession of higher tops and bottoms practically guarantees that the trend is upward. And bearish suggestions for a reversal of position will not occur until the trend is actually turned down once more through development of successively lower tops and bottoms, which, in themselves, guarantee at least a temporary downward trend.

Even the decline following Point V did not actually exceed the bottom at Point P. Minor suggestions were bearish when V broke below T, but there was no very definite signal at that point. As a matter of fact, the stock recovered slowly

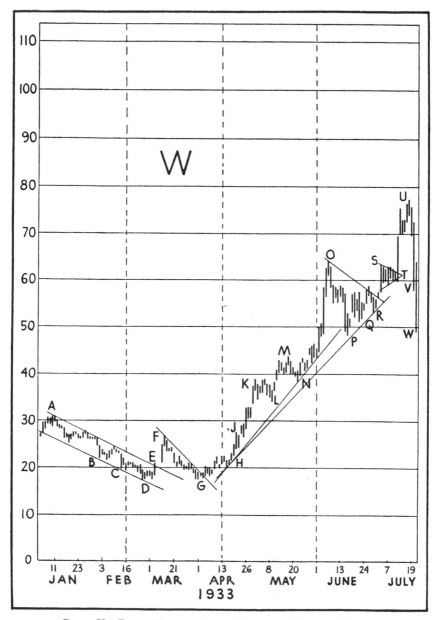

PLATE V. DAILY VERTICAL-LINE CHART ON WESTERN UNION

Showing the gradual upward turn in the Spring of 1933, and the major upward
move which followed.

and irregularly but again turned down before a new high was made and drifted on into the reaction of late Fall in 1933.

Valuation of Dow Theory Principles

Thus we have learned how at least important portions of one of our oldest and earliest technical theories may still be applied to practical market operation, not only for the long pull but also for intermediate trading profit, and its greatest recommendation is the simple fact that it is constructed on our practical foundations of trial and error, subjective logic and objective logic.

We have spent considerable time in consideration of these primary principles, not only because of the recent renewed publicizing of the Dow theory, but also because it illustrates so well our basis of objective logic, because it is often useful in short-term technical trading and also because it constitutes perhaps the broadest catalog of technical theory which is currently dignified with an inclusive title.

"Pattern Theory" or Line Method

There are plenty of other technical theories which the author considers more useful and practical, but they do not fall so easily into popular or complete classification. Perhaps the broadest heading would be under the "pattern" theory, or the line-chart method of analysis, though the author has never attempted to apply any all-embracing terminology to the work which he himself has done in this field.

We have already explained at some length the impracticability of attempting any complete catalog or detailed description of such theories in this volume, but we may at least mention the most important principles, and even examine a few of them in connection with the chart on Western Union already noted, as well as in connection with our new theory of objective logic.

Some Major Patterns

So far as the average operator's interest and profit in short-term trading are concerned, perhaps the most valuable of such theories have to do with technical chart patterns like the common turn, the head and shoulders formation, the large family of triangles, multiple tops and bottoms, complex tops and bottoms, flags, pennants, horns and the entire group of "area" patterns, together with such additional considerations as comparative analysis, trend lines, gaps, volume of trading, etc.

For full and detailed study of such theories, and indeed the entire field of technical science, the interested reader may simply be referred to other writings by the author.[1] Suffice it to say that practically all of such technical factors concern themselves almost entirely with the action of security prices, as represented on graphic charts, and are also based directly or indirectly upon our previous foundations of trial and error in experience, subjective logic and objective logic.

Conventional Analysis of Western Union Chart

For quick but specific consideration of a few of such principles we may turn once more to Plate V, on page 141, showing the chart on Western Union through the July reaction of 1933. From Points A to E we have a fair example of

---

[1] See p. 132.

parallel trend lines, forecasting technical continuation of the bearish movement until Point E was reached. Here the trend indication reversed abruptly from bearish to bullish as soon as the trend line A–E was broken on the up-side. From Points F to G we have an example of the single trend line, which was also bearish until broken at Point G, after which it immediately reversed its position to one forecasting further advance.

Once this advance got well under way we had the new single, upward trend line, H–N. This was broken at Point P and there was a short period of indecision so far as the trend indications were concerned, though it is only fair to say that other detailed theories suggested continued advance. It is also fair, however, to note how objective logic came into play. Temporarily the trend-line suggestion was bearish, because the market had begun to decline. As soon as the advance was resumed, however, technical theory lost no time in reversing a position against the market trend. Immediately following Point R the new trend line H–R was quite properly instituted, with the technical trend-line forecast again bullish.

Practical Application of Trend Lines

Point V, breaking this new trend line, gave another bearish signal which might well have been heeded, though there was still room for the later placement of still a third trend line. This latter line would have been placed at a more reasonable angle, in fact, through H–W, and would not have been broken until the more serious decline got under way in the early Fall of 1933.

Trend lines, therefore, based upon practical logic, serve also a highly useful purpose, in " limiting losses and letting profits run," and in marking the intermediate trend for the shorter-swing operator.

A somewhat similar aid may also be found in consideration of the flattering trend reversal pattern. This is nothing more than a logical observation of an approaching gradual turn in any previous trend, offering perfectly clear and simple evidence, through study of the price movement, either that buying power is gradually overcoming selling pressure, or that selling pressure is gradually overcoming buying power.

Flattening Trend Reversal

In the chart under current observation, for instance, we see buying power overcoming selling pressure all the way from Points C to J, illustrating the technical theory of the flattening trend reversal. Note the definite and regular down-trend from Point A through Point C, evidencing, as nothing else could, the certainty that selling of Western Union was still stronger than buying. But note also how the downward trend becomes less regular and begins to round off, to flatten out, following Point C, and especially around Point E.

Logic of Conventional Analysis

By the time Point G was reached there was no mistaking the flattening trend, or the fact that buying power was gaining strength and was gradually but surely overcoming selling pressure and reversing the previously weak technical situation.

If the entire trend to Point H is compared with the previous trend only as far as Point C, there could hardly be room for doubt, at the latter point, that the technical forecast had turned from bearish to bullish.

No such definite application of this particular condition is apparent at the extreme top of the move in Western Union, near the end of the current chart. But the recovery which followed, in the late Summer of 1933, afforded a very good example of this gradual turning down of the trend, following on into more serious recession.

The flattening trend reversal is thus seen to be another important aid for the short-swing operator, and to be based largely upon our practical hypothesis of subjective technical logic.

The Pattern Technique

Or we may view the technical picture from the standpoint of various "pattern" theories, many of which are simply more definite and specialized formations of a reversing trend. We have already mentioned the reversal pattern known as the head and shoulders figure and also its relative, the complex formation.[1] We may briefly describe this latter pattern, since it is well exemplified in our chart on Western Union in Plate V.[2] The complex formation is made up of the simple head and shoulders outline, but with a double, or multiple, top or bottom as the head instead of only one such extreme of the price movement.

The entire technical price formation from Points B to H may be considered a good example of this complex, or double head and shoulders, bottom. The previous trend had been downward in Western Union. At Point C we find the left shoulder of our head and shoulders bottom. At Points D and G we have the two bottom extremes, at practically the same

[1] See p. 143.   [2] See p. 141.

level, in the form of a "double bottom," which gives the formation its character of a "double" head and shoulders bottom. At Point H we find the right shoulder, which completes the picture with its bullish forecast for the future movement.

A double bottom is often suggestive of a reversal in price trend. A head and shoulder bottom is even more reliable as an indicator that the previous downward movement is reversing into an upward movement. The double head and shoulders bottom, a combination of both of these signals, is almost always a strong indication of bottom reversal or upward turn. No such patterns, of course, are ever perfect as they appear in practical market trading, and this illustration is far from it. But it was sufficiently well-defined and suggestive to prove a valuable aid in detecting the bottom turn in the early Spring of 1933 and the profitable advance which followed.

Practical Analysis of Pattern Formations

Through Points O–P–Q–R we have a fair example of the symmetrical triangle, with another and smaller one at Points S–T. The triangle family is one of the best known and most valuable to the student of technical market action, and this particular type of triangle usually denotes a continuation of the preceding trend after the apex has been reached, a forecast which was well borne out in both of the examples here noted.

Around Point U there were plenty of market indications which suggested danger and the possibility of intermediate reaction but it may fairly be admitted that there is no technical pattern formation in the chart on Western Union which was of any great definite aid at this juncture. It is worthy of note, however, that the July reaction, at W, did not penetrate the previous support level at P, and that the ensuing recovery, though not included in the present chart, returned to within six points of the previous extreme high. And we have already noted that at this latter point the rules of technical pattern theory did give a clear signal for the longer reversal of trend which followed, and which carried the stock back to around 40 by mid-October.

Volume of Trading in Technical Analysis

In our entire study of Plate V we have given no consideration to the factor of volume of trading, though this is another highly important and valuable angle of the technical approach to short-swing trading.   We shall not go into the details of this branch of technical theory here, except to note that high volume of trading at the beginning of a new move, shortly after the price trend has left a congestion formation, suggests *continuation* of the new trend; while high volume after a comparatively long and substantial movement suggests *reversal* of that trend, especially, of course, if it accompanies the formation of what appear to be our usual reversal patterns and other confirming technical indications.

CHAPTER VII

THE PROPER USE OF STOCK CHARTS

Vertical-Line Charts vs. Other Forms

Thus far in our consideration of technical action we have used as our pictorial basis for study what are generally termed line charts or vertical-line charts. This type of chart seems the most simple, the most easily understood and the most practically valuable for the average operator. But enough public interest in other chart forms has been generated by recent publicity and promotion to justify a short consideration of them in our current discussion.

Perhaps the most recently publicized of such alternate forms for technical chart study is one which is variously known as the point chart, the figure chart, the unit chart or the minor-move chart. The late Richard D. Wyckoff appears to have used this type of chart theory as a basis for his publicly-circulated course of technical market study, and Victor de Villiers has written extensively in practical exposition of the system.

The Point and Figure Chart

Its most important deviation from the vertical-line method of presentation is that the figure chart does not show actual high and low ranges for any designated period of time, but charts the course of price movement by swings of a designated extent, regardless of time interval. A one-point figure chart, for instance, will show no change until the price of the charted stock moves up or down one full point or more, no matter how many days it remains stationary before such a move occurs. Conversely, such a chart might move up and down four or five times during a single day's trading, following alternate full-point moves of the stock, while the conventional vertical-line chart would show merely the extreme high and low for that single day.

Another point of deviation in construction is that the figure chart generally uses figures or squares to designate the price movement, instead of vertical lines. In this regard it differs from still another form of minor-swing chart usually called the geometric type. Both types are shown in Plate VI on page 153, and practical illustration is the easiest method of comprehending such forms. The first portion of the chart in Plate VI shows the geometric design while the second portion illustrates the figure, or unit, type.

Chart Examples of the Unit System

In order to simplify our study, both charts are based upon the Western Union chart in Plate V, on page 141, and are, as a matter of fact, constructed from that previous chart, covering the same time and price movement. For our illustration in Plate VI we have selected the three-point minor-move as the basis for charting. In other words, no move of less than three full points in Western Union will show up on the geometric and figure charts. In these particular examples, however, the converse rule of this technique is not entirely true, because it is at least possible that not all of such three-point moves do appear on the charts presented herewith.

We have just noted that our current examples have been made up from the vertical-line chart on Western Union, shown in Plate V. But we have also noted[1] that such a vertical-line chart shows only the extreme high and low prices of each day and not the intermediate, or intra-day, swings. If Western Union is shown on the vertical-line chart with a daily range from 70 to 60, for instance, as occurs around Point V in Plate V, we cannot be absolutely certain from that chart how many three-point reversals the stock made during that particular day.

Plotting the Intra-Day Moves

Western Union might have dropped from 70 to 65, and then recovered to 69 during the morning, for instance. In the afternoon it might have declined to 64, then recovered to 67 again, and finally sold off to a low of 60 at the close. Both the geometric and the figure charts should technically show these intra-day movements of three points or more, but we should not be able to trace them by a mere reference to our daily vertical-line chart, showing only the high and low for that day.

A Technical Chart Liberty

This is perhaps a technical fault in the construction of such minor-swing charts from daily vertical-line charts, but the author considers it practically a negligible drawback. In the entire period covered by our geometric and figure-chart examples there would be perhaps not more than a few discrepancies. They would be minor ones and we shall note in our later consideration[2] the offsetting advantages which recommend this less exact, but more practical, method of construction.

[1] See p. 150.   [2] See p. 156.

Ignoring Fractional Moves

Another difference between the geometric and the figure chart may also be noted. The usual method of constructing the figure chart is to ignore fractions completely and consider only the whole, or even, figures of a stock's price in making the chart. The geometric chart, however, at least as the author has always used it, takes full consideration of such fractions just as does the vertical-line type of chart.

Taking our full three-point moves from Plate V, therefore, we find that Western Union started from around 27, moved up to 31, and then started its long decline to below 18, at Point D on all three of our charts. Between Points B and C, however, in Plate V, the price recovered from 21½ to 24½ in an intermediate movement. Our geometric chart, using fractions, shows this intermediate move of three points. Our figure chart, however, does not disclose this intermediate movement, because it ignores fractions. The previous low, on the unit basis, was only 22 and the ensuing high only 24. The resulting move thus being only two points, instead of the three necessary to reverse the chart price movement, the figure chart must ignore this intermediate movement.

The Geometric Form

Having all three of the finished charts before us, we may examine briefly their comparative advantages. It may be both assumed and frankly admitted that the author favors the vertical-line chart for all ordinary and general purposes of technical analysis. He uses such charts almost entirely in his work along these lines, having experimented with the others many years ago, tested them all over various periods

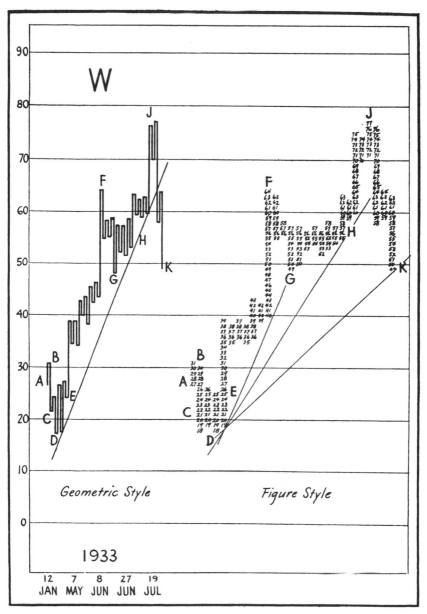

PLATE VI. GEOMETRIC AND FIGURE CHARTS ON WESTERN UNION

Showing three-point technique in both styles, with data taken from the conventional line chart on page 141.

and still holding the vertical-line type of construction superior.

There seem, however, to be two major advantages in the alternate forms which it is only fair to point out, the first being one of space economy and the second a truer picture of intra-day movements. The author does not subscribe to the argument of "figure-chart enthusiasts" that technical analysis should ignore a stock except when it is in process of movement. Quite often the mere factor of long hibernation or of narrow congestion offers helpful aid in technical analysis. But he does admit that, in the majority of instances, the basis of plotting only one-, three-, or five-point moves is adequate for general analysis. And the saving in chart space, as well as the compactness of the resulting picture, may be noted by comparing the charts in Plates V and VI. The three-point figure chart takes up only about half as much space as the vertical-line illustration, and even more space would be saved, of course, on a five-point basis.

Advantages of Geometric and Figure Charts

The second advantage is perhaps more theoretical than practical, but it is an advantage none the less. Technical analysis is based upon the pictorial representation of the trading history of any stock or group of stocks. The vertical-line chart, as we have already noted,[1] does not offer quite so full and detailed a picture of such intra-day history, as do the geometric and figure types. To that degree, and in rather exceptional circumstances, therefore, this "minor move" basis for charting is a little finer and more detailed than the basis of charting only the daily range of high and low prices.

[1] See p. 151.

Disadvantages of Geometric and Figure Charts

With these two admitted exceptions, however, the balance of value and advantage appears to be decidedly with the vertical-line method of charting. Technical analysis deals with price movement, but it also takes into valuable consideration both time and volume, neither of which factors is considered in either the geometric or the figure chart.

The geometric and figure charts ignore volume of trading completely, and they also ignore all but the broad generalities of time. It is impossible to detect definite dates in examining the historical record of price movement on such charts. And it is also impossible, without closer reference to additional and more basic data, to tell whether a congestion area on geometric and figure charts has lasted for a few hours or a few months.

One-Point vs. Multiple-Point Charts

Nor does this author approve the ignoring of fractions, which is almost always done in constructing figure charts, and which is often done when constructing geometric charts. This practice may not matter so much on one-point charts of this character but it can matter considerably on three-point, five-point, or ten-point charts. We have already seen an example of this defect [1] at Point C in Plate VI, where the three-point figure chart failed, by fractions, to register an important intermediate movement.

Without going into details, it may also be noted in passing that the author does not subscribe to the claim, often made for figure charts, that they reliably forecast the price

[1] See p. 152.

objectives for future market moves. The so-called "count system," often used in figure-chart forecasting, was experimented with many years ago by the author. His conclusions still stand today, that this "system" is misleading more often than useful, and that its inconsistent record makes it impractical for regular trading purposes.

The overnight gap is another important technical factor which shows up to full advantage in vertical-line charts but which is quite thoroughly ignored by the geometric and figure-chart technique. One result is a too-favorable distortion of trading theory when the student "works back" a hypothetical rule. One of the publicized trading practices with such charts is a rule, slightly reminiscent of the Dow theory,[1] in which the trader buys or sells when certain previous extreme levels are violated. It is difficult to trace the exact price execution under such principle with the minor-move chart, since such penetration on one day is often followed by a considerable gap at the next day's opening. Such less favorable execution would probably be missed, or ignored, by the student working with geometric or figure charts.

Time and Expense in Figure-Chart Approach

Our final objection to this type of chart, however, relates to the time and tools required for its use. Vertical-line charts may be constructed easily, quickly and efficiently for the price of one newspaper per day. In order to construct geometric or figure charts exactly, however, it is necessary for the student either to watch the ticker all through the day's trading, to have the entire day's tape available for his later study, or else to subscribe to some service which

---

[1] See Chapter VI, p. 136.

watches the intra-day changes for him, and reports the material which he must use to keep his charts up to date.

The latter is the only practical course for the average operator who insists upon the dubious necessity for having his figure charts absolutely exact. And the fees thus collected by the promoters of such "services" might well be suspected of providing at least an indirect incentive for their insistence upon the use of such methods.

Comparing Various Types in Practice

The author has tried to present fairly his own ideas on the relative merits of the charts which we have been discussing. The reader who is at all familiar, by this time, with technical method may judge for himself, by further comparison of Plates V and VI, whether the geometric and figure charts are more easily interpreted for technical analysis than the vertical-line variety.

The trend lines appear to the writer to stand out more clearly, and to be more practically useful, in the vertical-line chart, though there would not have been so many cases of necessity for redrawing them in the case of the geometric style. The double head and shoulders bottom shows up well in all but the figure chart, yet even in this picture the double bottom is marked.

The entire formation, A–B–C–D–E, in the figure chart of Plate VI, represents a powerful congestion area, suggesting the upward reversal which was confirmed at Point E. We have seen why the left shoulder of the bottom figure did not show up clearly on this figure chart,[1] but it may be noted that it would have done so if we had used the one-point move basis instead of the three-point construction.

[1] See p. 152.

Reviewing the Practical Charts

The flattening trend reversal shows up on the vertical-line chart only, but the triangle pattern is evident at Points F–G–H on the figure chart and may even be roughly perceived at the same points on the geometric construction. At the short top of the entire move, formed around 77, the geometric and figure charts prove superior to the vertical-line chart, since they suggest more of a top congestion.[1] On the recovery following the July break, and subsequent to the scope of the charts presented, honors were fairly even, all three of the forms showing strong suggestion of the ensuing down-turn. But only the vertical-line chart, of course, showed the special aid of the flattening trend reversal.

From such preceding discussion of various technical rules and theory, somewhat more lengthy than we had promised yet still but "a scratch on the surface," it may be hoped that the reader is not only more familiar with the usefulness of such technique, but that he may now better understand the practical basis for that usefulness, through our hypothesis of objective logic. He may now see why the technical student, who uses the tools of general chart science, protects himself against the huge losses which might otherwise be allowed to accumulate against him.

Back to the Basic Logic of Technical Analysis

One more glance at Plate V, on page 141, should guarantee the clearness of our argument. At Point H, technical theory had already turned bullish because the market had started up. But let us suppose that this view proved erroneous, that

[1] See p. 151.

the market soon reversed once more and went on down to new low levels. As soon as such a decline broke below Point G the technical operator would sell out or reverse his position, because technical action would immediately take back its bullish forecast on such a decline and would signal weakness once more.

The operator would take a loss but it would be a small and unusual one, compared with the loss that might be taken by the operator who was not " chart minded." With the stock already down to 17 one may argue that there was little room for further great loss in this case, but the same principle would work at 100 as at 17, and with much more practical benefit, of course.

Objective Logic on the Major Swings

The technique worked with particularly valuable results, for instance, during the bear market of 1929–32, as may be noted by reference to Plate I, the Frontispiece. As the market started to decline in 1929 it touched off one bearish signal after another for the technical operator. There were literally scores of bearish chart indications even preceding the rapid phases of the panic. But even if they had all been ignored, the technical student could not help but " get out " and cut his losses short as the ensuing decline carried below one previous point of support after another.

Technical action merely interpreted the logical conclusion of the market itself — it was going down: " get out." How many operators who thought their current losses too great to take, who hoped for " just one more good recovery," spent the next few years wishing they had taken those comparatively small losses, as technical analysis would have commanded them to do.

How Market Reverses its Own Technical Forecast

Or, take the intermediate recovery of the Winter of 1930–31. There were plenty of arguments for considering the bear market over at that time, and there were plenty of operators who bought heavily. Even from a technical standpoint alone it is easy to see the head and shoulders bottom formation which also suggested a long-term bottom.

Purchases were justified, from both a fundamental and a technical basis, through the first three months of 1931. They *might* have been the bottom — but they weren't. The " fundamentalist " was much more likely to hang on than was the technical student. What happened to the bullish technical forecast when the market began to sag once more? As soon as the new recession approached those support levels of the previous December, the technical forecast switched from bullish to bearish. Technical action is not proud. It knows full well that its dictates are not infallible, and it is willing to switch its forecast with utter equanimity — and with valuable speed.

Cutting Losses Short

The operator who did not know technical rules might easily have continued to hold the stocks he bought early in 1931, on the rather plausible basis (at that time) that the bear market ought not to go much farther or last much longer.

That operator would have had a paper loss of around 80 per cent inside of two years, and he would also have had plenty of sleepless nights, to say nothing of constant regret and perhaps even a nervous breakdown in the bargain. And, finally, he would have had no free funds to purchase stocks at their lower levels when the true time for purchase came in 1932.

The technical operator, on the other hand, would have stepped aside early in April of 1931, answering the automatic dictates of technical analysis. He would have taken approximately a 10 per cent loss, at the worst, but he would have kept his capital free and intact, ready for the real opportunity when it appeared later on. And he would also have kept his poise, his good judgment and his peace of mind during those intervening years.

An Example in Long-Term Analysis

Or, if we care to study briefly still another example of the value in technical analysis, we may take the early Summer months of 1931, when there developed still another strong bottom formation. Fundamentals turned temporarily bullish and for a time public opinion veered sharply to the thesis that we had finally passed the bottom of the depression and were at last headed upward into prosperity once more.

For a period of about six weeks, technical analysis suggested that this might well prove to be the case. But when the market turned down again in July and August technical analysis reversed its forecast with valuable promptness and decision and turned bearish once more.

There was no room for hope, for wish-thinking, for pride of previous opinion, for costly stubbornness or for delay in action. It was not until months later that public opinion again resumed its pessimistic and hopeless attitude. Many long-swing investors, watching the slow-acting fundamental factors, were "caught," and had to carry their stocks and losses through, if possible. But the technical operator was

" out " in a hurry, with only a small loss, if any, and with a clear conscience and protected capital.

The Daily Average Chart

Since the Dow-Jones monthly average in Plate I is on too small a scale to show the fine details of this critical period we may spend a few profitable moments of study in consideration of the daily chart on this same situation. For the sake of versatility we may also switch to another important stock index, the New York Times, or Annalist, average of 25 industrials and 25 railroad stocks combined. Plate VII, on page 163, shows this average index daily from the end of April to the middle of September, 1931, and from it we can follow the daily movements during that period.

The long bear-market trend enters our picture at Point A and, based on its objective logic, if on nothing else, the technical forecast had been bearish for at least several weeks.[1] The market continued to decline rapidly and sharply to its swift double bottom at Point C. By the time Point E was reached there was some basis for near-term optimism but the figure B–C–D–E was not a very strong or convincing bottom for a long bear market. And as soon as prices began to slip again, declining at Point F below Point D, there was no further doubt of continuation of the major downward trend.

Pattern Formations Applied to Major Movements

The major bottom, however, was formed at Point J, and we soon had a striking head and shoulders formation, with H and K as the two shoulders. At Point L the bullish forecast was strengthened by the development of still another

<hr>

[1] See p. 160.

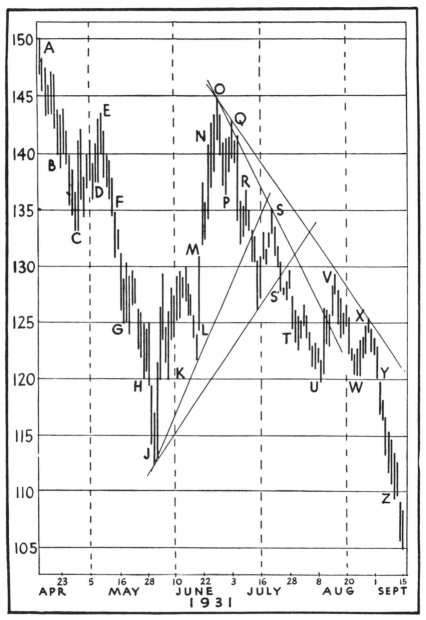

PLATE VII. TIMES DAILY AVERAGE OF 50 STOCKS IN 1931

Showing details of the intermediate recovery and later resumption of the bear market.

pair of shoulders, at Points G and L. The right shoulder at the latter point was too low for a perfect figure but the intermediate reaction held well within normal 50 per cent limits.

The technical operator who had accumulated stocks across G–L, or lower, would have held them so long as K was not violated. The sharp break-away gap following Point L indicated further rapid advance and, together with the second gap at Point M, gave a " technicast " that the move would extend to around 144, on a basis of the multiple gap theory.[1] The move actually ended at 144¾.

Around Points N–O–Q, therefore, we had numerous suggestions of reversal, including an area formation, the multiple gap theory, some semblance of a symmetrical triangle or even an imperfect head and shoulders top, with the added forecast on the Dow basis of lower tops and bottoms. Point Q was below Point O, and when the market broke below Point P, at R, another bearish signal was offered.

Distinguishing between a Reaction and a Reversal

However, there was still no certainty that these were signals for anything more than a mere intermediate reaction. Even if we had actually passed the long-awaited bottom of the bear market and had started on another new upward cycle, there was still perfect justification for an intermediate reaction from the strong resistance levels across the price band extending from Points B to N.

The important point to watch, from a technical angle, was the character and extent of this secondary recession. To maintain its intermediate character and continue faith in a new major upward cycle, we might have postulated at once that the intermediate reaction should not go back more than

---

[1] See " Technical Analysis and Market Profits."

one-half to two-thirds of the preceding advance. If it did not hold and reverse upward once more around the G–L level, then we should have to give up our new hopes for a final turn and anticipate rather the further continuance of the major bear market.

Applying Trend Lines to the Average Chart

Our first trend line, J–L, was easily broken but it was too steep anyway for a major upward trend, and was by no means a significant or final bear argument. When our next trend line was broken, at Point S', however, the action was significant and we had real basis for beginning to turn bearish once more on the major trend. The decline at Point U was deeper than should have occurred in merely an intermediate reaction, and the forecast was assuming a definitely unfavorable aspect.

Our first downward trend line, O–S, was broken, but the more dependable one, O–V–X, was not broken. The weak recovery to Point X and the ensuing tendency to sell off once more was practically conclusive that the recovery which started at Point J was not a new bull market but merely an intermediate recovery in the long bear cycle, which was now resuming its deflationary course.

When the reaction broke through the G–L level it gave a definite bear signal. But when it broke below the long support level across Points H–K–U–W–Y, technical action spoke most conclusively. Even the veriest neophyte at technical forecasting should have sold his speculative long commitments at Point Y. And if there were any slight doubt remaining on the bearish forecast it must have been dispelled before Point Z was reached, when the new declines penetrated below the previous turn at Point J.

Long-Term Success vs. Perfection

It would seem quite unnecessary further to mark the advantages of technical science in this particular illustration. The chief point for the long-swing investor, as well as for the short-term trader, was simply the suggestion that the major trend had turned upward, with long commitments justified anywhere around Points G–L, and then the rapid and dogmatic withdrawal of that suggestion, with forecast for new weakness, which developed all the way from Point Q to the end of our chart.

The author would not insist that the long-term technical student would have made a profit on this picture, though, as a matter of fact, it was easily possible. Even granting the worst probable judgment from a technical standpoint, the operator would have bought at Point M and sold at Point Y. He would have lost an average of about 10 points on this extreme supposition. But the important observation is that he would actually have gotten out at Point Y, taken his modest loss and protected his capital from the terrific further declines which accrued to the operator who was not familiar with technical science and the advantages of its objective logic.[1]

Technical Record in History of Major Trends

The author did not construct these examples of the values which lie in the mere basic logic of technical action. The market constructed them. Nor did the author "hand-pick" these short samples. They are the only ones in which we shall indulge for our current volume, but the reader may be

[1] See Chapter VI, p. 134.

assured that practically every important and profitable turn in the stock market over many years has either been " called " in advance by technical action or has been dealt with by the rules of technical science in such a way that losses have been cut short while profits have been allowed to run.

The author contents himself merely with stating this as a fact in the present volume, but the interested or skeptical reader may find plenty of practical proof in his more purely technical writings.

Summary of Technical Advantages

For the purposes of this volume it is sufficient if we have developed a fair basis for understanding what the technical approach to market operation is, and the purely logical basis on which its value rests.

Turning for one final glance at our previous introductory basis for its value, we find that technical theory is profitable, first, because it has been founded upon practical success in past history and because it may be assumed that such theories will also hold in the future: Second, because it is based upon subjective logic, bending its forecast to the natural expectations which plain common sense would anticipate from a knowledge of market forces. And, third, because it is based upon objective logic, assuming continuation of the current trend and thus making provision for rapid shifting of an incorrect forecast, automatically cutting losses short on such improper deductions, and conforming quickly and automatically to the " judgment of the market-place " and to the actualities of price movement, rather than trying to fight them or indulging in the human frailties of hope and the pride of personal opinion.

The Defects in Technical Approach

What, then, are the defects of technical action? We have spent considerable time and consideration on its value, but what are the drawbacks? This is almost like asking a fond father to criticise his own child. There is little temptation, however, to answer " there ain't none." The author has devoted many years to preaching the advantages of technical analysis, has often preached them in what seemed " the wilderness," but he has tried never to allow a dogmatic devotion to overcome a proper sense of humility, conservatism and balance, or to blind his eyes to the practical dangers which lurk in the one-track mind of the so-called " chartbug."

In spite of this constant aim toward moderation and fair thinking, the author must reply with the assertion that the greatest disadvantage, the most potent danger, in technical theory lies not so much in the theory or the science itself as in the individual who uses it.

Weaknesses are Largely Personal

If the operator approaches technical trading with the idea that it is perfect, that it is infallible, that he can use it in place of hard work, study and clear thinking for himself, then there is so much danger that the author would advise such an individual that technical science holds absolutely nothing for him. He had better spend his time and study on perfecting perpetual motion or on a new method for unbending paper clips. Technical study would be exceedingly dangerous for such a man, yet the drawbacks would be more with him than with technical science.

Chief Danger is Over-Confidence

In spite of all the complimentary things we have said about technical theory in this volume, in spite of a lifetime devoted to its study, development and use, and in spite of utter personal faith in its efficacy, the author has never claimed, or considered, that technical market analysis is an exact science or an infallible one.

It is merely an aid in proper composite market judgment. It fails perhaps as often as many of the other general rules and theories which we are attempting to study in this volume. But, along with them, it provides an additional tool, the mastery of which should make our future market judgment more accurate, and our practical operations, especially from the shorter-term standpoint, more profitable and more successful.

If we grasp this point of view, then we have successfully avoided what the author considers the greatest drawback to a study of technical action, and its greatest danger in practical trading. To turn our idea into its seeming paradox, technical analysis has no real drawbacks if the individual realizes that it *does* have them. Inconsistent as this may sound, it is the prime and necessary basis for a successful approach to technical forecasting.

Simple and Basic Rules Overcome the Dangers

Such a proper attitude is achieved, of course, not merely by closer study and experience with technical action but by repeated application of our introductory and general rules against over-confidence, against trusting any single theory too far, against over-enthusiasm and all of the allied evils of human nature.

If such rules are properly mastered and respected, then the chief danger in technical science would appear to be safely negated. For these dictates of common sense will guard the individual from falling into the more specific error of concentrating on this one angle of market forecasting alone, to the exclusion of other factors which may be highly important in the composite judgment. They will guard, in short, against making one what is often termed a " chart-bug."

The " Chart-Bug "

Perhaps the greatest element of popular and general skepticism with regard to " stock chart " and affiliated studies results from contact with this deadly species. He is the dogmatic type, with a one-track mind, and is likely to be almost a fanatic on the subject of his own specific theories of technical, or chart, action. The reader has quite possibly met up with at least one or two of such types. The author has had to see so many that they are a tragedy and not a joke to him.

They come from all parts of the country, bringing their pet theories. They are, almost without exception, totally sincere. But they are, also almost without exception, shabbily dressed and unsuccessful. Most of them are seeking not merely encouragement but financial backing.

If they are perfectly frank, they will admit that they have lost money on a basis of their pet theory, but they are just as quick to explain that it was not the fault of the theory but simply a stroke of bad luck, or faulty application, which has led to temporary failure. All they need is capital, or an " angel " to pay them for managing someone else's large speculative account.

Beware of Dogmatic Faiths

There is little use in attempting to reason with such people, or to dissuade them from pursuing their dogmatic ways. They have already violated the cardinal rules of broad-mindedness, humility and compromise. Their very make-up is such that they would probably never be successful in market operation, either with or without the aid of technical science.

The author has been approached by so many of this type that it is almost difficult for him to admit that they are extreme and rare examples, but that is undoubtedly the case. It is fortunate that they *are* rare, for they are living evidence of the fundamental danger in allowing oneself to become a " chart-bug."

The reader is probably in no such danger, but we have drawn our extreme picture merely as a warning. Chart theories often have an insidious habit of working almost perfectly for the beginner, and in such case he must guard himself carefully against over-confidence and thinking he has found a sure and easy path to rapid riches. In technical science he will find a trustworthy and profitable friend, but he will not find a substitute for study, common sense and the other virtues of the consistently successful operator.

Exploitation of Technical Science

Somewhat related to this over-confidence in charts and technical science is another danger which appears to have assumed growing importance in the past few years, and which may quite possibly continue to grow. That is the promotion and publicizing, by various " authorities," of untried or questionable theories of technical action. The author welcomes new contributions to the technical catalog of learning, but only provided that they are the genuine results of conscientious research, and not a basis for exploitation of the rapidly-growing public interest and enthusiasm for additional knowledge in the field.

Sensational advertising and extravagant promotion claims are perhaps the most easily apparent characteristics of financial exploitation in the technical field, just as they are in most other lines. In like manner, the field of technical science would seem to hold its own law of diminishing returns, and the mere fact that a form of chart or theory is new and intricate does not guarantee that its results will merit practical application.

Dangers of Too-General Familiarity by Public

Such tendencies toward exploiting the rapidly expanding interest in technical action lead naturally to a consideration of the dangers that confront any general theory when it becomes too widely known and used in practical market operation. Here we have a danger which the author must admit is not a subjective one, nor yet an unimportant one.

Just as "the insiders" may use fundamental factors of news to mislead the public, so it seems quite logical that if enough of the "public" learn and use the principles of technical action the insider may find it also to his advantage to attempt misleading moves in this direction.

Such Dangers not Serious for Technical Theory

Happily, however, the danger of such a development does not appear serious, not because the insider would shrink from trying it, but because the basis of technical science makes it extremely difficult. In order to " cross " the public, the insider need merely sell when the public is buying and buy when the public is selling. Such inside, or manipulative, operations do not affect the fundamental picture but they most certainly would affect the technical picture.

It is simply impossible for the insider to manipulate security prices without either buying or selling. And as soon as he does either, he immediately exposes his hand to the student of technical analysis. The technical forecast is always closely in line with the market trend; if the insider decides to "fool" the technical student by buying when the technical forecast suggests selling, then the insider's buying immediately tends to turn the technical forecast toward the buying side once more, and Mr. Insider will soon find technical action barking at his heels again.

Most Probable Future Danger is " Whip-Sawing "

As a result of such basic principles of technical action it does seem possible, however, that manipulative efforts along such lines would tend to " whip-saw " the technical student trying to play too close to the minor moves. They might also result in temporarily incorrect technical signals at eminently critical points.[1] But the incorrect signals should be no more than temporary; technical action would quickly switch to the proper forecast as soon as the insider had turned his own tactics into the proper trend channel.

While it must be admitted, therefore, that the future may see efforts to manipulate prices in such a way as to mislead the technical student, the danger will be more for the minor-trend operator than for the longer-swing investor. And

[1] See Chapter VIII, p. 204.

even so, the danger must be largely discounted because the basic theory of technical science leaves little room for any serious or long-continued deception, and the minor difficulties may usually be overcome through proper use of stop-loss principles.[1]

Dangers of Government Regulation

Recognition of such possible "inside manipulation" leads us naturally to one final consideration regarding the value of technical theories in the future, and that is on a basis of the growing disposition for Government to restrict by law the free operation of organized security markets.

Personally, the author considers that there is little danger to technical science from such an angle. If we conscientiously felt that legislation could thoroughly accomplish its apparent aims, then we should consider recent threats more dangerous.[2] But so long as human nature remains essentially unchanged, it is difficult to conceive that over-strict Government regulation of security trading would succeed in its basic aims with much greater success than did the "noble experiment" of prohibition.

Effects on Technical Value Practically Negligible

We have already noted in a previous chapter [3] the personal elements in security movement and public trading, and they underlie all such activity. Regulation of security trading by law may tend to flatten out the curves of business and security cycles to some degree but not enough, it would appear, to detract appreciably from the advantages of technical science.

[1] See Chapter IX, p. 224.   [3] See Chapter II, p. 31.
[2] See Chapter II, p. 35.

Regulation of speculative and pool operations by law may also tend to diminish such activity, but it would seem extremely difficult to extinguish it entirely. The most definite danger in legal regulation would appear to be that the Government may attempt to eradicate the "evils" of organized security markets by killing the markets, while the "devils" simply reappear elsewhere in another, and perhaps more insidious, form.

Even Restricted Operations Need Technical Basis

Once again, the author must hasten to explain that he is by no means out of sympathy with efforts to rid organized security exchanges of certain and definite evils, unfair deceits and dishonest machinations. He simply feels that, so long as such markets are allowed to keep open for the free meeting of buyers and sellers, for fair fixing of prices based upon equitable operation of demand and supply, so long will technical science prove a valuable and profitable aid for the average market operator.[1]

Concluding Summary for the Technical Approach

In closing our lengthy consideration of this great subject, therefore, we may merely repeat what the reader should by now completely understand for himself. The science of technical action is no rose-strewn path to quick and easy profit. It is not infallible and it is not to be relied upon to the exclusion of all else. But it does constitute one of the most important aids in consistently profitable operation for the average individual, whether he be long-swing investor or short-term speculator.

[1] See Chapter XII, p. 324.

If he is willing to become familiar with the rules and theories of the science, he will also become familiar with the basic conversation of the market itself. He will have brought himself about as close to "intimate converse" with market movements as he is likely ever to get in any other way. He will set himself in tune with those basic elements and they will speak to him through technical action, guiding him without fear or favor in the true path of market movement, simply because they are based so closely upon the "stuff" of which market movements are made.

We may thus listen to the "voice of the market-place," from which there is no appeal, through study and familiarity with technical theory. We shall not close our eyes and ears to the multitude of other factors which help us. We shall welcome them, just as we welcome technical action. For all of them will add to our repertoire of market science and will assist us to that composite judgment which is so important as our basis for future independent action, proper decision and practical market success.

CHAPTER VIII

MARKET PSYCHOLOGY

From Technical to More Simple Consideration

In outlining our approach to market success, at the beginning of this volume, we promised the reader that it would be a fairly simple approach, depending more upon the fundamental basis of pure logic and common sense than upon the seemingly more popular study of higher mathematics, science and involved technical theory.

In the last few chapters, we may appear to have departed somewhat from this opening premise. But the author considers the more technical field, just covered, so basic and important that a simple outline of that method seemed necessary even for the average, "non-technical" education in practical market activity.

Psychology Seldom Applied to Market Operation

Having made our brief excursion into this technical field, however, we are ready to come back again into the more simple realm, in order to give consideration to an aspect of successful approach which seems to the author just as neglected in present-day study as it is important. In his opinion, there is most definitely a broad field for the application of simple, elementary principles of psychology in security analysis and operation. In many respects, it appears to be a field quite as important as others on which much research has been done and on which many volumes have been written. And yet, this psychological aspect has been almost totally neglected in modern market analysis.

The reader need not become fearful of being led through an intricate maze of involved psychological theory in the present volume, if for no other reason than that the author does not pretend to be an authority on such a broad and specialized field. Furthermore, it seems quite unnecessary to apply any very involved principles of psychology. A mere consideration of some well-known and easily-apparent aspects may serve our practical purpose.

The Author's Simple Definition

In fact, the author is not certain that his own definition of psychology would be allowed by real authorities in that science. For it must be admitted that he has chiefly in mind his own attitude toward psychology, as the study of how the human species reacts to various stimuli. We shall thus merely attempt to analyze these human reactions to certain ideas and circumstances, placing ourselves in perhaps a better position to profit from the knowledge of such characteristic human behavior.

If we grant such a basis for our psychological approach, then its value is made clearer at the very outset. If there is any fundamental tenet in the workings of the security market which our previous chapters should have made clear, it is the fact that all such workings are based primarily on the action of a great many human beings who are no more mysterious, no more difficult to fathom, than are we ourselves. Especially is this the basis for such technical theories as we have studied in the last few chapters. Technical science is at bottom merely the attempt to analyze, through consideration of stock charts and trading data, the changes that are taking place in the activities of human beings, whose individual actions go to make up this thing we call market movement.

Logic of Psychology as Applied to Market Forecasting

We speak perhaps too glibly about "the market" going up or going down, and we think too little about the human reactions which are at the bottom of such movements. Prices never rise or fall by themselves, but only as a result of the buying and selling balance established through the meeting and balancing of the operations entered into by thousands of individual human beings.

They all have their own personal doubts and fears and reasons for buying or selling. And if we can approach some understanding of the characteristic manner in which such reasons develop, then it seems quite logical that we shall also be approaching a new aid in deciding what the bulk of such individuals are thinking, what they are planning, what they will do regarding their security operations in the future, and therefore what we ourselves ought to do to place our own operations in the best position to profit from those future trends.

Detecting Changes in the " Public Mind "

Our study of technical science was based largely on an attempt to discover the changes in market sentiment, in the balance between buying and selling, while they were in progress or in process of reversal, by a study of the price movement itself. Through a psychological approach, it seems reasonable that we might detect such changes in sentiment through pure analysis of the stimuli that market operators are receiving, and by deciding in advance, through the application of psychological principles, how they are going to react to such stimuli, even before they have had time to register such reaction in their stock market operations.

Even the layman, with no very clear ideas of psychology at all, would have no difficulty in analyzing very simple applications of such a theory. In fact, we have already done so, without special regard for the psychological basis of our conclusions.[1] When we noted that the usual tendency was for the public to buy when the good news was out, we made use of this simple theorem.

The psychological reactions of the so-called "public" are, indeed, usually fairly simple of analysis. The public buys on good news and sells on bad news. To the extent that the public rules market movements, therefore, it would be quite safe to assume, on our simple basis of psychological stimulus and reaction, that when a stock's dividend is increased, or higher earnings are announced, the public will buy and the stock will advance.

Why Pure "Public Psychology" Doesn't Work

Unfortunately, we have also seen [1] that market psychology is not quite so simple as this — chiefly because there are other elements in the market besides the public, and these other elements are quite often large enough and powerful enough to exercise greater influence on market movements than does the public.

We went still further into our theory of psychological reaction, therefore, when we noted [2] that the officers, directors, even employees of such a company, together with "insiders" who also had advance information, might well decide

[1] See Chapter V, p. 108.   [2] See Chapter VI, p. 128.

to buy the stock in advance of public announcement that the dividend had been raised or that earnings were increasing, and then would be likely to sell the stock again at just about the time that such news finally became public information.

The Factor of "Crossing" Operations

This is an extremely simple example of psychological application, for it is the first stage of "crossing" operations, in which one group of operators "crosses" another group by planning its operations so that they are exactly the opposite of the other group's activities. The insiders "crossed" the public, by buying the stock early and then selling the stock when the public was buying it on the publication of favorable news.

We have just said that such a situation is an example of merely the *first* stage of crossing operations. This is true because, as we progress still further into the details of this same psychological approach, we may discover additional possibilities of profit in further stages of crossing, in double-crossing, or crossing the crossers, and so on to the limit of practical profit.

This principle of crossing operations is at the very basis of our profitable consideration of psychology in market success, and it is therefore advisable that we understand clearly the implications of such crossing activities, the logic behind their use and the profit motive which brings them into being.

The Theory of Crossing Activity

It is the basic motive of market profit, as a matter of fact, which does make this entire practice of crossing practical, and thus makes our study of psychology in market operation a useful one.

In clearly establishing this logical basis, it will perhaps be necessary to offend the illusions or tenets of our more sensitive readers, but the author can see no alternative. And the sooner the reader admits the logical basis for our hypothesis, the sooner will he place himself in a position to take advantage of the implications.

This basic hypothesis is that no one can make money in the market except at the expense of someone else. This statement need not be particularly shocking, because it is theoretically true of any business, activity or exchange where profit and loss are involved, whether it be in the buying and selling of stocks or of mouse-traps.

From a purely theoretical angle, the man who buys a mouse-trap and then resells it at a profit has derived that profit through depriving someone else of it — either the man he bought it from or the man he sold it to. If the man he bought it from had held it, he might have made the profit and, therefore, he may be considered to have lost the profit by selling it too soon. Likewise, the man who bought the mouse-trap at the higher price may be considered to have lost the difference in price, because he might have bought it at the lower price earlier and from the first seller.

One Man Gains, Another Loses

We need spend no further time on such purely theoretical discussion, however. The point is that in the stock market the hypothesis becomes more clearly distinguishable and, unfortunately, more culpable from the popular point of view.

The man who buys a stock for 20 and sells it for 40 has made a profit of 20 points. But he could never have made that profit unless he had found someone who was willing to sell the stock to him at the lower price and then later have found someone who was willing to buy it from him at the higher price. On the basis of pure theory, therefore, the first seller lost the 20 points profit which was taken by the principal in our illustration. He did not *actually* lose the 20 points, perhaps, but he at least lost the opportunity of making the 20 points. The same theoretical loss might be traced to the final buyer, also, for he bought at 40 the same stock that our principal originally bought at only 20. He thus lost the chance of buying 20 points lower than he did buy.

Buyers vs. Sellers

But the really important point, for our current argument, is the fact that our principal cannot be considered alone in the transaction. It is not a complete report to say that he bought the stock at 20 and sold it at 40. He was not the only individual concerned in the transaction. In order to make his trade and take his 20-point profit, he first had to buy from someone else, and later had to sell to someone else.

For every buyer of stock there must be a seller, and for every seller there must be a buyer. And our basic hypothesis may thus be further expanded to state that the only way anyone can make a profit in the stock market is by doing the opposite of what someone else wants to do whose judgment is not so good and who will suffer by doing it.

A Practical Example

To say that the "other party" in a successful trade is the "sucker" and is losing by the trade is a bald statement which does not consistently hold true, by any means. The man who sold our exampled stock at 20 might originally have bought it for 10 and might thus be making a good profit. But he might have made more. Likewise, the man who buys the stock for 40 may eventually sell it for 50, thus also making a good profit. But he, also, might have made more.

And so, somewhere along the line in every series of market transactions, resulting either in price rise or decline, there must be a theoretical loss for every profit made. If we expand our example to take in a subsequent fall in the stock as well as a continuous rise, then our theorem becomes even plainer. Suppose our friend who bought the stock at 20 and sold it at 40 had paid all that it was really worth. Suppose, also, that the man who bought the stock at 40, later realized his mistake and was then willing to sell it back to our friend for only 20. Then it is perfectly easy to see that our good friend's profit was paid directly by the loss of the man who temporarily thought the stock was worth 40.

Crossing Necessary for Market Profit

But the primary point which we are trying to get at is the necessity for this crossing type of operation in order to realize a profit. Our operator bought the stock at 20 because he bought it when someone else was selling it wrongly. Likewise, he was able to sell it at 40 because he acted on the opposite side of the market from someone who was buying. In other words, he made his profit not simply by buying and selling, but by crossing, first the previous seller and later the subsequent buyer.

And since he made a profit of 20 points by buying first and selling later, it seems logical to assume that his ability to make this profit resulted from poor judgment and theoretical loss, first by the man who sold him the stock at 20, and later by the man who bought it from him at 40.

Gains and Losses Cancel Out

Therefore we emerge to the inescapable conclusion that in order for one individual to be correct in short-term trading some other man must be incorrect. If we multiply our example by several thousand individuals, we shall approximate the understanding which the author is attempting to convey with regard to the basic crossing operations which make trading possible in securities.

If we find that 2,000,000 shares of stock were " traded " in the market yesterday, then we may be sure that 2,000,000 shares of stock were bought and 2,000,000 shares were sold on the same day. And if we could trace the subsequent history of each one of those trades we should be likely to find that resulting profits and losses were about evenly divided. Perhaps the buyers were the smart ones who saw a profit in a few days, while the sellers were the stupid ones who lost out by selling, or vice versa. Perhaps the profits might ultimately have been fairly evenly divided between buyers and sellers on that particular day but, in the long run, it is logical to assume that the bulk of individual profits and losses are cancelled out.

The Professionals Must Make a Living

Having granted the logical thesis that, in individual trades, one party makes a profit at the expense of the other party, and having further granted that this individual rule is also applied to the market as a whole, we need not go much farther in our reasoning to postulate that there may be certain groups of individuals whose judgment is so keen, whose influence is so powerful, that they do not profit on one trade and lose an equal amount on the next, but rather that their operations are consistently correct and profitable.

If we grant this one additional theorem, then we need simply call this habitually successful group the "insiders." But the theorem has its inescapable corollary — and this is perhaps the shocking part to the gentle reader. All of our preceding, and perhaps tedious, theoretical argument leads us to the logical conclusion that if there is a group of such "insiders" who are consistently successful in drawing fairly regular profit from the market, then there must also be another group of operators whose buying and selling brings them more loss than it does profit. Because we have seen that, theoretically at least, a profit in trading can result only from doing the opposite of what someone else is doing whose action will either bring him definite loss or at least deprive him of a profit that he might otherwise have had.

Who Pays the Professionals?

The reader should now be prepared for the statement that "there is no Santa Claus." Simply call this unsuccessful group of operators, trading opposite to the "insiders," the "public" class of lambs, and the picture is complete. It is the author's theory, therefore, that the "insiders" are consistently successful in their market operations, at the expense of the opposite "public" group whose fairly regular losses pay for the insiders' profit.

While the foregoing is largely theory, it appears to be logical theory, and it becomes even more logical if we examine the business of individuals or groups who draw their chief livelihood from the stock market. By far the majority of the people who trade in stocks do so as a side-line. Many make it a hobby, but to the "public" class it is often an expensive hobby — subtle and disarming in its mixture of only gradual loss and constant hope.

Professionals vs. the Public

Yet over against this class we have fair grounds for believing that there exists a much smaller group of operators who do not dabble in the market as a relaxation from a successful dental practice or grocery business, but rather who depend upon market operations for their daily bread. Security trading is their business. They live on it. They *must* make a profit from it or they would no longer continue in that business. They are the group whom we label the "insiders," or the successful professionals. And the "public" pays them their profits.

The "Business" of Making Profits

The author has not embarked upon this long exposition simply to make cynics out of his readers, to shock them or to discourage them, but rather to open their eyes to the real basis for differentiation between consistently successful operation and consistently unsuccessful operation.

As a matter of fact, there is no true necessity for the reader to be shocked. We have already noted that something of the same sort of theory holds true in any business. The point is that if the stock market student is truly desirous of making his market operations profitable, then he ought to realize that there is such a thing as the serious "business" of market operation, and align his own attitude toward the market accordingly.

The "Insiders" Reap Consistent Profit

Nor need the reader assume that such a statement means he must either go into the market as a business or else stay out entirely. If that were true, then there would be no point in the writing of this volume. The aim of our study, throughout all of our composite consideration, is not to teach the reader to make a business out of market operation, in the usual sense of the word, but rather to bring his own "part-time" market occupation into proper alignment and consonance with the "insiders" who *do* make it their business to be correct.

The reader may note that we have defined the opposing groups of successful "insiders" and unsuccessful "public," but we have not described their individual memberships. Therein lies our point. It is both impossible and unnecessary to state definitely that a certain operator is an insider because he makes market operation his sole business, and that another individual is a "lamb" because he does not give the bulk of his time to market study and operation.

How to Join the Successful Group

The term "insider" may logically be applied to those successful operators who do make the market their business. But anyone who takes enough time to study the market and align his operations with successful trends may just as logically remove himself from the "public" class of lambs and enter this indefinite but successful class of "insiders."

"If it were not so" this book, and many others, would not have been written. The grocery-store clerk in a small village of the Middle West may quite conceivably make himself just as successful, comparatively, as the professional operator. But in order to do so he must first realize the boundaries and definitions of the two classes which we have been attempting to illustrate. Being fully aware of his task will be his first and most important step in accomplishing that task.

The Problem Summarized

Having thus exposed the problem, it may happily be said that the reader is already on his way to its solution. We need not define the insider as one who makes market profit his sole business, but rather as one who gives his operations enough study, common sense and thoughtful consideration to draw from them a fair and consistent profit, whether that be his sole business or merely an interesting and a valuable side-line.

All of our studies and considerations in this volume are pointed directly toward a conscientious attempt to attain just such a successful attitude toward the market, without the necessity for giving up all of our time to market plans or to the study of intricate theories and formulae.

So far as our current method of approach is concerned we may now gather together the wandering threads of our study. We are not planning to go into business with the insider, but we can, in point of fact. We do not intend to put as much time and study on the market as he does. But we *can* become co-partners with him, by studying his methods and by studying means for detecting his probable future course of action. We need not have as much capital as the real professional to accomplish such a purpose. Logical thought, common sense and an understanding of simple psychological elements may serve as our most valuable aids.

The Simple Solution

We have already granted that the insider makes consistent profits from his market operation. We have also seen that in order to do this he must take the opposite side of the market from the public. That simple fact establishes the logical basis for the professional " crossing " the public in his average operations. And it also leads us back to our primary consideration of market psychology.

The successful insiders cannot make money by buying stocks when the public is also buying them, or by selling stocks when the public also wants to sell them. The most successful basis for inside operation is for the professional to anticipate the public desire in advance and then cater to it when it appears, by taking the opposite side.

On such a basis it is easy to see why the corporation officers, or insiders, bought stock in advance of the bullish information on earnings or dividends.[1] If they waited to buy only when the news was out, they would be competing with the public. But if they buy in advance, then they will have no difficulty in finding someone to sell to when the good news *does* come out.

Why We Must Understand Professional Operations

Our whole theory of anticipating fundamentals[2] was based upon this same type of psychological " crossing " operation. The operator who decided that a broad public demand for automobile replacements would develop in 1933 would not have reaped a very large profit if he had waited to buy motor stocks until that demand had actually ap-

[1] See p. 180. [2] See Chapter V, p. 117.

peared. Because by that time the balance of trading would be definitely on the buying side, and he would be competing on the same side of the market with everybody else.

His proper course was to " cross " the balance of trading, which was on the selling side in 1931 and 1932, thus making it easy for him to buy. Likewise, his proper course was to sell and take his profits when the public turned to the buying side on actual development and public realization of the revival in motor demand.

Two Types of Professional Crossing

Such examples of anticipating future demand or supply for stocks, and crossing them in advance, are simple ones and do not depend upon proper psychological analysis quite so much as the more professional type of crossing. This professional type may be divided into two distinct classes, the first one where the impetus is provided by public psychology and the second where the public impetus is supplied by professional psychology.

Examples of the former type are almost infinite, but a single recent one should suffice for our purpose of illustration. In Plate VIII, on page 193, we shall find a chart showing the daily movement of the New York Times, or Annalist, average of fifty combined railroad, utility and industrial stocks, from 1932 on. The market trend was strongly upward through all of January, 1934, and into the early days of February, even though "inside" news from Washington had threatened a strict stock market regulation bill for many weeks.

It is not the purpose of this volume to discuss the possibility of "inside" advance information on such a bill, but the market had a sharp decline for the full week preceding its publication.   Then, on the morning of February 10, 1934, the original draft of the Securities Exchange Act was made public, in all the seriousness of its unexpected limitations.   Probably most of those who read the bill or gave serious thought to its implications were " scared stiff " at the opening of that day's market.

An Example of Public Psychology

Even the public knew enough about it to precipitate a mild panic of selling, and the public did most certainly dump stocks overboard that morning.   Without the psychological background which we have been discussing in the current chapter, the average operator might well have expected a considerable decline, and dumped his own stocks with the rest of the public.

But the basis of psychological approach, combined with our knowledge of the necessity for professional crossing of public impetus, might have prepared the thoughtful trader for what happened.   Stocks did not decline far.   They opened off several points, it is true, but the panic was short-lived.   Why?   Simply because the insiders could not afford to sell when the public was selling.

The unfavorable news from Washington, perhaps largely unexpected at that time even by the inside element, had brought a psychological stimulus to public operation whose only reaction could be anticipated heavy selling.

Psychology Naturally Generated

But the insiders could not profit from selling when the public was also on the selling side.   They had to make their profits by *crossing* the public.   And so they bought stocks as

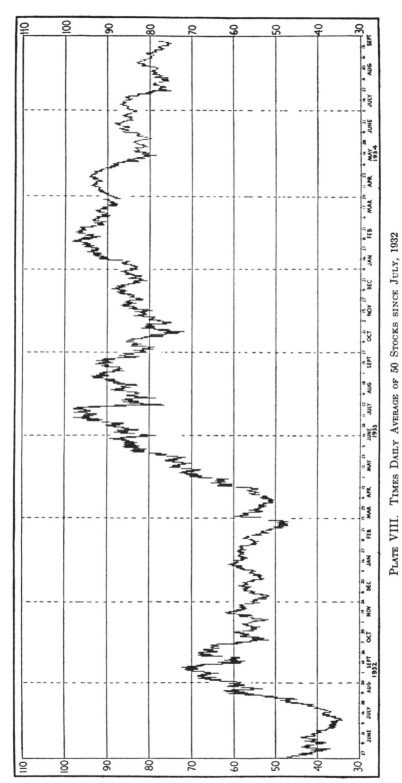

PLATE VIII. TIMES DAILY AVERAGE OF 50 STOCKS SINCE JULY, 1932

Showing the final turn of the long bear market and subsequent movements.

the public sold, contrary to current reasonable stimulus, but exactly in consonance with the dictates of psychology.

And, as usual, the insiders won. The market advanced steadily through the following week and it was only after the " public " had been reassured by this strong recovery and had begun to buy back (at higher prices) the stocks it had dumped overboard in panic, that the insiders again turned safely to the selling side once more, thus continuing to make their professional profits by crossing the stimuli and psychological reactions of the public.

Psychology Artificially Generated

Thus, in our first example, the public furnished the basic stimulus which gave the insiders their proper psychological cue in crossing operations. The other major type of professional crossing is that in which the insiders, themselves, appear to originate the public impetus, in order to make their crossing operations possible and profitable.

It is not so often that the general market offers satisfactory examples of this type, but we may illustrate our point by reference to the same Times index chart on page 193. We have no definite grounds for suspecting a deep-dyed plot on the part of the professional element, but it was at least logical to anticipate a good business recovery early in 1934. It was thus necessary for the insiders to accumulate stocks in advance of such recovery, and then sell them out when the recovery became public knowledge.

But the accumulation could only be carried on profitably if the public was first induced to sell, so that the insiders could cross by buying. How much of it was " manufactured propaganda " and how much actual fact is problematical, but it is true that, during the market decline of September and October, 1933, there was plenty of public news of a bearish and unfavorable character. The Autumn business recovery had failed to materialize as well as expected. Government was investigating, chastising, castigating business at every turn; the NRA codes were increasing wages and reducing corporation profits. Labor troubles threatened constantly. Fourth quarter and annual earnings were to be extremely disappointing. Inflation was dead as a basis for higher prices. And so on.

Psychology Directly Connected with Crossing Operations

The public, reading such disappointing news, fact and forecast, sold a considerable volume of its stock, but it is fairly apparent that the insiders were again crossing this tendency by accumulating their own lines. The market made its bottom on October 21, 1933, and then proceeded to advance quite consistently and materially until its intermediate top early in February of the following year.

By that time the public realized that corporation business and earnings were gaining. Certainly it was so informed by the bullish news advices. Probably many traders came back in and repurchased (at higher prices) the stocks they had sold out on the bearish outlook of the preceding Fall. But, while the public was finally turning to the buying side, the insiders were again switching their own operations, to keep them at proper opposites to the public. Now that the good news of improving business was out, they had customers who would buy from them the same stocks they had previously sold. The professionals crossed once more, and sold stocks as the public bought.

Much of this reasoning, of course, must be based upon pure theory. But it is logical theory. And it would have been profitable for the insiders once more, for just about the time that business figures were turning up the market made its high, in early February, and began a substantial intermediate decline.

Government Regulation No Obstacle

Our best examples of this type of inside crossing, however, are to be found in the cases of individual issues, usually where insiders, or even manipulative pools, are at work. Nor does it seem probable that Government regulation will change such situations very drastically.[1]

Whether due to such manipulative operations or not, for instance, Plate IV, on page 115, will show the reader how slowly the activity and interest in National Distillers Products picked up during the early part of 1933.[2] Not much was heard about the stock until the volume of trading got really heavy in the early Summer. Then, indeed, the public press and brokerage letters took notice of its splendid opportunities for profit on prohibition repeal.

But by that time the stock was already near its high point. It seems quite logical to suspect that the " insiders " who bought the stock quietly at the beginning of the year were crossing the avid public by selling out that stock during June and early July, when the price shot rapidly up to 125, and then dropped precipitately back to 65 in a few days.

A Practical Example Suggestive of Inside Crossing

Or, if we care to glance ahead at Plate XI, on page 269, of Chapter X, we shall find another individual stock movement which may illustrate our theory. Along with many other corporations, Paramount Famous-Lasky had been ex-

[1] See Chapter VI, p. 125.   [2] See Chapter V, p. 116.

panding considerably during the "new era." It is logical to assume that at least a few powerful and keen-minded insiders had the perception to suspect that some of this expansion was dangerous, and might, in fact, prove disastrous, if business declined, or if the market for the company's stock did not hold up above certain contractual levels.

During the Panic of 1929 Paramount broke sharply from around 76 to 35, suggesting perhaps the inside realization of the company's danger. But there came the logical time when the public began to sell the stock also, probably between 35 and 50. That meant that the insiders could no longer offer their own stock for sale without unduly depressing its price. If they were really scared, if they really wanted to sell, they could not do so successfully in a weak market, with the public also selling, for then there would be nobody to sell their stock to.

Public Psychology in Paramount

The logical thing to accomplish was a new building up of public confidence in the issue, thus providing a popular demand for the stock which would supply the "other side" of the deal and would absorb their own selling. In the Spring of 1930 the general market staged a technical and intermediate recovery from the Panic, but a glance at any average will show that the recovery was by no means suggestive of a new bull market. Most of the accredited indexes came back up barely halfway to their 1929 peaks.

Not so, Paramount. The stock was one of the strongest in the list and, accompanied by enthusiastic rumors and favorable reports for the future, it shot back up not only to equal its previous 1929 top but actually to exceed that previous high mark by several points.

What was the result? Just what it would be logical for the insiders to hope for and work for, if they wanted to create a public buying demand to absorb the stock that they themselves had to sell. Strong-arm buying sent the stock up so rapidly and so high that many short-sellers were "stopped out" and joined the public demand, whether they believed the bullish stories which were whetting popular buying appetites or not.

Theory vs. Proof

The result is history, even though it must be theoretical history. The insiders created the public market for their stock. As the public bought, they themselves sold. Near the top of the move to 87½, in March of 1930, volume of sales reached a high record volume of around 85,000 shares a day.[1] Major distribution covered a wide period of perhaps three months. And then the stock began to break more rapidly than the rest of the market. Early in 1933 the company went into receivership and the stock sold for less than 50 cents a share.

It is, of course, much easier to formulate the logic of such an "inside crossing" example, with the whole chart history before us, than it was to see the danger signals in 1929 and 1930. The author does not claim to have foreseen all that followed in Paramount, for the indications were by no means clear or simple. But there were plenty of technical and fundamental suggestions of danger at that time. And when these were coupled with our current consideration of market psychology and inside crossing operations, then the bullish propaganda of early in 1930 might well have given basis for question and cynicism at that time.

[1] See Chapter VI, p. 148.

Attitude More Important than Precept

Our individual examples in the present chapter, however, are offered not so much as a basis for ironclad detection of psychological deception, as they are to instil into the reader's consciousness the common sense and logic of our psychological approach to the problem of future market forecast.

When we have fully realized the fundamental fact that successful insiders must usually take the opposite side of the market from the public in order to be successful, then we are ready to understand also the plain logic of the fundamental corollary that the market seldom does the obvious, or takes the course that the public expects it to.

The Practical Application

And with this theorem, our complete basis of psychology may begin to clarify itself. If, through the use of psychological reasoning, we can evaluate the factors which are being reflected in the public mind, then we can also anticipate the manner in which the public will react to such mass stimuli. And we can then turn to the opposite side of the situation and investigate more fully the logical grounds for anticipating that the market may do just the opposite of what the public is doing and expecting the market to do.

We have admitted that our current illustrations are fallible.[1] They have been offered more to induce the psychological point of view than for the value of the theories in such practical instances alone. That is because this factor of psychological approach which we are considering is not

[1] See p. 195.

one which stands out by itself the way many of our other theories do.

Needless to say, it is not a very definite avenue of approach. But if we become familiar with its reason, with its logical basis and with its general importance, then it may well become part of our growing catalog of tools for market profit. And it will do so, not because it is complete in itself, but because it gives us just one more useful aid in our approach to that composite market judgment toward which we are pointing our study. Often the thesis will be practically useless. But there will be other times when it may become the critical consideration between success and failure.

Why the Market Seldom Does the Obvious

Such a broad psychological approach is hardly a rule at all. It is more a state of mind, an attitude toward the market, toward the news that affects it, and toward the popular ideas about the market. From it, the operator should begin to see that there is little merit in following the crowd, in putting blind trust in gossip, in widely-circulated rumor, in newspaper propaganda, or even, at times, in official corporation reports. It should teach him why the market so seldom takes the obvious course of movement, and why there is little hope for the operator who always does the obvious in his market trading.

The psychological attitude is one which may often best be applied to the future movement of the market as a whole, in its broad intermediate trends. Perhaps its most valuable aspect is merely to instil the importance of changing one's general attitude toward the market, from one of the public reaction to current stimuli into the psychological tendency of the professional.

"What Would the Insiders Be Doing Now?"

After all, there are only two possible courses of action in these broad, sweeping trends of market movement. The operator should either sell or he should buy. The psychological approach will lead the individual away from the obvious conclusions, and will lead him to pause in his analytical considerations every now and then and put himself mentally in the shoes of the professional.

"What would the insider be doing in a market like this?" "What would the professionals and the powerful traders be up to under current conditions and current public stimulus?"

Such questions will lead naturally into a much more profound, a much more professional, and probably a much more successful, attitude toward these intermediate swings. They will tend to restrain the individual from blind and panicky selling on publication of unfavorable news. And they will lead him just as surely to a healthy cynicism of rapid advances on publication of good news.

Why Prices Move Counter to Reason

They will lead him to calculate for himself the most profitable course that the inside professionals might adopt if they wish to accomplish certain aims. If the individual's careful analysis indicates, for instance, that there will be less favorable market factors developing four to six months from now, then he will not jump to the simple conclusion that selling should begin in volume at the present time. He should rather suspect that the market will be advanced in the meanwhile, be made to look strong, that favorable reports and prospects will be published, that the insiders will do all in their power to encourage public buying, in order that their own selling, on the crossing principle, may be done in volume and with profit.

He should not be misled by a rather enthusiastic advance in the market toward the close of the week, or just before a holiday, when the public will have spare time to read the financial pages more carefully and place their buying orders. He should not be misled by all the artifices which his own psychological considerations can conjure up to increase public buying. He can perhaps do some valuable thinking on the subject of whatever theories the public holds most closely to heart, no matter how unorthodox or treasonable such thinking may seem at the moment.

Crossing the Technical Indications

And the author does not close his eyes to the fact that such thinking might include a consideration of technical signals as well as fundamental ones. If the perusal of widely-circulated forecasts, financial columns and brokerage-house letters, for instance, should indicate that the up-side penetration of a certain point on the market averages would signal further wide advance, then the psychological student may well reason the logic of professional efforts to engineer such a penetration, simply because public attention has been called to it.

And the author would have no objection to the reader's discounting such ordinarily useful signals under these circumstances, and substituting the thought that when that occurs and the " public " buys, he might well be on the lookout for inside selling and an early reversal of the favorable " technicast."

Most technical theories are not widely enough known or used to prove dangerous or misleading in such regard, and the bulk of such theories probably never will be. But there are certain simple rules (like a "double top," for instance) which become popular enough at intervals, if talked about in the press or in brokerage circulars, to discount their usual value, simply on this psychological basis. The point is that the individual who is attempting to align his own psychology with that of the professional insider, will keep his eyes open for individual theories which do become common enough to make crossing operations profitable.

Crossing the Fundamental Indications

The fundamental field, however, is of course the more fertile of the two, and it is here that the best use may be made of the psychological approach. We have already discussed the proper cynical attitude toward such fundamentals as reports of increased earnings, dividends, better business, etc.[1]

By far our most valuable use of the psychological approach will come, however, from a broad and general mingling of all factors which affect the public mind, whether they are technical, fundamental or what not.[2] Around the middle of January, 1934,[3] for instance, general sentiment shifted strongly bullish over the week-end as a result of inflationary gestures from Washington and other news factors.

The market opened up sharply on the morning of January 15th, after vacillating gently up and down for many weeks. The previous picture was still in the public mind, and even

[1] See Chapter V, p. 108.   [3] See Plate VIII, p. 193.
[2] See Chapter XI, p. 289.

the general consensus of good Wall Street opinion was that the rise was too sharp to hold. Psychology said, however, that, if that was the general opinion, then it was the best reason for expecting that the advance *would* continue, until these " doubters " became convinced that the rise was genuine and turned from selling to buying. And the advance did continue for just about that long.

Some Specific Examples

And again, the technical point of view entered in. Many widely-read commentators had been preaching for some time that, on the basis of the Dow theory,[1] penetration of the market through the previous July tops of 1933 would be exceedingly bullish. Enough publicity was given this theory to suggest that if the insiders wanted to create a demand so they could sell stocks, their best way to do it was to attempt such penetration. The author does not claim that such penetration was deliberately engineered by professional manipulation, for there were plenty of bullish news factors. But it might easily have been " abetted " by insiders. Or, if we assume that they had nothing to do with the advance and with encouragement of public buying, such demand nevertheless tempted professional selling on the " crossing " basis.

As a matter of fact, the railroad average did not confirm penetration of the industrial index, so the Dow signal was not genuine, but the bullish tendency was present nevertheless. Now, temporarily, the public construed the gold dollar devaluation act, passed at that time, as bullish. But it tended toward dollar stabilization, which was also a less apparent, but bearish, factor. Also, it was common knowl-

[1] See Chapter VI, p. 136.

edge that some sort of security market regulation bill would soon be announced,[1] which would probably also be bearish.

The psychological thinker, faced with such a situation, might well have suspected that the insiders were selling stocks as the public bought, and that at least an intermediate reaction was not so far off. As a matter of fact, it materialized in less than a week, and the subsequent decline was both wide and persistent.

The Summer Declines of 1934

Crossing psychology of somewhat the same sort, but in reverse, might have been suggested by the market declines in the Summer of 1934. For nearly a year, general sentiment had been decidedly bullish for the long term. The services and professional advisers were consistently recommending purchase, and the public had been steeped in " inflation " psychology and the theorem that the market simply had to go up. Once again, psychology suggested that a logical action would be the crossing one, and stocks declined sharply in the late Summer and early Autumn months.

Back to Common-Sense Thinking

At bottom, of course, this psychological method of approach is really nothing more than the old basis of our entire volume — good judgment, common sense, some real thought and logical consideration.

Toward the close of 1933,[2] for instance, Government sympathy and encouragement for labor led to constantly growing employee difficulties, resulting in threats of serious strikes and tie-ups. Public reaction was generally fearful

---

[1] See p. 192.   [2] See Plate VIII, p. 193.

and bearish. But it was merely common-sense reasoning to anticipate that such strikes would not have been possible if orders and business had not been on the increase, and also that the same Government which had encouraged labor and which was working so hard for industrial recovery would not countenance any long-drawn-out interference with industrial production or the bases of business recovery.

But perhaps the most bullish argument for the immediate future was that thus far there were chiefly only *threats* of serious strikes. Our postulated attitude of putting oneself in the other fellow's place led to the inescapable conclusion that the mere threatening of such strikes, with implication of possible difficulty in obtaining future deliveries, would lead business men to place rush orders immediately and to buy ahead, thus giving a powerful, even if temporary, impetus to industrial activity.

Following Logical Lines of Market Reasoning

Such theoretical reasoning is never open to definite proof. But it seems logical to suspect that such factors had considerable to do with the quickening of business operations over the next few months and the early reversal of stock prices into a fairly substantial recovery which followed. The public, acting on the usual immediate fear instilled by press stories of threatened strikes, sold stocks and made it easy for the longer-visioned and more astute insiders to buy them for the ensuing profit.[1]

From a more fundamental angle, likewise, the sharp gains in business indexes during the early Summer of 1933 were not so bullish as they might have appeared to the public. The operator who was looking ahead might have suspected

[1] See also p. 195.

that sudden gains on heavy speculative and advance buying resulted largely from impending Government codes and processing taxes which would make it more costly to buy later than at that time. There was bound to be a considerable reaction in business when such·codes and taxes finally went into effect and when the heavy purchasers could coast along on their advance buying without further current demand. The author would not argue, of course, that such reasoning accounted fully for the reactions late that Summer, but at least it added a factor of natural logic, based largely on psychological analysis.

How Psychology Ties in with Basic Rules

And so, in closing our excursion into the psychological paths of approach, we may see once more that, while our individual theories are not totally infallible in themselves, or even always very definite, they may often add to our store of general knowledge and may bring us some valuable aid in composite judgment for proper forecast.

Our consideration of the psychological attitude should teach us the basic logic of cynicism regarding popular market expectation. It should show us why the market so often does the unexpected, and why we should shy away from purely obvious and easy forecasts. It should teach us to attempt the attitude of the successful professional and to question the attitude of the public. It should disclose the fundamental advantages of forward thinking and clear reasoning,[1] in order that we may join the insiders in anticipating future developments. Thus, through our own crossing operations, we may be in a position to take our profits when those future developments do occur, instead of joining

[1] See Chapter V, p. 111.

the public in merely initiating our trades at the obvious moment.

Results of the Proper Attitude

And, finally, our psychological considerations should teach us the necessity for courage when once we have followed through our logical analysis for the future and made our calculated decision. It is much easier to follow the crowd than to buck it. It takes courage to align oneself with the successful insider, for it means that we shall often be buying when popular sentiment is the blackest, and shall be selling when sentiment and general conditions seem most generally promising.

Such courageous bucking of the apparent, easy, and obvious path has its dangers, of course, and should usually be protected by mental limitation of possible loss. It *will* bring losses at times, but they should be small ones. And they should be almost negligible compared with the profit which can come to the individual who realizes the psychological "facts of life" which we have considered in this chapter, who is willing to use common sense, logical reasoning, sound thinking and mental courage in deserting the easy, public attitude and aligning his approach with the reason, foresight and profit of the professional contingent, whose hallowed ranks he joins by that very course.

CHAPTER IX

COMMON SENSE AND FORESIGHT IN TRADING

Continuing the Logical Approach

If the reader has gotten as much out of previous chapters as the author fondly hopes that he has, then he may well feel that the present chapter heading might be applied to many other chapters, and to most of our previous consideration. As has been noted so often, the entire approach which we have been attempting to master herein is the combination of some basic rules of logic with a healthy utilization of one's own native thought.

Our current chapter is therefore merely a continuation of the attitude which we have been considering in all that has gone before. But there is still room for more specific attention to previous suggestions as well as some new angles of successful trading, on this important and valuable basis of plain common sense and foresight.

More on Conservatism

One of the most important of such factors is that of conservatism in all trading and market policy. And with this virtue we tend to return to the less positive, more preventive approach to practical success. In our opening chapter we considered some of the cardinal rules for general market profit, such as warning against over-confidence, against hasty action and against ever holding too dogmatic views on future trends of the market, all of which are closely aligned with our current arguments for conservatism. In succeeding chapters, we have concentrated our main attention on the more positive aspect of successful operation, seeking out the proper methods of approach, the more basic, successful and simple rules for assuring the consistent accuracy of our own composite judgment. Having studied diligently the most useful methods for making our trading successful, we may take further steps to protect ourselves on those occasions, rare ones we may hope, when our judgment turns out to have been wrong instead of right.

By insisting upon the importance of such protective technique, through repetition and fuller consideration, the author is not suggesting any lack of faith in the efficacy of our positive rules for success. What he has tried to stress through our entire study, however, is that the mere knowledge of such positive rules is not going to insure permanent infallibility in our market judgment. Such theories and practical methods of approach should most certainly increase our successful trades and diminish our unsuccessful ones, but the sooner the reader gets rid of any notion of infallibility the nearer he will be to the properly humble approach to successful market practice.

Back to the Protective Technique

As we noted in our opening chapter,[1] it is not the correct market commitments which try our mettle as successful traders, but the incorrect commitments. Anyone can be successful if he is on the right side of the market. But his profits on many previous successful trades may be entirely wiped out and turned into tragic loss if he does not know

[1] See Chapter I, p. 19.

how to handle one single unfortunate and unsuccessful situation.

And so, in returning to our basic consideration of such defensive tactics, we may emphasize once more the importance of conservatism in practical market operation. It is no difficult feat to be a market "plunger." It requires no greater analysis, from a theoretical standpoint, to risk a million dollars on any single market decision and the resulting commitment, than to risk only $500 on such a commitment. From a market and judgment standpoint the results will be the same. Either the judgment is correct and a profit results, or the judgment is incorrect and a loss results. The only basic difference in mental activity is nerve. And the only basic difference in physical activity is the added energy which it takes to write " 1,000 " shares on a brokerage order pad instead of only " 10 " or " 20 " shares.

Plunger vs. Conservative

Wherein lies the difference, then, between the plunger and the conservative operator? The difference lies in personal attitude toward the market, in psychological strain and in a certain element which we may rather inaccurately call chance.

The personal attitude of the plunger is likely to be one of daring. He risks so much of his capital on a single trade that he is also likely to risk much more in his judgment and analysis. He is likely to be abrupt, dogmatic and prejudiced in his analysis, if not actually slipshod in his methods. The very traits which lead him to risk such capital lead him also to substitute risk for knowledge, chance for study and a thorough weighing of the situation. And the results are much more apt to be disastrous on that account.

The psychological strain is perhaps ordinarily not so great for the plunger as it would be for the habitual conservative. But in most cases the fact is that the plunger does not worry until his over-commitment goes wrong. Then, however, with terrific and misguided losses piling up, he is just as likely to break under the strain and lose any semblance of sane thinking and calm judgment as is the conservative trader.

The psychological point is that no operator can think as clearly when he is worried or scared as when his risk is small enough and his campaign sufficiently well mapped out to allow him to concentrate on the proper method of limiting his loss instead of worrying about it.

Advantages in the Conservative Attitude

But the third advantage of the conservative trader over the plunger is just as important, even though it is perhaps more theoretical. The neophyte may well ask, "Well, after all, if I'm going to be successful, why not multiply my profits? If I'm a flop, why prolong my interest in unsuccessful operation?"

The most pertinent answers have been given in the paragraphs above. But the element of chance must also be considered. Success in the market does not mean the complete absence of loss. It means that there will be a greater number of profitable commitments than unprofitable ones. It means that profits on successful campaigns will be larger than losses on unsuccessful ones. It means that success in market trading is not measured by one or two spectacular trades but, rather, that profits are greater than losses over a long period of time, that success comes from average performance in many trades.

The Basic Theory Involved

If the individual is going to be successful over the long-range period, then he might expect perhaps seven profits out of ten tries, and three losses out of ten commitments. But the plunger may happen to take his three losses first. They clean him out and he is rubbed from the picture before he had a chance to get started. Or else his capital is so depleted that his judgment is already warped when the time comes for his seven profitable ventures.

Or, perhaps his seven profitable commitments come first. His plunging results in large gains, but the result is likely to make him even more reckless than when he started out. He is apt to increase his commitments even more carelessly than before and thus lead to much greater than proportional loss when the time comes for his three unsuccessful commitments.

The conservative trader is free from all such dangers. He avoids the psychological handicap of over-strain or worry on his unsuccessful commitments. He builds his self-confidence and his judgment slowly. He is not so prone to dogmatic and swift conclusions. And his operations work along with the law of averages in much more satisfactory manner than those of the plunger.

How it Works in Practice

If we look at the matter from a purely practical angle of experience, we shall reach the same conclusions. The annals of Wall Street personalities are marked by the records of many plungers and many conservatives. The success of the conservatives is perhaps less spectacular, but it is certainly more consistent and lasting.

The successful plunger may make a great name for himself for many years, on account of his huge profits. But by far the majority make just as great names for themselves, and far more tragic ones, by later failure and disaster. No names need be mentioned but the reader is probably familiar with those great meteors of past market fame who have gone through one bankruptcy after another, and who have finally died in poverty, loneliness and despair.

" One out of a Thousand "

Let the reader ponder this basic fact. Out of a thousand individuals who enter the market, he may read in the newspapers of two, because of their practical success. One of these will be a conservative and will be consistently successful and happy. The other will be a plunger and will very likely get later publicity because he has lost the fortune that he previously made.

We are more interested, however, in the other 998 traders. Perhaps half of them are plungers and half are conservatives. The conservatives do not win public fame because their profits are slow and reasonable, but they continue to profit and to be satisfied. The plungers are not mentioned either. Why? Because they were not successful in their first experiences and were wiped out. They seldom get a second chance. They are the " down-and-outs " who nobody ever knows were plungers.

Plunging Success Rests on Luck

Just as in business, therefore, the plungers who are successful come to public attention. The ones who go down to defeat are never heard about. It is largely a matter of luck in market plunging as in business plunging. The plungers are by no means smarter or more capable than the conservatives. They are usually less so. The chief difference is that we hear of the successful plungers, whereas we are not so likely to hear of the much larger number of successful conservatives. The plunger takes a greater risk for the chance of fame and fortune. One out of several hundred may be successful, and it is he that we hear about. But his example should be no invitation to plunge, for the others, who did not have luck on their side, are never brought to our notice.

Let the reader be convinced, therefore, that conservatism is his best market policy, certainly until he has tested his ability for several years. The proper approach, and the one which this volume has stressed in perhaps tedious fashion, is moderate but consistent profit, rather than spectacular but fleeting profit. One of Wall Street's truest adages is that at times the bull may profit and at other times the bear may profit, but the pig never profits.

The Cardinal Theory of Compromise

Another aspect of common sense and foresight in market trading is our gospel of compromise, and it is the best companion virtue to conservatism.[1] It is also a protective factor, rather than a positive one. But it may easily be proven of positive importance and profit through practice as well as theory.

It goes hand in hand with conservatism because there is no denying that conservatism may be carried to an extreme, especially if the individual is characteristically inclined in that direction. The writer is prone to preach the protective

[1] See Chapter IV, p. 96.

gospel of conservatism at length because his experience has shown that most individuals need strong arguments. But there is another group, smaller but still definitely extant, which carries this virtue to such an extreme that it becomes the opposite vice of indecision, constant worry and constant procrastination. This type of individual is careful and meticulous in his analysis. He is likely to be correct and successful. But his native conservatism leads him to constant doubt of his own ability, with the result that he delays his proper commitment until it is too late to be profitable, and then spends the rest of his time regretting the delay.

How to Correct Market Timidity

This type of personality and approach is more to be desired than the plunger type, but both must be corrected. The advantage for the conservative is that correction is easy and simple, through the doctrine of compromise.[1] If a definite judgment is arrived at, but actual trading is held up on account of doubt and conservatism, then the simple and effective way out is compromise. Everyone has a fairly definite commitment in mind while considering a stock. Very well, if the proposed commitment is 100 shares, simply cut it down to 50 shares, and the doubts and conservative tendencies melt away. If the originally-conceived commitment is only 20 shares, then procrastination may be overcome by cutting the actual trade to only 10 shares.

The practical result of such compromise method is, first, to spur the individual to practical action and, second, to reduce the risk so that there will be psychological satisfaction no matter how the trade turns out. If it is profitable, then the conservative may well be glad that he overcame his fears

[1] See Chapter X, p. 254.

and bought even only 10 shares. If it is unsuccessful, he will still be glad that he did not buy the originally-conceived block of 20 shares. In either case, practical market trading is combined with mental satisfaction and that, after all, is one of our desired qualities in operation.

How to Treat Indecision

But the compromise theory is not designed alone for the conservative. It is a positive aid to any operator, large or small, both from a practical and from a psychological angle. It offers the sane, simple and logical answer to any and every circumstance of doubt, worry or fear in market operation.

It has always been a puzzle to the author why the average individual, when his market trades worry him, cannot see the logic of this compromise solution. He frets and stews over one difficult question, when the simple and easy answer lies in breaking his problem down into several easy questions. He lies awake nights trying to decide whether or not he shall get out of 100 shares of Steel at a two-point loss, being utterly unable to decide whether Steel is going up or down. His whole attitude is subconsciously based on " 100 shares or nothing." How simple the proper step is made by the principle of compromise. The logical answer is simply to reduce the risk, in such a case of indecision, and to sell half of the commitment only, or 50 shares.

How to Avoid Worry

This may seem like a weak answer, akin to begging the question or to improper vacillation. The answer is that it is only resorted to when the individual has already begged the question. His very indecision indicates that he does not know the proper answer to his question of whether to sell the full commitment or not. Selling half of the commitment, and compromising on the problem, is no further step toward vacillation or indecision. It is the proper and logical answer to such indecision, for it reduces the risk of possible loss in such a troublesome situation, gratifies the desire and necessity for action, and supplies also the practical certainty of mental relief for the present and psychological satisfaction for the future.

The mere fact that the individual is worrying over his commitment is sufficient grounds for considering it dangerous and therefore advisable to reduce the risk. And the same psychological satisfaction is almost bound to result as we have already observed to be characteristic of the compromise principle. If the stock goes down still further, the trader is glad that he sold out half of his commitment, and he is in better position to deal intelligently with the balance, even resorting to successive scaling down on the same principle if doubt is renewed. But if the stock advances, then he will not regret overly much the fact that he sold out 50 shares, because he will still have the satisfaction of not having sold it all, as he had considered doing.

Importance of the Stop-Loss Principle

Another comforting instrument that is aligned with common sense and foresight in trading is the stop-loss principle. It may be assumed that the reader is familiar with this automatic device for trading, and he is probably also familiar with its advantages and disadvantages. A short argument for its use is not out of order, however, for there are plenty of operators who are on bad terms with it.

As ordinarily used, the stop order is designed to have a buying or selling order in any stock executed if it touches a certain stated price level, and without further attention from the trader. It transmits, in practice, the duty for action, under certain conditions, from the shoulders of the individual to the responsibility of his broker. In broader conception, however, the stop principle is merely the decision on the part of the individual that if his stock pursues a certain course of price action, he will either buy or sell it at such future time. Thus, the "stop" can be purely mental and need not be transmitted to the broker in advance.

Mental vs. Actual Stop Order

There are, in fact, advantages for the mental type of stop order over the actual transmission of such an order to the broker in advance. Brokers are sometimes not overly anxious or willing to accept all types of stop orders. Furthermore, efforts toward Government regulation of the security markets indicate that its use is frowned upon, as providing potential danger of sharp acceleration in market movements when bunches of stop orders are caught and executed in volume. Finally, while there is no proof that floor-traders "gun" for such stop orders if they can discover where they lie on brokers' books, there *does* exist some suspicion along these lines and with fair logic, especially in the case of large blocks of stock.

If one's stop orders are mental, therefore, there exists no possible danger from such an angle. In the case of mental stop orders, there is the disadvantage, of course, that the individual runs the risk of having the price drop straight through his mental stop limit during the day unless he is watching the market himself. But the chances are not great that such an occurrence would be at all common, or serious in its results.

Automatic Limitation of Loss

The stop order is valuable, in the author's opinion, chiefly because it is the easiest and most certain method for following our basic rule to limit all losses.[1] It has its disadvantages and no dogmatic rule for its constant use can be set up. But the author is convinced that the majority of those crippling losses that play such havoc with the average operator's capital, to say nothing of his morale, could be avoided, easily and simply, by the use of stop-loss orders, be they actual market orders or merely mental limits on risk.

We have already referred to the use of such protective instrument in our introductory chapter[1] in connection with the advantages of planning one's campaign and weighing the risk in any transaction before the commitment is made, rather than afterward. This is fundamental, both from the standpoint of practical market success and for psychological peace of mind and freedom from worry. The stop-loss order is the bosom friend of the conservative individual, but it is also the need of every trader, whether he realizes it or not. The conservative, who hesitates in carrying out his analysis because of fear or timidity, may reduce his risk, as we have already noted.[2]

But he may also choose the alternative course of limiting his risk, through the simple expedient of the stop protection. If he hesitates in buying 100 shares of Steel at 100 because he is not quite certain it is going up, he may buy only 50 shares and thus reduce his risk. Or he may buy 100 shares at 100, and immediately enter his stop-loss order to "sell

---

[1] See Chapter I, p. 22.   [2] See p. 216.

100 shares at 97 stop, good till cancelled," thus limiting his risk of loss to only 3 points. Or he may, of course, use both methods of protection, by buying only half of his projected commitment, and then stopping that smaller block at a three-point maximum loss.

In Harmony with Basic Rules

Whether he is in the "conservative" class or not, however, the average operator may also find much value in this protective use of the stop order, particularly in short-swing trading. Its chief merit lies in practically "forcing" him to get out of a commitment if it does not work out in accordance with his previous analysis. There is no room for hope, for procrastination, for waiting one more day on the chance of a rally, for carelessness or forgetfulness. He should be *made* to get out, with his small and limited loss, in order to avoid a much larger and more serious loss. For possibility of the latter is definitely enhanced by the very fact that the market is not following the operator's analysis or previous conclusions, and has already started to move against him.

The greatest danger of serious market loss, especially in short-term operation, is found once more in the purely human element of wish-thinking, of hope and pride of personal opinion. A man buys Steel at 100, for the short-term, not because he thinks it is going down, but because he thinks it is going up. If it goes down even only a few points, then his original judgment has already been proven faulty. His judgment on that commitment is wrong. His new judgment, in the light of the modest decline, is just as likely to continue being wrong, and he had best get out while the getting is good, and limit his loss.

The Dangers of "Holding On"

Yet how common, and human, it is to cling to one's original analysis of advance. " Nothing but a technical reaction — purely temporary — only down two or three points, anyway — probably come back up tomorrow." Perhaps such mental calculations are correct. But, then again, perhaps they are not correct. The first calculation has already been proven wrong. That makes the chances just so much greater that the current calculations will also prove incorrect and that delay will result merely in piling up a greater loss.

Tomorrow the stock may drop another three points. Then the real worry begins. " Too late to sell now — should have sold yesterday — six points too big a loss to take — wait for a recovery and then sell, even at two or three points loss."

How Small Losses Grow

But " tomorrow " may bring still another decline, instead of that hoped-for recovery. Then the jig is up, unless the operator has sense enough to get out immediately and take his licking. Such a licking of even 10 points or more would be money well spent if he really learned his lesson. But anyone who has had any wide experience in the market at all knows how often the greatest tragedies, with results that linger for years or a lifetime, start with such innocent beginnings in short-term, speculative operation. The stop-loss order, placed with the broker at time of purchase, or the mental stop order which is carried out conscientiously and bravely, are the best practical means of protection against such crippling catastrophes.

Stop Principle in Short Trading

If the stop order is advisable in speculative long commitments, then it is practically indispensable in short operations. The author has no objections to short selling,[1] provided it is legal. It would seem both unfair, inconsistent and dangerous to suppress it. But it may readily be admitted that it is exceedingly dangerous for the average trader, unless every short commitment is conscientiously and immediately protected by the automatic use of the stop order, either mental or with the broker. No further consideration need here be given to this point,[1] but the author may simply repeat, as an axiom, that no short commitment should ever be made without establishing at least mental stop-loss protection before the original sale is contracted.

The author is quite willing to admit the indictment that stop-loss orders are often caught by only a fraction of a point, during false moves or shake-outs, after which the market proceeds to do the expected, but without the stop-user aboard. Everyone has had such experiences and they are exasperating. But it may also be said that they often result from the improper use, or improper placing, of such stops.[2]

Disadvantages of the Stop Principle

Even with the best judgment and greatest care in the placing of such stop orders, however, the operator must expect to be " taken in " once in a while, by execution of his stop order and desertion of his commitment, with a small loss, just before a reversal which would have brought him a

[1] For full discussion, see " Stock Market Theory and Practice," Chapter IX.   [2] See p. 224.

large profit.   A moderate proportion of such experiences is perfectly normal.   And the operator should consider them merely a fair price to pay for the valuable protection against large and crippling loss which the principle affords him.

If such losses become too frequent, however, then it is likely that the student is not using the principle correctly. He may be placing the stops too close to his commitment price.   He may be using them at the wrong time, or placing his original commitments at the wrong time, which amounts to the same thing.   There are many cases where stop-loss protection is excessively dangerous and that is one reason why the author is not dogmatic in advising its *constant* use.

But certainly in the case of the beginner one should pass up the temptation to trade on such situations which do not lend themselves naturally to use of the stop protection principle, and should wait patiently for the ideal situation where the principle is properly justified.

Proper Uses of the Stop

The logical test for measuring whether any given situation is open to use of stop-loss protection, either mental or actual, is a simple one.   It is any case where future execution of one's mental stop order would automatically reverse the market analysis which has led to the original commitment. In other words, the ideal situation for stop protection is one where all indications point to a certain definite movement in the immediate future, but where the indications will promptly and automatically be negated if the actual market movement is in the opposite direction from the current forecast.

A specific illustration is perhaps the quickest way to certain understanding of this principle, and we may glance first at Plate VII, on page 163. There are almost constant possibilities for use of the stop-loss principle in this chart, but we shall select only a few basic examples. At Points B–C–D, for instance, we have a fair suggestion of a technical bottom formation,[1] and a long position was justified at Point D, between 138 and 139.

Here was an ideal situation for the use of automatic protection. If the trend continued upward the picture would remain bullish. But if this favorable forecast was not correct we should very soon know it. For if the market turned about and declined only to a level of about 136 then our bullish forecast would be reversed into a bearish one and we should make haste to liquidate our long position. The proper commitment was purchase at around 138, with at least a mental stop-loss level at just under 136.

Examples in Actual Trading

By use of this simple and logical formula we could practically guarantee that, no matter what happened, we should not suffer a loss of much over two points on the average. We should assume that the market's bullish forecast would bring us a good profit. But if the forecast, or our interpretation, were faulty, then we were automatically protected against any undue, or crippling, losses.

There was a fairly rapid advance of about five points and we might have taken profits around 142, retired our commitments and dismissed the stop-loss protection. Whether we did this or not is immaterial for our current consideration. The important point to be noted is that just as soon as the average dropped back below 136, we sold out and cut our losses short, because that decline had already reversed

---

[1] See Chapter VII, p. 162.

the previous bullish implication into a new and definitely unfavorable forecast.

The reader may see for himself, in the subsequent rapid decline of 24 points, whether it was worth while to avail oneself of this opportunity for automatic protection against "bucking" a technical market trend.

Operating on the Master Index

At around Point Q there is another good opportunity for use of stop-loss protection, this time on the short side, or at least for selling long holdings. The technical picture was bearish enough to justify sales at around 141. Stop-loss levels were around 144, thus insuring that if the market did not actually go on down, as it had already suggested it should, we would in no case lose more than three or four points. As a matter of fact, of course, such action would have proved highly profitable on the ensuing major decline.

Still another illustration has already been studied in some detail: the broad and critical support levels across the approximate level of 120 on this same chart.[1] Certainly the bulk of trading commitments on the long side should have been thrown overboard when that final level was eventually broken, following Point Y. In this particular case a stop-loss order "with the broker" would have saved about three points, since prices broke rapidly as they went through the 120 level. The operator who was not watching the market during the day, and who had merely a mental stop-loss order in this case, would have had to sell at the next day's opening, at around 117. But he would still have had reason for thanking the principle of automatic protection. In little more than a month the same average had broken below 80.

[1] See Chapter VII, p. 165.

The Positive Uses of Stop Protection

It is not necessary, however, to consider the stop-loss principle useful only in the case of unsuccessful campaigns. In a somewhat indirect way, it may often lead to very successful profit, chiefly through the theory that, when a commitment is adequately protected by the stop-loss formula, the operator is justified in taking wider and more frequent chances for profit.

In practical terminology this theory is known as the coupled-order formula. It is hardly a new theory[1] but it is a valuable one, and there seems no reason to suspect that it will lose any essential value in the near-term future, in spite of Government disapproval of the stop-loss order. The latter is an important part of the coupled-order formula, but we have already noted[2] that stop-loss protection may be utilized just about as successfully on a mental basis as though the order were actually placed with one's broker in advance.

The Coupled Formula

We have also already noted the ideal situation for the use of stop-loss protection, where a forecast has been given but will be reversed if the close protective level is violated. Thus we buy if the current forecast appears favorable, but we protect ourselves against large loss by the automatic stop-loss level. But in all such cases, we do not actually anticipate that this stop-loss order will be executed. We expect the market to continue upward in pursuance of its bullish forecast, or we should not buy. The stop-loss

[1] See "Stock Market Theory and Practice," p. 543.
[2] See p. 219.

order will only be executed in those properly rare instances when the previous forecast, or our judgment, shall be proved faulty.

Granted that we are to be offered a profit on most of such commitments, therefore, the next practical decision to be made is when to accept such profit. The coupled formula is merely a simple expedient for suggesting when to close out this type of commitment, either with a loss or with a profit.

Having established our stop-loss level in advance, we know where we shall sell if the result is to be a loss. Where, then, shall we sell if the result is a profit?

Use in Successful, as Well as Unsuccessful, Trades

The coupled theory merely suggests a proper and logical combination of two possible selling levels, the one to take a profit, the other to take a loss. The profit-taking level must be judged with respect to each individual commitment, just as is the stop-loss level. But the coupled theory offers the logical suggestion that our profit-taking level should be so placed as to offer a greater profit, if the commitment is successful, than the possible loss would be if the commitment is unsuccessful.

It is simply an arithmetical manner of increasing the chances for profit as compared with the risk of loss on any transaction. Let us suppose, for instance, that a stock gives a bullish suggestion at 50, and we consider buying it there. We decide that 47 is the proper level for stop-loss protection, so that we already admit the possibility of a three-point loss if our judgment is incorrect. How much profit would be necessary to make the risk worth while, compared with this possible three-point loss?

The Basis in Logic and Common Sense

The coupled formula suggests that, other things being equal, the logical profit possibility ought to be from one and one-half to two times the possible loss. In other words, our risk of a three-point loss on this commitment will not be worth while unless we can see the probability of a profit of from 4½ to 6 points, if the campaign is successful. If we buy, therefore, at 50, with a stop-loss level at 47, the transaction is not attractive unless we may expect a profit of at least four or five points if it *is* successful. On such a basis, we should plan to take our profit, if it materialized, at around 56.

Once more, our most certain guarantee of clarity is the examination of a specific illustration. Plate IX, on page 231, shows the daily vertical chart on American Can from September of 1933 through the Spring months of 1934. Following the decline from Points A to B, the recovery to around Point C is normal but should not go much above 95. If we sold here, we could place definite stop protection at around 98, showing a loss of three points if we are wrong. In order to make the risk a fair one, therefore, the coupled theory suggests that we ought to have a potential profit in sight of from four to six points if the stock declines as we anticipate.

Increasing the Chances for Profit

The suggestions were for a decline to at least 90 which would show us a five-point profit, and thus make the coupled campaign logical. So we should sell at around 95, with at least the mental provision for repurchase at either 98 or 90,

whichever level was reached first. We risked a three-point
loss for a five-point profit. The market movement was in
accordance with its suggested forecast and with our own
judgment, and we should have accepted the anticipated five-
point profit.

There was no very favorable situation, or forecast, for the
theory until the technical trend had been reversed into an
upward one at around Point G. Here we might have bought
the stock at 91, with stop-loss protection just under the upward trend line, D–F–G, at perhaps 89. We should have
wished for at least a three- or four-point profit to make this
chance worth while, and should have sold out at 95, accept-
ing a four-point gain.

A Practical Illustration

We might possibly have bought again at 95, around Point
H, again with a stop just under the upward trend line, perhaps at 93. The two-point loss would have suggested the
necessity for the chance of a four-point profit, and we should
have taken such a profit at 99.

But the profits are not always so obligingly consistent.
When the first upward trend line was broken, to Point K,
followed by the recovery to Point L, a sale was justified at
the latter point around 98, with stop at 100 or 101. This
trade would not have proven successful. We should have
had to wait for a low of under 94 to take the proper profit.
That low point was not reached and our stop-loss order at
100 would have been caught almost immediately. If we had
selected a stop-level of 101 it would have been caught on the
subsequent advance to Point M. But our loss would not
have been greater than three points, compared with a profit,
thus far in our theoretical trading, of 13 points.

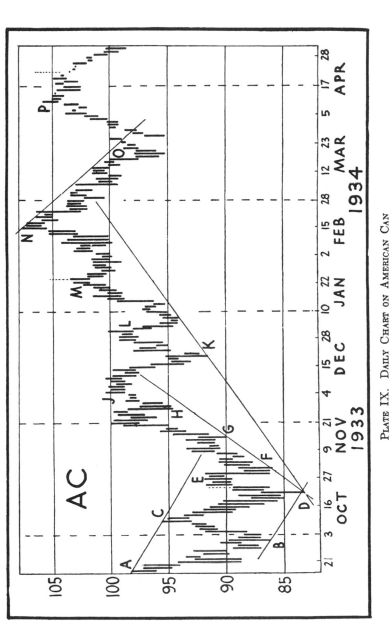

PLATE IX. DAILY CHART ON AMERICAN CAN

Illustrating detailed trading movements from the close of 1933 through the Spring of 1934.

A Speculative Campaign in American Can

The trend had now been turned upward once more and we had a good trend line through Points D–K. We might, therefore, have been ready to buy at 98, following Point M, but the stock did not get low enough for such purchase on the minor recession. Even in spite of the temporary upward trend line, however, there was sufficient suggestion of technical reversal,[1] following the top at Point N, to justify sale at around 105, with stop protection at 108. This would mean a possible three-point loss, and therefore the necessity of a possible five- or six-point gain on the suggested decline. The fact that such a profit could not have been taken without breaking the upward trend line made this a dubious risk and we shall not consider it a logical or conservative one. As a matter of fact, however, the trend *was* reversed downward, as suggested by the top at N, and we should have taken our profit had we proceeded on the suggested theory.

Risking Small Losses for Large Profits

At around Point O we had a sufficiently definite downward trend line, through N–O, to justify a somewhat radical risk in selling at 98. Though radical, the risk was a fair one because stop levels were so close — at par or even less. Doubling this possible two-point loss, we needed a four-point decline for profit, to around 94. But it did not materialize, and we soon took our second loss of two points, making a total loss of five points, against a profit of 13.

At Point P, the intermediate recovery was close enough to the preceding top level, at Point N, to suggest at least

---

[1] See Chapter VI, p. 143.

short reaction. Sale at 105 was justified, with a stop level at 107. We should, therefore, set a profit-taking level of 101 for our double profit of four points. And we should have accepted such profit at an early date. Thus our record, in this practical illustration of the coupled formula, is six trades, four of them successful and two of them unsuccessful.

But the important point is not so much the *number* of gains and losses as the *amount* of such gains and losses. Our judgment should make the number of gains larger than the number of losses. But even if their number is equally divided, the theory of coupled commitments is such that the gains will overbalance the losses. For, in every case, we refuse to risk a commitment unless our chance for possible gain is close to double our chance of possible loss. Thus we find that we had one gain of five points and three gains of four points each, or a total gain of 17 points. We also had one loss of three points and one of two points, or a total loss of only five points, against the gain of 17 points, leaving us with a net gain of 12 points on the entire six trades.

Practical Success of the Coupled Method

It is easy to see, therefore, how the theory of the coupled formula offers a simple, practical and highly logical method for increasing the winning risks and decreasing the losing ones, through the basic use of the stop-loss principle and its automatic protection.

The theory is much more exact, of course, where actual stop-loss orders are entered. If these are impractical and mental stop orders are used, then profits might be cut down moderately, but no more than moderately. As a matter of fact, they would actually have been increased in the illustration just studied. For, in each case of loss, an order executed at the next day's opening would have turned out more favorably than if an actual stop-loss order had been entered in advance with the broker.

Summary of Stop Advantages

From such illustrations it is easy to see not only the logic of the coupled-order formula, either mental or actual, but the advantages of the entire principle of stop-loss protection. As previously noted, it is by no means necessary to have one's stop-loss order placed with the broker in order to utilize this theory. Government regulation may make such advance placing of stop-loss orders entirely impossible, and in any case we have also seen [1] that it is better strategy to keep the exact stop-level a personal secret rather than publishing it to the broker and specialist far in advance.

The fundamental basis of the entire stop principle is not so much the entering of such orders with the broker, as the mere future planning which it entails. It guarantees not only that the operator will consider carefully both sides of the possible future outcome of his commitment, before he makes that commitment, but also that he will calculate, also in advance, the exact amount of loss which he is willing to risk, for the chance of his more probable, but still not certain, gain.

Some Corollary Rules

The stop-loss principle guarantees, in theory at least, that the individual who enters a commitment will have at least a mental level in mind at which he will promptly and decisively "get out" if his speculative campaign goes against

[1] See p. 219.

him. He will take his loss, but he will cut that loss short
and avoid the possibility of any further unfavorable eventuality in that particular campaign.

Two points stand out on such a basis. First, so long as
such a stop level is definitely decided upon, it is not necessary to use the actual stop-loss order as it has been generally considered in the past, namely, the actual entering
of such an order with one's broker. Second, the individual
must be firm, conscientious and strict in his mental discipline. He must play absolutely fair with this theory or
it is of no practical use to him at all. This is especially
true, of course, in the case of setting a purely mental protection level instead of placing an advance order with the
broker.

Play Fair with the Theory

If a stock is bought at 100, with a mental stop protection
at 95, and the stock drops to 94¾, then the operator is
morally and practically obliged to sell, without quibbling
with his conscience, without deciding to " wait awhile and
see," and without dropping his mental stop to 94, for
instance.

The principle is purely an automatic one, in essence. And
where the stop level decided upon is a mental one, the individual must force himself to act upon it just as automatically as the principle implies, and without consideration
for hope, fear or personal opinion. There will be exasperating losses, as previously noted, and the principle need not
be applied to purely long-term investment.[1] But it does
have a practical and valuable place in short-term, speculative policy.

[1] See Chapter IV, p. 80.

Another Important Principle of Success

One final point of common sense and logic in practical trading may be mentioned before we close our current chapter. That is the proper and necessary restraining of enthusiasm and eagerness, especially on the occasion of rather sharp daily market moves in an anticipated direction. Once more, we may recall our introductory warning [1] against over-enthusiasm, but we may now enlarge upon such warning and seek out a more specialized application.

It often happens that market trends have been lethargic and irregular for a time but the student's analysis leads him fairly definitely toward a bullish forecast, let us say, for the future. He does not act upon such personal judgment because of his proper conservatism, because the prospects are by no means definite, and because there have been intermediate and minor declines from time to time, which have contributed to this lack of personal confidence in the bullish and logical forecast.

The Market Confirms Previous Analysis

But suddenly, one fine day, the market turns strong and starts up. Most of the intriguing leaders show closing gains of from fractions to several points. Such an occurrence, by no means uncommon, is especially trying because of the psychological forces involved. Such a day of general strength will almost certainly add the appearance of practical certainty to the bullish picture which the student has been watching in individual stocks. It will provide the final argument for conclusive bullish forecast in his mind. And,

[1] See Chapter I, p. 13.

what is more, the apparent confirmation of his previous analysis and wish-thinking will so excite him that he is prone to rush headlong into the market next morning.

There are two dangers in such a situation. The first is the practical certainty that, if market orders are placed, the individual will pay fancy prices at the opening of trading next day, followed almost as surely by at least intermediate, or minor, reaction. The second danger is that the operator, excited by the sudden and long-suspected upturn, and fearful of losing profits on a correct advance analysis, will discard his usual conservatism and buy too heavily.

Meeting the Dangers in Such a Situation

The author would not argue for a purely indifferent attitude toward this kind of a situation, but merely warns against over-enthusiasm and losing one's proper perspective. We have already seen [1] that in special cases, when there is unexpected news foundation, or when too many people are anticipating minor reaction, the move may continue rapidly and sharply upward, without the usual intermediate correction. But it may also be said that such occasions are the exception and not the rule.

The individual would be perfectly justified in buying a *few* stocks at the next morning's opening, even on market orders, simply to guard against such an unusual exception as we have just noted. But once more, he should fall back upon the gospel of compromise. [2] Let him limit such market purchases on strength to a few stocks, preferably those which have advanced the least, and resist the perfectly natural urge to " plunge." Then let him wait, at least for a few hours, if not a few days, before taking on additional risk, to

<hr>

[1] See Chapter VIII, p. 203.   [2] See p. 216.

see whether the too-abrupt rise is not corrected by later reaction.

The Proper Course to Follow

He will usually find that such sharp one-day advances *are* disappointing to follow, especially if he ascertains that the show of strength was largely a burst of buying during the final hour or so of trading. If the usual intermediate reaction develops, then he may step in and add to his opening purchases, but still only moderately, until the picture is further verified, perhaps by resumption of the advance into higher ground than on the first upthrust.

To wax even more practical, we may suggest that the operator is entitled to three methods of buying, in such a situation and in accordance with the principle of compromise and common sense. He may enter buying orders for a few stocks at the opening and at the market. He may also enter buying orders for some additional stocks at the opening, but at limited prices, to attempt catching even only a short-lived technical correction during the day following the original show of strength. And finally, he may watch for a further correction, in the course of the next few days, and buy more stocks during such temporary reaction.

Restraining the Tendency to Plunge

But even all three of these buying methods should not account for any volume of purchase at all tending toward the "plunging" vice. For thus far we have considered only the possibility that the first day's strength was a true corroboration of the previous bullish analysis. Yet such is by no means universally the case.

It is almost more likely to have been simply a short false move, possibly engineered for the very purpose of enticing buyers into the market, to create a demand for stock and to provide the outlet for professional selling, and later reaction. We need merely recall the psychological crossing principles which we learned in our preceding chapter [1] to suggest the possibility of such manipulation on a basis of inside crossing operations.

Let the operator consider carefully, therefore, the preceding psychological implications of the past price trend. Let him ask once more, "What would the insiders do in a case like this if they wanted to liquidate stock in preparation for later declines?" No categorical reply may here be offered, of course. But it is at least possible that the honest reply would be, "Why, they would do their best to make the market promising, would engineer a short but attention-getting upward move, simply to attract public buyers to whom they could sell the stock they wanted to unload."

Buy on Weakness, Not on Strength

Such mental gymnastics may sound rather confusing and involved, but the point of our entire illustration is that the student should have been buying on *weakness* instead of on strength. If his analysis, even though incomplete, led him to expect a bullish move in the future, he should not have waited for the sudden corroboration of those views but should have commenced moderate buying during the preceding period of quiet irregularity.

Instead of being scared out of his own well-based analysis by the intermediate declines, he should have had the courage to buy on such minor dips. He need not have

[1] See Chapter VIII, p. 202.

bought heavily but at least sufficiently so that he could look with equanimity upon the sudden advance, content with having a modest stake in it if it continued, but not being rushed into an unsettling excitement and fear that the market was starting up without him.

Don't Let a Fast Market Hurry Personal Analysis

One of the best safeguards against this tendency to let one's temporary and suddenly-kindled enthusiasm run away with oneself is simply the common-sense cultivation of an unhurried, unruffled discipline. There is no greater danger of unsound market action in such a situation than where the element of haste in arriving at practical decisions is added.

The longer time interval the student allows himself to "cool off," to regain his proper poise, to study and consider the careful analysis of such new data, the less likely he is to commit costly errors in judgment. But if he allows himself to be hurried in his market decision on such an occasion he is almost certain to regret it.

The principle is somewhat the same as the psychological one which is so often used by the fake stock promoter and salesman.[1] His constant effort is to hurry the decision of his prospect, because he knows that longer thought and consideration will generate more mature and logical judgment, and will probably result in his losing the fraudulent sale.

The same tendency toward improper decision when in haste applies to the legitimate field of listed stock operation. If the student comes home from the office at six o'clock in the evening and has a "date" that night, he can almost

[1] See Chapter XI, p. 301.

certainly save money either by cancelling the date or by refraining from giving the "quick-decision" orders which would almost certainly result, especially after a day of sudden strength such as we have postulated.

The Proper Time for Regular Analysis

The author's habit, and one which has always seemed reasonable, is to formulate and place brokerage orders only while the market is closed, except in unusual circumstances. He usually gives market analysis his main attention after the close in the evening and formulates any orders at that time. Unless the operator is a professional or has nothing else to occupy his attention, it is much more advisable to get into the habit of such leisure time for consideration, rather than accustoming oneself to "keeping in touch" with the market during the day. The latter habit not only interferes with attention to other work but is also very likely to induce the hurried and excited judgment which we are attempting to avoid.

Cancel the "Date" or Cancel the Order

There are plenty of occasions, of course, when evening appointments leave only a comparatively short time for such intensive market consideration. If no great change has taken place in the market that day, all well and good. Probably there will be no necessity for prolonged consideration or for new orders. But if such a full evening conflicts with study after a day of sudden activity and a possible change in market action, then let the student beware. Let him guard against excitement and haste. Let him dismiss especially any feeling that he can control his analysis so closely as to do several hours of thinking and observation in a half-hour, write out his market orders and still have time to dress, dine and be on his way to the evening's rendezvous.

Such an attitude is almost infallibly fatal to sound and mature judgment and to profitable action. There are two sensible alternatives — either cancel the date, or cancel the orders. With no attempt to belittle the importance of proper market judgment, the author would usually prefer to suggest the latter or at least refraining from formulation of any definite orders until more time is available.

That is, of course, not a dogmatic statement. Much would depend upon the " date " and other circumstances. Our suggested preference is merely based upon the feeling that sudden activity on such days as we have been considering is more likely to be misleading than genuine, that the average trader is likely to over-estimate its importance, and that even unhurried judgment on such an occasion might not be so successful as was anticipated.

Don't be Afraid to Change Your Mind

A useful point in this connection is the cultivation of willingness to change one's mind, if further consideration suggests that first judgments were made too hastily. Vacillation and indecision are to be avoided, of course, but there is no weakness in cancelling previous orders if they later seem to have been formulated impetuously.

If, in spite of our previous argument, the operator does attempt to analyze a spectacular or switching market in a short time, writes out his orders and mails them on his way to the evening date, and then begins to doubt their wisdom later in the evening, he need not be afraid to 'phone his broker before the market opens next morning and cancel them. Especially would such a course be logical if the feeling of impropriety develops along with a " cooling off " stage after the initial excitement and enthusiasm generated by the sudden developments in the day's market.

A Cancelled Order May Mean Profit

The author has often gone home from his office rather elated over the day's sudden action, only to have such a feeling "wear off " and give way to doubt and more mature skepticism. In such a case, there should be no hesitation or shame in cancelling any orders that may already have been dispatched to one's broker. The average order-clerk or customer's man will take it in good grace. But, in any event, the trader need not shrink from silent, and perhaps merely imagined, scorn of a busy and disgruntled broker. The cancellation may cause him inconvenience and some additional clerical expense, but he is being well paid for his services in the interest of the customer. And the customer may save himself a tidy sum by cancellation of orders formulated on a basis of excited and immature judgment, provided he realizes the situation before the next day's opening.

CHAPTER X

DIVERSIFICATION OF RISK

Reasons for Lack of Diversification

Why it is that many so-called investors prefer to load themselves up with several hundred shares of a single stock, when that is all they can afford to buy of any stock, is difficult of ready understanding. Yet the author's contact with problems of "the average investor" indicates that such procedure is far from exceptional.

The reasons for such a tendency, while not directly important to our study, are yet clearly based, once more, in the plain frailty of man's normal, human nature. The first common reason is not so readily admitted by the individual, but it springs from plain ignorance and laziness. It is much easier to "get the dope" on only a single security than on many. Likewise, it is much easier to follow, and manage, a single security than many.

Usual Human Weaknesses Involved

A great many individuals, whose field of experience and knowledge must be rather limited, seem able to interest themselves in only a single set of facts. They think in terms of only one set of conditions at a single sitting. And by the time they get through deciding to buy one security there is no further energy or enthusiasm for studying another.

The second reason for lack of diversification probably results from this same mental characteristic. For it is a strong tendency toward a great many of the vices which we are attempting to eliminate from our market practice, including over-enthusiasm, general impatience, and lack of conservatism, all of which lead naturally into the habit of "plunging." [1]

Such individuals, concentrating on their *one* security, not only grow too worn out by that application to take up another security, but they also get themselves so utterly enthusiastic by their single study that they think it bootless to look further for their million-dollar profit. " Here it is. Here is the one perfect security for big profit."

Allied with this vice of over-enthusiasm, of course, is the equally disastrous tendency toward greed. The investor has found a good stock — or he thinks he has. Very well; he immediately calculates his profit if it doubles, let us say, in price. If he uses his total investment fund properly, with good diversification of risk, he should probably buy only 10 or 20 shares of this good stock, and then buy equal amounts of many other good stocks.

Over-Enthusiasm on Profit Possibilities

But the profit on 10 shares of Galvanized Toothpick, now selling at 10 (" and bound to double in price ") would be only $100. The trader actually has $1,000 to spend. So why not forget about any other stocks and concentrate on this one that looks so good. He proceeds to put all his $1,000 in Galvanized Toothpick, and buys 100 shares instead of only 10, thus calculating immediately an early profit of $1,000, instead of only $100.

In point of fact, of course, Galvanized Toothpick looks particularly good to such an individual because he has not

[1] See Chapter IX, p. 211.

taken the time or energy to study additional stocks he might buy. If he went on he would probably lose interest in Toothpick. But he does not go on. And so, the human elements of laziness, over-enthusiasm, incomplete analysis, credulity and greed, all combine to lead the unthinking individual toward " plunging," which usually means simply the lack of a proper and reasonable diversification of risk.

The Average Trader is Not Immune

The reader will perhaps bridle his mane and retort that such an illustration is extreme, and applies only to an individual who is too inexperienced and lacking in good sense to deserve anything better than the loss of his entire $1,000 capital in Galvanized Toothpick. Perhaps the illustration is a bit over-drawn, but let the individual hesitate before he dismisses himself entirely from such a group.

Almost everyone interested to any degree in the security market is bound to have his own favorites and his own pets. We shall not quarrel with such a natural tendency, provided only that the favoritism is merited, that it is based upon long and constantly-alert analysis and not on the fact that previous experience in this one issue has been successful. And provided also, that concentration on such a favorite issue does not over-balance the general investment policy and destroy the proper degree of diversification.

Logic of Diversification

For the principle of diversification of risk is not only one of the simplest and most logical rules of consistent market success, but it is one of the most important and useful ones as well. And we have already noted that it is often overlooked, perhaps because of its very simplicity.

The fundamental basis for diversification is laid partly upon the factor of chance and partly on the practical theory of protection against heavy loss in case of incorrect analysis. The man who stakes his all on the purchase of a single security, no matter how sound his analysis and judgment, is running the risk that one unforeseen, and unforeseeable, factor may arise which will just happen to hit that one security and cripple his entire market policy.

The man who divides his market capital between 20 different securities, on the other hand, runs only one-twentieth as great a risk if one of his stocks should be hit by such an unforeseen development. He runs a somewhat greater risk that one *will* be hit, of course, but he stands to lose only one-twentieth as much in such a case, and conservatism thus argues for the policy of diversification.

The Element of Misfortune

If the reader did not know it before, he should certainly be vaguely aware, by this time, that there are a great many unexpected but not-so-unusual factors which may enter into any market picture, to upset previous calculations and to turn an anticipated profit into an unexpected loss.

Quite often such factors affect the entire market, but just as often they strike at individual securities and groups of stocks. But even if they do affect the entire market, all stocks do not react so rapidly or widely. And the man with 20 stocks has just that much better chance of cushioning his loss than has the man with only one stock.

But whether the basic factor be chance — unknown and unknowable in advance — or whether it be an improper personal analysis by the investor, the results are the same, in practice as well as in theory. The man with his capital well-diversified over a great many individual securities, all of which his analysis dictates to be sound risks, is in immeasurably better position, in case of disappointment, than is the man with all of his capital concentrated in a single security or one compact group of securities.

The Element of Good Fortune

Nor are the advantages of diversification confined only to the disappointing and unsuccessful experiences. If we allow consideration of the element of chance, then we must also allow that it may work for profit as well as loss. Good news and fortunate developments — also unforeseen and unforeseeable — may strike only a handful of stocks, perhaps even only one single stock. Once again, the man with 20 stocks has a much better chance of the good news striking one of his issues than the man with only a single stock. And if the unexpected factor raises the entire market, we also know that all issues will not rise correspondingly. Here again, the man with broad diversification has a material advantage over the one with no such diversification.

Or, if we discount chance and stress the just rewards of painstaking analysis, we may still be assured that the man who takes 20 shots, carefully aimed as they may be, has a much better chance of hitting the bull's-eye than he who puts all of his ammunition into a single charge.

Diversification vs. Concentration of Risk

The argumentative reader may suggest, of course, that such reasoning is paradoxical, and that if the investor does pick a winner, then his profit will be much smaller if his capital is diversified than if he had concentrated on that one issue. Even if we reduce our theorizing to approach the pure chance of roulette, however, the practical results are generally better — certainly less dangerous — in playing "blanche et noir" than in concentrating one's chips on individual numbers.

But the stock market cannot be compared with pure chance on such a basis. It is open to entirely different approach, to compromise, to limitation of loss, to logic, thorough analysis, and a thousand other elements which cannot be applied to pure chance. And they all argue for diversification of risk rather than concentration of risk.

Diversification in Depression Markets

Especially practical is the diversification principle toward the close of any long period of market liquidation and industrial depression, such as in 1931 and 1932, when scores of stocks were selling at or near receivership levels. It was not only possible, but quite practical and profitable, to make up a list of as many as fifty of such low-priced issues. They *might* be forced into receivership if the depression continued long enough, but they also seemed in good position to emerge without insolvency, and they offered opportunities for tremendous percentage profit if they did come through into recovery.

In spite of careful choosing of such a list, it was entirely probable that a few of the issues selected would indeed go bad. But it was unthinkable that all 50 of them would and it was very improbable that more than 10 of them would, at the most. There were plenty of border-line risks, but even if these were included, as they should have been, it was also practically impossible to forecast in advance exactly which 10 out of the 50 would fall by the wayside.

The man who insisted on buying only one of the 50, or only a few of the list, and staking all his market capital on the one security, was running a terrific and altogether inexcusable risk. But the man who bought equal amounts of all 50 stocks was not only diversifying his risk through the protection which such a principle offered him, but he was almost guaranteeing his campaign an attractive eventual profit on the entire portfolio.

A Practical Example in History

That such an illustration is not pure theory may be substantiated by the record of a group of 62 low-priced speculative issues which the author recommended in his published articles as late as February of 1933.[1] At the end of three months exactly three of these issues showed a loss, while the average profit on the remaining 59 amounted to more than 70 per cent, after deducting the losses of the three unsuccessful issues. Inside of a year the average profit was well over 150 per cent.

Without diversification over a broad list, the purchase recommendations might conceivably have been concentrated on those three disappointing issues. But, through the principle of broad diversification, it was practically certain that the profits would more than make up for any individual losses.

Minimum Limits of Operation

It may thus be hoped that the reader is convinced of the practical advantages inherent in this important principle of risk diversification. And the author has perhaps justi-

[1] Forbes Magazine, February 1, 1933, p. 26.

fied by this time his dogmatic assertion, on all occasions, that he would much prefer to have the average investor own only 10 shares each of 10 different securities, than 100 shares of only a single security.[1]

So long as minimum commission rates remain at their current high levels, the practical minimum base for such diversification in medium-priced issues is in 10-share blocks.

Larger Commissions Money Well Spent

The author would by no means subscribe, for instance, to the apparently short-lived propaganda which was used several years ago, urging the purchase of "stock bundles," including one share each of many different stocks. The advertised theory of diversification was laudable, but the practical factor of commission charges, if the individual stocks were ever sold, made the plan highly impractical. It would have cost more to sell some of such "bundles" through a broker than the entire portfolio was then worth in market price.

In individual cases, a minimum commitment of as low as only five shares of any one issue is allowable, but the more satisfactory limit is the 10-share minimum.

Once the investor becomes convinced of the soundness in our rule for diversification, then its actual achievement is not difficult. There may be a slightly higher percentage expense in brokerage commissions, and there will quite probably be a greater outlay of security analysis. But neither of these additional elements is substantial when compared with the valuable protection and the practical increase in consistent profits which the diversification principle offers, particularly, of course, in long-swing operations.

[1] See Chapter I, p. 13.

Diversification in Groups as Well as Individual Issues

But broad diversification of risk means not merely the purchase of a greater number of stocks in any single group. It means also the diversification of risk in many different groups of stocks, and also in other security classifications. The principle, as the author uses it, is a very broad one, in fact. It branches out to include the spreading of one's personal risk over as many different types of general financial medium as appear justified by the advantages of such medium and by the dictates of the general situation.

The man, for instance, who has many stocks in many different groups of stocks, is not properly diversified, in the author's estimation, if his diversification does not also extend into preferred stocks, bonds, cash and even possibly into other mediums like commodities, real estate, insurance, etc.

The Degree of Risk in Selected Groups

And each of these specific groups, in turn, must also be broken down into its own individual classification, according to the degree of risk involved in the individual issues that may be purchased. In practically every one of such groups we shall find varying possibilities of profit or loss.

It is no new theory, of course, that the general category of common stocks, preferred stocks and bonds must be further labelled according to whether the individual representatives are speculative, medium-grade or high-grade. But the same differentiation is not only possible, but advisable, in such additional mediums of investment as real estate, bank deposits, building and loan interests, commodities, foreign currencies, and even hoarded domestic cash.

A few moments of thought will serve to clarify the logic of this view for the majority of such classifications. The less-apparent cases are bank deposits and actual cash, but even here there are varying degrees of risk involved. Bank deposits must be valued on such a basis according to the rate of interest received and, more especially, on the basis of safety. Such consideration was especially true in the dismal days of 1931 and 1932, during the epidemic of bank failures. But the improvement in this factor, together with Government insurance of such deposits, hardly does away entirely or permanently with the advisability of such considerations.

Variable of Theoretical Safety

It might be maintained that actual cash is the final extreme of safety and that this financial medium is, therefore, not open to varied degree of risk. But even here the lodging place of such cash is, in itself, a variable as regards safety. Certainly the hoarding of cash in one's home carries greater degree of risk than if it were lodged in a safety-deposit box. And even in the latter case, it is quite conceivable that there still exists some slight degree of varying risk, according to the location of the vault, the quality of management, etc.

Such considerations verge, of course, on the boundaries of quibbling. They are perhaps not important for the average investor during normal times. They have been noted simply to justify the author's statement that diversification of financial risk is a broad term, applying to varying degrees of speculation not only in stocks and bonds but in any and all advisable mediums.

In point of actual practice it is seldom that all of the varying types of medium would be utilized. But the important point is that they must all be considered, at least in the theory of proper long-swing diversification.

Compromise Principle in Diversification

And the fact that they would not all be used in actual practice, certainly not at the same time, leads us to further consideration of the principle of compromise in diversification.[1] We have already discussed this important factor in the formulation and management of broad investment policies[2] and need spend no great time on it now.

But it does come into valuable use in connection with the principle of diversification. There can never be a time when it is safe to say that all of one's funds should be placed in common stocks, to the exclusion of all other mediums. And there exists no individual sufficiently clairvoyant to guarantee that, at a certain stage, all of one's funds should be in bonds, or cash, or commodities, to the exclusion of all other groups.

Gradual vs. Headlong Shifting of Risk

Diversification of risk, therefore, must depend in large measure, not merely upon economic conditions, not merely upon personal analysis, but also upon this doctrine of compromise. That very principle suggests, in itself, the *gradual* shifting of risk, and not the headlong or dogmatic switching from one group into another. If economic conditions

---

[1] See Chapter IX, p. 215.   [2] See Chapter IV, p. 96.

and personal analysis suggest the growing attractions of bonds over common stocks, then the percentage may gradually and slowly be shifted in such a direction. But the move should not be a sudden one, nor should it be a decisive one. It should be a tendency, rather than a clear-cut or headlong rush.

And it should mean merely a tipping of the scales a little farther in the direction of bonds in comparison with stocks, and by no means a complete desertion of all stocks and a complete shifting to bonds. So the principle of compromise and the gospel of diversification go hand in hand, to furnish another element of practical assistance in the successful direction of investment operation and the management of broad investment policies.

Importance of the " Tendency "

As should be quite apparent from our previous discussion, then, it is quite impossible to offer any definite or precise rules for the formulation of certain percentages of diversification in the various types of investment medium. That depends upon too many elements in the constantly changing economic outlook, to say nothing of the individual needs or opportunities of the investor himself.

No one would suggest, for instance, that the widow, without additional means of support, should follow the same percentages and mediums of diversification as might be quite justified for the active business man who has a large, independent income and who would not be greatly harmed if speculative operations proved unsuccessful.

If the reader understands fully, however, that no iron-clad formula may be laid down for any and all individual policies, then the author is inclined to offer at least a sample,

or skeleton, formula for such total diversification, simply
to illustrate his own broad views on the practical subject.

Formula for Diversification

Such an illustration is, therefore, offered in Plate X, on
page 257. It is a concrete illustration of the theory, because it is taken from an article which the author published
early in 1933, for the general guidance of the average investor group.[1] This large class is divided into four smaller
groups, according to the individual degree of risk which each
might be justified in assuming. We have (I) the "widow
and orphan" trust fund class, where the risk undertaken
must be kept at a minimum; (II) the retired investor class,
where a slightly higher degree of risk is allowed; (III) the
average business man class, where considerable risk may
be assumed; and we have, finally, (IV) the speculative class,
where the maximum risk is justified.

Classes of Investment

We then break down the most common and useful investment mediums into nine different groups, including (A)
savings, bank deposits and cash, (B) foreign exchange,
foreign securities and international credit, (C) high-grade
bonds, (D) speculative bonds, (E) high-grade preferred
stocks, (F) speculative preferred stocks, (G) high-grade
common stocks, (H) speculative common stocks, and (J)
commodities.

Such categories are merely in rough outline, of course,
and no attempt is made to go into further detail, such as

[1] See "An Investment Policy for Every Pocket," Forbes Magazine,
April 1, 1933.

PLATE X

TABULAR REPRESENTATION OF A SAMPLE DIVERSIFI-
CATION FORMULA IN FOUR BROAD INVESTMENT
CLASSES

(Per Cent. of Capital in Various Groups of Medium)

I — THE WIDOW AND TRUST FUND CLASS

A	B	C	D	E	F	G	H	J	Total
10	5	60	10	5	5	5	—	—	100

II — THE RETIRED INVESTOR CLASS

A	B	C	D	E	F	G	H	J	
5	5	40	20	5	10	5	10	—	100

III — THE AVERAGE BUSINESS MAN CLASS

A	B	C	D	E	F	G	H	J	
—	5	20	20	5	10	5	30	5	100

IV — THE SPECULATIVE CLASS

A	B	C	D	E	F	G	H	J	
—	5	5	30	—	15	10	45	20	130

GROUPS OF INVESTMENT MEDIUM

A Cash (savings & bank deposits)

B International credit (foreign exchange, foreign securities, etc.)

C High-grade bonds

D Speculative bonds

E High-grade preferred stocks

F Speculative preferred stocks

G High-grade common stocks

H Speculative common stocks

J Commodities

might advisably be done by including the various degrees of risk in commodities or in adding specific groups for medium-grade security issues. No consideration has been given, for instance, to many other mediums such as annuities, insurance, real estate, mortgages, building and loan commitments, etc. Government bonds, however, might be included in Group C, strong bank stocks in group G, ordinary investment trusts in group H, and so on.

The chief point which the reader should note, however, is that no individual, no matter what broad class of investor he falls into, is justified in placing too much risk in any one group of investment medium. In the table itself, we show, for each class, the suggested percentage of total funds which might properly be allocated to each individual group of investment medium. Thus the total of such percentages adds across to a full 100 per cent, except in the case of the speculative class. In this latter group the total is 130 per cent of the investment fund, indicating that this class may assume the additional risk of borrowing money and operating on conservative margin.

Classes of Investor

Let the reader note, for instance, that all four of the individual classes of investor have at least part of their funds in such major groups as bonds and stocks. But the widow and trust fund class is mostly in high-grade securities, while the emphasis on this group diminishes, down through the other three classes, until we find the speculator with by far the bulk of his funds in the speculative groups of investment medium. The widow has 60 per cent of her funds in high-grade bond issues, and none in speculative common stocks. The speculator, on the other hand, has only 5 per cent in high-grade bonds, and the majority of his risk is in speculative bonds and common stocks.

As has previously been noted, of course, this example is cited merely for purposes of illustration and might not be practical under all conditions. The table shows that all four classes of investor, for instance, had moderate commitments in foreign exchange or international credit, but this suggestion was by no means a permanent generalization. It was justified, in the Spring of 1933, by the indications for devaluation of the American dollar, a factor which, it may be hoped, shall not be a recurring one for investment policy.

Policy of Risk Constantly Changing

One of the fundamental bases in any such outline, as well as in the entire principle of diversification, is balanced judgment on the comparative attraction of risk in investment. It is by no means always true, for instance, that the greater the risk the greater will be the profit. At the time when our current illustration was formulated it seemed reasonable that the greater profits would accrue in the more speculative categories. But the principle of diminishing returns often enters into this consideration of balance.

Theoretically, of course, the greater risk which the investor assumes, the greater return he expects if the commitment is successful. But there is a variable degree of attraction in risk, based upon many individual factors, but chiefly upon the future prospect for business and security prices. In 1933, the widow might have envied the speculator his capacity for assuming risk, since greater risk seemed likely to bring greater gain. Yet in 1929, the speculator might well have envied the widow her comparatively conservative position, for she stood to lose much less than he did. In fact, of course, no such emphasis on speculation would have been placed in a diversification formula in 1929. But at least a moderate degree of diversification would still have been present, as required for the different capacities of risk assumption. The change would have been one of shifting *gradually* the bulk of speculative percentage commitments from one group to another rather than a sudden closing out of certain groups.

Dangers in Over-Reaching the Class Boundary

Since the fact remains that, on balance, the greater risk would seem entitled to the greater profit, it will probably always hold true, however, that the individual aspires to assume a greater degree of risk than he should. The widow and trust fund class will probably always envy the speculative class and, unfortunately, will always strain at the leash to get through the fence into a more speculative policy.

It should be almost unnecessary to call attention to the basic dangers inherent in this tendency. It is perhaps a merely normal and human one, but it is dangerous, none the less. Without going into concrete and individual examples, it may be said that the best way to test one's ability to assume risk is through utilization of our rule for future loss calculation.[1] The individual should calculate just how much money he or she is able and willing to *lose* on any venture or investment policy, and not concentrate attention on how much *might* be made. And, needless to repeat, this weighing of the risk, and the ability to assume such risk of loss, should be thoroughly studied *before* the commitment is made, and *not* afterward.

[1] See Chapter I, p. 24.

Listed vs. Unlisted Securities

One additional point may be noted in regard to practical diversification policy, and that is with respect to listing. We already know [1] that it is not enough to select the proper group of security. We must also diversify within each individual group, and must bring proper attention, knowledge and analysis to bear on each individual possibility in the group. But in a more general aspect, the author must needs offend certain " interests " by here suggesting his habitual rule on marketability.

It has been taken largely for granted, thus far in our volume, that the investor is interested only in securities or investment mediums which have a ready market. The author is particularly dogmatic in stressing this necessity for just about every individual investment policy. In the average case, and for the average operator, we should much prefer a fair risk in a listed security than a seemingly splendid risk in a security which is either unlisted or has a narrow and indefinite market.

Advantages in an Active Market

Especially in formulating total investment policy, the individual will only too often be tempted, usually by personal friendship or good salesmanship, to include in his portfolio some securities which are not actually listed or actively traded. The author would avoid such temptation in almost all cases, no matter how close the friendship or how attractive the profit offered — unless the individual is perfectly willing to run the risk of having such assets " frozen " at some future date.

[1] See p. 252.

The "interests" previously referred to include all companies sponsoring securities which are not thus listed. They have criticized the author for such utterances before, and they probably will do so again. Their arguments are that such an attitude automatically rules out what may be exceedingly strong securities in many banks, investment trusts, insurance stocks, real estate holdings, and so on.

Limits of Investment in Unlisted Issues

The author is fully aware of such an implication. And he is also aware of the unquestioned merit and profit inherent in many of such vehicles. But he has already made allowance for *some* such securities by refraining from making his suggestion iron-clad or final. There are some individuals who can afford to place a fair share of their total funds in such unlisted securities of various corporations, whether they be large ones or merely local enterprises. There are also some circumstances where the author would not object strenuously to including a considerable amount of such securities in even the average portfolio.

" Keeping Control " of the Personal Policy

But the important point is that such cases are the exception and not the rule. For the average investor, not more than a few of such should be included, and then for no greater risk than perhaps 5 per cent of total funds. For the purely average portfolio, we may simply repeat that one of the fundamental tests for any potential security investment is the test of its marketability.

And the term " marketability " does not mean merely the glittering promise of a glib salesman that, " Oh, yes, this stock will be listed at an early date." The investor should concentrate only on those securities which are *already* listed, which have had a broad and active market for at least several years, and preferably, of course, on the New York Stock Exchange or the New York Curb Exchange.

Then, no matter what happens, he at least has the basic advantage of knowing exactly what he can get for such security at any time. Regardless of the fact that such active trading, at a publicly listed price, is one of the investor's best aids in purely technical analysis, it is also a decisive benefit in assuring adequate regulation, statistical information, collateral value and, by no means the least important, in assuring him of the ability to " get out " if he wants to do so, even at a loss.

" Averaging " Operations and Diversification

So simple and logical is our general principle of diversification that it should really be unnecessary to lecture against one of its chief corollary violations, that of "averaging down." Whether because the investor does not think of his averaging operations as a violation of diversification, or whether he has simply ignored the broad and general principle, the fact remains that " averaging down " in the same stock or group is one of the most common fallacies, and therefore one of the most common bases for loss, with which the garden variety of investor is afflicted.

Averaging operations, of course, are simply the process of adding to one's previous commitment in any security after the original commitment shows a loss. An individual buys 100 shares of stock at 100. It drops to 50. He thereupon buys another 100 shares of that same stock, figuring that he is thus reducing the average price of his 200 shares to only 75 and that he can now get out even if the stock recovers to only 75 instead of to his original purchase price of 100.

Misleading Attractions of Averaging

Perhaps the apparent logic of this assumption is one of the reasons for the prevalence of such averaging operations. On this particular basis of theory, of course, the plan sounds quite reasonable. But let us also consider such action from another standpoint. In the first place, the fact that the stock has already declined from 100 to 50 is just as likely to be an indication that it is going on down to 10 as that it is going to recover to 75. The stock has already shown weakness — why load up with more of a commitment which is behaving unsatisfactorily?

In the second place, the decline which has already taken place is ample proof that the investor's judgment and analysis on it were incorrect in the first place. It is simply another suggestion that his future and continued judgment on the same stock may be just as incorrect. He unquestionably left out of his original consideration an important and unfavorable factor. That factor may easily still be important. And the individual may still not know what the factor is. Or he may not value it importantly enough, if he does know what it is.

Arguments Against Averaging Down

But the final argument against averaging operation is that it violates the primary dictates of the principle of diversification of risk. The greater the possibility of loss — the greater the speculative degree of risk — in any situation, the greater need is there for proper diversification. Now, when his stock has already declined 50 points against him, has lost half of its purchase value, there seems no further question but that the situation involves a high degree of risk.

The purchase of more of this same stock, therefore, is contrary to the justified dictates of logic, to say nothing of the principle of diversification. Averaging operations, when carried on in the same stock, directly violate the dictates of this principle. They increase the risk and narrow it down, concentrating the speculative danger, instead of diversifying it.

Logic vs. False Logic

The above considerations are perhaps a bit theoretical, but if we desire practical arguments against averaging then we have plenty of them. And the reader need perhaps not go far beyond his own personal experience for such examples. Especially during a long bear market such as that of 1929–32, the actual disasters that result directly from averaging down are legion. But they are plentiful in any type of market and at all times.

The author, in his professional capacity as a general "practitioner," is almost constantly receiving letters and requests for advice from investors who have caught themselves in what is already a major financial tragedy, or is well on the way to becoming one, simply by this stubborn policy of averaging down in some pet issue. The stock, at least in the extreme cases, has been declining fairly steadily and consistently for perhaps a number of years. And probably justly so, due to some special tendency or development which is affecting the company adversely, and even suggests eventual receivership or reorganization.

How it Works

But the investor has " always liked the stock." Or, he has "put so much money into it" that he cannot let go now. Or, the " bears are attacking the stock temporarily." So he goes on buying more, thinking it a greater and greater bargain as it declines in price, until finally the awful truth begins to dawn, that the stock has always been too high, that it is just beginning to approach a level in line with future prospects, that his long favoritism has been sadly misplaced, and that he stands to lose all of the money he has ever put into it.

The final tragedy in many of such practical cases is that the financial analyst, or investment adviser, does not hear about the averaging operations until the investor is "in extremis." Then, finally, when he is far over his head, when he has made his own bed of financial ruin, when the stock is already near receivership levels and most of the harm has already been done — he comes for advice. He unfolds his particular tale of misplaced judgment, of over-confidence, of stubborn tenacity or of speculative " plunging," and asks what he shall do.

Averaging Down to Catastrophe

How much simpler would have been the answer if he had come a year or more ago, before he built his ruinous policy, instead of afterward. Often there is little that can be done in such extreme cases except to hope. It is no exaggeration to say that the cases are by no means isolated, where a misled investor has averaged down in the same pet stock from 100 to receivership levels below five, until practically his entire capital has been eaten up in this one tragic situation.

It is difficult to advise throwing the whole commitment overboard at such a level. For there is always some basis for hope, forlorn though it be. Pure common sense would sometimes counsel retention of the stock, in fact, based upon its low selling price and on the fact that the investor has so much more to gain than to lose if it *should* come back. But it is a sad case for the adviser as well as for the investor, because the fight is so nearly lost before the battle is even begun.

Practical Example of Averaging Misfortune

Definite illustrations might be selected from practically any stock which has " gone bad " in recent years, after once having found a fairly broad and active public following. The case of Paramount Publix Corporation common stock may serve as a single practical illustration. Its price is charted on a monthly high and low basis, in Plate XI, on page 269, through the years 1929–33.

We have already noted the " psychological crossing " operations suggested by the advance into new high ground in 1930, following the Panic decline of 1929.[1] Let us suppose that a hypothetical investor is favorable toward Paramount from the beginning of 1929, starting with an original commitment of 50 shares at 60. For most of the year his judgment appears good, and he may even be led to take on another 50 shares at 70, buying " on a scale up." Following the Panic of 1929, he sees the stock recover rapidly. It does " better than the market " through to Point C on our chart, giving such a convincing performance that our

[1] See Chapter VIII, p. 196.

theoretical investor takes on another 50 shares at an average of 70.

The Psychological Temptations

The stock declines to Point D, but it is still doing better than the market. Our "investor" now has 150 shares of Paramount at an average price of around 67. But the stock has dropped to around 60. If he buys another 50 shares now he reduces his average price to 65, only five points above the current selling level. It looks like a good bet, and he now has 200 shares at an average price of 65.

But, instead of going back up to 70, the stock proceeds to drop back to its 1929 panic low around 35. That has the investor worried, but only for a time, because the recovery to around 50 is fairly prompt. Now he has a "double bottom" support level, earnings are still reported good, the general market seems to be recovering. Maybe the bear market is over. Anyway, the stock looks cheap now, for he can buy another 50 shares for only 40, a full 30-point reduction from his previous purchase price. "It must be a bargain"—so he takes on another 50 shares, and reduces his average buying price on the entire 250 shares to only 60.

Too Big a Loss to Sell?

But again the market fools him. The stock drops away from Point E, around which he made his most recent purchase, and continues on down to about 20, at Point F. Now matters are growing serious. Our "investor" has 250 shares of Paramount, at an average cost of 60, with a total investment of $15,000, whereas he started with an original commitment of only 50 shares that cost him a meager $3,000.

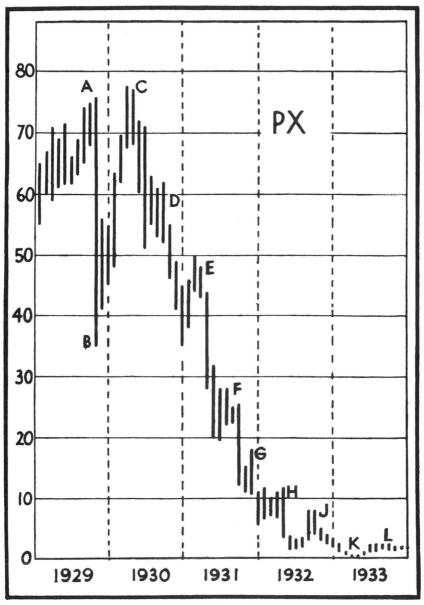

PLATE XI. MONTHLY CHART ON PARAMOUNT PUBLIX

Showing the almost steady depreciation in price, and illustrating the
dangers of "averaging down."

With the stock down to 20, and his investment now worth only $5,000, he is losing sleep as well as money. He can hardly afford to lose that $10,000 anyway. Moreover, the stock is so cheap at 20 that it can hardly be expected to go much lower. And, if further temptation were needed, he can now buy another 50 shares for only $1,000, instead of $3,000 or $3,500.

It doesn't seem likely that the stock will recover to his average level of 60 in the early future, but by purchasing another 50 shares at 20, he can reduce that average price to only about 53, which doesn't seem so far away, after all.

Deeper and Deeper

But the final and critical argument is that "some day Paramount will be back up there again," and that if he holds on patiently enough, and even buys more stock while it is "cheap," then the mathematics of averaging will work for him. And when the depression is finally over, he will have a big lot of Paramount at a low average price, and will be "sitting pretty once more."

So he takes on another 50 shares at 20. Exactly the same arguments are used to take on still another 50 shares at 10, around Point H, except that now it is a matter of "life and death." He cannot let go. His "all" is tied up with this one stock. He has been so intent upon "averaging down" in Paramount that he has had no time for analysis of other issues, no money for diversification.

Perhaps he might even buy some more of the same stock at Points J, K or L, but we shall close our eyes after his last purchase, around Point H, at 10. Our investor now owns 350 shares of Paramount at an average cost of only 47, compared with his original price of 60. He has an accumulated cash investment of $16,500, compared with his initial investment of only $3,000.   But it is also true that his current commitment of 350 shares is actually worth only $3,500, compared with his $16,500 investment.   He has a current paper loss of $13,000.

$16,000 vs. $43

Now this entire policy of averaging down would not be bad — in fact, it would be very good — if Paramount were going to "come back" with the rest of the market, as our hero has expected it to do.   The tragedy of the whole policy is that Paramount goes into receivership in the early part of 1933.   The stock does not recover with the rest of the market.   It drops to 12½ cents a share.   Now our investor's block of stock is worth exactly $43.75, if he wants to sell for such a price, less commissions, exactly the same thing for which he paid a total of $16,500!

Great Losses from Little Ones

If he holds on, no one may say that he will not some day get more than $43.75 for his 350 shares.   But it is a fair certainty that he will never get back any *great* portion of his entire $16,500 investment.   In point of fact, Paramount certificates were selling back up around $4 a share in the Summer of 1934.   The point is that they had then recovered barely 5 per cent of their long bear market decline, while the accredited stock market averages, representing fair diversification, had recovered around 30 per cent.

Even that is not a fair comparison, however, because if our investor had "averaged down" on the general market, instead of only in this single stock, he would have had an average purchase price, on the "averages" of only about 175, compared with average levels in the Summer of 1934, of around 85, showing a recovery to nearly 50 per cent of the average purchase price. But the average of the Paramount commitment was 47, compared with a 1934 level of four, showing a recovery to less than 9 per cent of the purchase price. The general market, therefore, showed a performance, or recovery, approximately five times as favorable as the performance of this single stock.

The reader may suggest that this is an isolated case, that no sane investor would have continued to buy Paramount. Neither of such arguments is valid. It is not a particularly unusual case. But even if it were, the mere fact that it "might have been" any one of a great number of issues should be a sufficient argument against averaging down in any stock. And there were plenty of perfectly "sane" investors who *did* average down in Paramount. It is easy enough to see their mistake now, but it was not so easy to see the handwriting on the wall prior to 1932.

Right and Wrong Way to Average Down

But our reference to the general market and hypothetical averaging operations on a basis of the "averages" brings us to the worthy consideration of a perfectly proper and logical method of averaging. While it is extremely dangerous, as we have seen, to average down in one single stock, or group of stocks, it is entirely logical to average down on the general market. The primary and fundamental difference is one between concentration of risk and diversification of risk.

We have seen that averaging operations are correct in theory, when postulated upon eventual recovery in price. The fallacy is that no one can be certain that a single, individual issue is actually going to recover to anything like its previous value. Therefore, averaging operations in a single issue are extremely dangerous. But one can be much more certain that the market as a whole *is* going to recover some day. Therefore, *diversified* averaging operations are entirely logical and proper.

If our hypothetical investor had averaged down on the general market instead of only in one stock, his position would have been perfectly justified. Every time the general market sold down to a new low level, and every time he found some additional cash for market operations, he might have diversified his purchases, buying first one security, then another, but never more of the same issue. In that case, he would have been doing a wise thing, instead of the foolish thing he did when he simply kept on buying more of the same stock.

Averaging on the General Market

We already know enough about the theory of diversification [1] to realize the theoretical logic of this statement. And we have just noted its practical truth, in our comparison of the general market and Paramount. We have seen that because our investor averaged down in only one stock, and that one happened to be a poor one, he had, in the Summer of 1934, a recovery of only 9 per cent of his average purchase price. But if we assume that every time he bought more Paramount, some other, more far-sighted and logical, investor bought 50 shares of "the averages," then the latter's average purchase price would have worked out to around 175, using the Times average of 50 combined industrial and railroad stocks.

[1] See p. 249.

This average had recovered to around 85 in the Summer of 1934, and would thus have shown him a recovery amounting to about 50 per cent of that average purchase price, a record which we have previously noted, compared with the 9 per cent recovery realized by the Paramount investor.

If we need one additional argument against averaging in the same stock and in favor of averaging on the entire market, through diversification, it may be found by the mere reversal of an argument against averaging in the same stock.

Averaging Combined with Diversification

We have seen [1] that the decline in an individual stock is a suggestion of weakness, and we had best buy no more of it at the lower price. Yet if the general market is declining, then it is no disgrace for our individual stock to decline also, provided only that it does not drop faster than the general market.

But if it drops no faster than the general market, then there is no advantage in buying more of that same stock. And if it *does* drop faster than the general market, then we again have our old argument of special weakness in this single stock, and the suggestion for its avoidance in future purchases. In either case, therefore, the logic of the situation calls for diversifying by purchases throughout the general market, during declines, rather than recurrent investment in a single security.

In other words, the only argument for averaging at all, is that the general market has declined, and such a factor calls for averaging in the general market, rather than in an individual issue.

[1] See p. 264.

Trading on Margin

One final consideration may properly engage our attention before we leave the subject of our present chapter. That is the practice of trading, or investing, on margin. No categorical advice may be given on this subject, but a few observations may aid the individual reader to decide for himself whether he ought to utilize marginal operation or not.

Naturally, one of the fundamental considerations must be the degree of risk which is assumed. In spite of Government regulation, there are still plenty of degrees ranging from conservative credit, which cannot harm greatly, to the speculative type of marginal "plunging" which can wipe out fortunes and bring sudden tragedy and ruin. Naturally, the latter extreme is to be avoided. And it will be avoided, if our previously-noted rules against over-enthusiasm, over-trading, plunging, etc., are properly and consistently followed.

The Element of Market Analysis

There is another element of risk, however, which bears on the propriety of marginal trading, because it bears also upon the amount of risk justified. That is the current analysis of the general market and business situation. No such analysis can ever be infallible, of course. But we may simply illustrate the point, in brief mention, by suggesting that marginal trading was most certainly justified in 1932 and 1933 to a greater degree than in 1928 and 1929. The limits of possible, and probable, loss were entirely different during the two periods.

And the adequate comparison and weighing of such risks, in the less extreme intermediate periods, is a valuable basis for judgment on the extent of conservative marginal operation.

The Element of Risk

Even more important, as a practical factor in such consideration, is the degree to which marginal trading will increase the investor's risk. The basic and decisive question to be asked, before embarking on any such marginal enterprise, is this: "Will the utilization of this credit in my trading increase the amount of my risk to a point where the maximum possible loss would endanger my personal life, my peace of mind and my capital estate?" If the answer is "yes" then the credit should not be undertaken.

In other words, we go back once more to our basic principle of conservative operation, to weighing the risk of loss *before* entering upon any commitment, rather than afterward. The use of margin trading means the utilization of credit in order to trade in a greater amount of any security than one's current free capital would normally permit. Very well. Does this additional commitment increase the risk beyond one's normal ability to withstand whatever loss might be entailed, provided that the commitment is unsuccessful, instead of showing a profit?

Dangers in Marginal Trading

Such a measure of risk capacity would preclude, as dangerous, the utilizing of credit to such an extent that complete collapse of the collateral would leave the investor unable to pay up his loan out of his other free assets, based upon normal analysis of the future value for those assets themselves.

Let us suppose, for instance, that our hypothetical investor has an estate in which his asset surplus is $100,000, calculated at a reasonable valuation and based upon reasonably definite liquidation values. Of this entire estate, he has only $10,000 in a fund available for market operation. His analysis is bullish, however, and he wants to buy, not merely $10,000 of securities, but $20,000 worth of securities. The answer would be that he is entirely justified in such a plan, borrowing the additional $10,000 which he needs, because even if he loses the entire $20,000, his loss will not cripple him or his estate.

But let us suppose that we now have a potential investor with $10,000 in cash and an estate of only $20,000 besides. This investor would not be justified in assuming the risk on an additional $10,000 loan because if his entire commitment of $20,000 were lost it would cripple his estate and adversely affect his entire future outlook and standard of living.

The Temptation to Over-Trade

Such examples are entirely general and theoretical, of course. The true, basic criterion is always the ability to *stand* loss. But the more practical factor is the ability to *limit* loss. From a purely practical standpoint, the man who could not stand a full loss of $20,000 would, under most circumstances, be justified in borrowing his $10,000 and operating on margin, provided only that he calculated in advance exactly how much loss he was able and willing to take, and then adhered to that calculation through the use of our stop-loss principle, studied in the previous chapter.[1]

This individual might calculate, for instance, that he was willing to lose his entire $10,000 of free capital, but no more

[1] See Chapter IX, p. 220.

than that. On such a basis, he could go ahead and borrow another $10,000, giving him a fund of $20,000, with which he might buy, let us say for the sake of simplicity, 100 shares of stock at 200. But now he must immediately consider that his risk is not merely his own $10,000, but is combined with the $10,000 which he has borrowed. If he is willing to lose only $10,000, then it must be his own $10,000 and not the $10,000 he has borrowed. For the fact remains, in spite of rather strange implications in recent governmental attitude, that the man who borrows money to speculate is morally responsible for its repayment, whether his speculation has been successful or not.

Use of the Stop Principle in Marginal Trading

Our trader, therefore, will have a stop-loss limit of 100 points on the 100 shares of stock which he has purchased. If he allowed any possible declines to run over 100 points, then he would have to delve into the balance of his estate in order to pay up the loan. But if, in case the stock should decline to 100, he carries out his original campaign promise with promptness and with courage, then he saves himself from further crippling loss. He sells out his 100 shares at 100, takes the $10,000 proceeds of the sale to repay his loan, and closes the entire matter.

If the penalty sounds severe, then let the reader ponder the fact that this man did not *have* to borrow the extra $10,000. He could just as easily have used only his own $10,000, bought only 50 shares of the stock at 200 and thus have cut his loss. His only logical argument for buying 100 shares on margin was to make double the profit. Hence, our oft-repeated emphasis upon considering possible loss instead of possible gain, when planning commitments.

Making Margin Trading Safe

From a more practical standpoint, however, the example should show us the usefulness of the stop-loss principle in margin trading. The author's chief objection to the use of credit in security operations is simply that it provides a temptation to over-trade, to assume too high a degree of risk. If we can avoid such tendencies, then there seems no great danger in margin trading.

And we have already seen that the stop-loss principle offers our most valuable and most practical protection against the assumption of too great a risk. If this principle is properly used, it seems not to matter very much how large or small one's margin. For, whatever it be, the individual will calculate in advance the total risk he is willing to undertake. And he will close out his commitments immediately and courageously, just as soon as his paper losses have reached the maximum figure which he is willing to lose.

The Impropriety of the Margin Call

The chief danger in marginal trading, therefore, seems to be the possible lack of a proper and definite advance campaign, coupled with the temptation to stretch the assumption of risk as the losses grow. The latter, of course, is usually fatal. We have already seen that the principle of stop-loss protection is of no use unless the individual abides by its rules conscientiously, promptly and courageously.

Such rules provide sound basis for the premise that the far-sighted and conservative operator should never receive a margin call, unless he has provided for it in his original campaign planning. The conservative investor, and even the

conservative speculator and trader, will be out of an unsuccessful commitment long before the loss is great enough to
worry a margin clerk.

Defense is the Best Attack

And thus we come to an end in our consideration of the
protective aspects of market technique. We have, it may be
hoped, gained considerable confidence in the helpful assistance of stop-loss protection, of conservatism and compromise. We should realize the necessity for weighing the risk
of loss as well as the promise of profit, for careful diversification of total risk and for using that principle of diversification in averaging operations, rather than concentrating additional capital on unsuccessful commitments.

In the consideration of such protective aids, we have been
obliged to concentrate for a time on the less optimistic side
of market analysis and judgment. But the reader need not
conclude that the chances are against him. If he has learned
properly how to handle the difficult situations, then the
others should prove simple. And then, in fact, the chances
for true market success and consistent profit are definitely in
his favor.

CHAPTER XI

MARKET COUNSEL — GOOD AND BAD

The Independent Approach

Through our entire studies thus far in the present volume, we have attempted to formulate the most useful principles of logic and common sense which may aid us in consistently successful market operations, entirely independent of outside advice or assistance.

The fundamental advantages of this subjective approach should by now be readily understood. They are founded on the fact that the majority of market operators, who enjoy only modest success, base their commitments on the same stimuli to which thousands of other traders are reacting in similar manner at the same time.

But we know that the successful "insiders" must cross all such popular market movements in order to be successful,[1] and that since the professionals usually are successful, the logical conclusion is that our own success must depend not upon following the crowd but upon acting independently and opposing our own individual judgment to that of the general public.

Does not Mean Being a Hermit

Our independent and individual approach seems clearly justified, therefore, in practice as well as in theory. But even such a purely subjective approach would be incom-

[1] See Chapter VIII, p. 181.

plete if it entirely ignored the validity of outside assistance. In point of actual fact, of course, it would be utterly fallacious to carry such a point of view to any extreme. We cannot shut ourselves up completely, within our own private shell of analysis, and ignore the outside world in which we live.

Even in our past consideration of subjective principles for success in personal analysis, we have had almost constantly to base such analysis on facts, figures and stimuli which came to us from basic information available to all. Our more logical approach is therefore based upon the fact that our attitude and our use of such public information is different from that of the public, rather than that we have access to any greater or more intricate mines of information.

Contacting the " Outside World "

And so, in the current chapter, we may spend some time profitably in consideration of the most important sources of "outside" stimulus and advice which are brought to bear on practical trading. These sources are the various public agencies which undertake organized or specialized counsel to the general investing and trading public, such services almost always being offered on some basis of financial remuneration.

It is difficult to trace very clearly or definitely the beginning of this great "business" of selling market advice. It had its most widespread beginning, probably, in the free counsel which the banker is generally glad to give to his client or depositor. But, at least in this country, the more specialized business of investment counsel for a fee is of comparatively recent origin.

The "Service Line"

It is definitely a "service line." It has developed as the wealth of our country has developed, as public interest in the business of investing has increased. And it is thus the direct answer to a special and insistent demand on the part of investors for authoritative aid and specialized counsel.

The more mature firms in this field have sometimes started out as plain statistical organizations, devoted more to the garnering, compiling and presentation of pertinent facts than to the analysis of such facts. And it may be said that such service is still one of the most important rendered in this field. Certainly the statistical organization has a definite place in our own theory of individual thought and personal analysis. A subscription to one of the better services in the statistical field is one of the logical and recommended tools in our own subjective market approach.

But by far the greater portion of the services now operating throughout our fair land have found it much less expensive, much easier and much more profitable, to concentrate upon the analysis of such statistics and upon the offering of advice rather than upon the efficient gathering of complete financial figures and data.

Classifications in Advisory Services

The strictly advisory services may perhaps best be classified for practical purposes according to the basis or emphasis of their forecasting approach. One large group, comprising chiefly the older service agencies, is inclined to base its analysis upon the purely fundamental angle. Another group, chiefly the newer entries, concentrates more on the technical aspect. Of these two great groups, the author would prefer to recommend the second, or technical, classification.

But there is a third, and fairly large, group which takes no dogmatic sides with either the fundamental or the technical approach, but watches and considers both, basing its final judgment and advice upon a combination of all angles. The superior agency in this third classification is the type which constitutes the ideal advisory service for the average market operator.

Discretionary Accounts

Most of these services operate almost entirely by mail, but some of them offer " wire " services also, whereby the client may receive special advice by telegraph. Many of them are also willing to accept " discretionary accounts," in which they agree to manage the client's brokerage account directly, simply informing him of the actions they take. Fees for such service are much higher, in theory, than the mere advisory service by mail or telegraph. In fact, the discretionary fees are very often based upon a percentage of the profit made for the client. This latter basis for fee-fixing has grown more popular in recent years, because it appears so logical and fair a proposition to the client that he is much more apt to subscribe.

It is perhaps not quite so fair as it sounds, however. The fee is usually paid monthly out of the profits for the previous month, but there is no redress, or drawback, in most of such schedules, for the months when a loss is shown instead of a profit. In other words, the client's profits are shared with his discretionary agent, but the losses are shouldered by the client.

Tricks of the Trade

No matter what the quality of the discretionary agent's judgment, he is almost bound to show a profit in some months, and thus make a profit in fees for himself. He need not worry, so far as fees are concerned, over the other months which show a loss, because he generally takes no fair responsibility for those losing periods.

Some discretionary traders and agencies have even overcome such an objection by agreeing not to take any percentage of the profits unless there is a net balance of profit over loss in the account. This is, of course, the fairest basis for fee-fixing. But even thus it does not always follow that the agent depends entirely upon the client's net profit for his own income. His client is constantly paying the commissions on all business transacted through his discretionary agent. And delicate methods may conceivably be found whereby the agent might be rewarded for trading through specific channels.

Supervisory Accounts

Many of the highest-grade advisory organizations have also established what are commonly termed " supervisory " accounts, or services. The basis for such service is the mere " watching " of one's personal investment portfolio by the agency. It advises changes from time to time in the client's investment policy, as changing conditions make switching advisable. The fees for such supervisory service, based on the total market capital involved, run fairly high, but they are usually applied only to the larger and more important accounts.

Although the investment trust is not primarily an advisory service, it does partake definitely of the " counselor " or management aspect, especially in the case of discretionary, flexible, or management types of trust. No lengthy or detailed discussion of this group is here necessary, since it is only indirectly connected with our study of individual market operation. It may simply be noted that the investment trust provides diversification for the small investor, and advisory management for all investors. But it also entails a fairly high charge for such service and interposes an additional, and conceivably unscrupulous, human element between the investor and his equities.

Investment Trusts

It may also be suggested that the two advantages are fairly well discounted by the disadvantages. The investment trust is quite logical and useful for certain types of individual, provided there is fair diversification elsewhere, and a definite limitation of risk. But, for the average reader who has found himself capable of, and interested in, following the principles of the current volume, it may be said that personal management of his own investment policy seems generally more to be desired than the "farming out " of such responsibility.

Having reviewed briefly the major types of advisory and counselor service, what shall be our proper attitude toward the field? In a general way the author considers such services as comprising a valuable and worthy institution. But there is the usual reservation in such a statement.

At the beginning of our chapter, we suggested the first basis of disadvantage, by reference to our study of inside crossing operations, the psychological aspect of public information, and the logical conclusion that it is better to play at least an individual hand, if not a lone hand, than to depend too much upon the same type of market news, information or advice which is available to the " public."

Dangers in the Market Advisory Principle

In point of fact, of course, the recommendations of such advisory services are not disseminated as widely as ordinary news. Subscribers are limited, but they are likely to be individuals whose operations are sufficiently important to provide " crossing fodder " for the professional. And, certainly in the case of a few of the larger services, the subscription lists reach fairly large proportions.

But if this drawback is kept in mind, if such services are not followed dogmatically, or blindly, or in their entirety, then they can be definitely valuable. The author has already recommended the use of some good statistical service for the average and fairly active operator. He can also recommend, with the reservations mentioned, the use of at least one good, and fairly popular, advisory service for the individual who is often too busy with other matters to keep up to date on current thought and trends, and who will use such a service with moderation and with logical common sense.

Advantages of the Service Subscription

One of the best methods for making proper use of the better advisory bulletins is chiefly as a stimulus to one's own personal thinking and personal analysis — as a basis, or a starting point, for one's individual thought. Many a time the author has refused to agree with the final forecast of such a service, but its perusal has been exceedingly useful, because some of the points or arguments therein had not been previously noted, and they suggested a fresh basis for the author's purely personal thinking and subjective analysis.

We have already mentioned that, in spite of our rule for individualism, the most valuable advisory service may often be the most popular and the largest, instead of the small and relatively little-known service with a limited clientele. Such advantage is based upon points already discussed. The larger service is more likely to give us these new ideas for our own thinking. And if we realize the psychological implications of wide circulation, then there is little danger that we shall be led astray into the too simple and easy paths of popular thought and action.

So far as the specific recommendations are concerned, we shall not follow them blindly, but merely as suggestions. We may, at times, decide that the reasoning and advice is good, and shall follow the recommendation, if the danger of thus following the public does not appear too great. But, perhaps more often, we shall use such advice merely as an aid in our own policy of "crossing" popular theories and popular trading action.

Crossing Operations and the Advisory Service

If we follow such a plan, then we would hardly act merely on the advice of any single service, but would find our crossing operations more logically based if we knew that quite a number of influential agencies were advising an identical course. Just as profitable a conclusion may often be reached, however, by considering the specific advice of only one popular service in connection with general public sentiment. If our own service, with a large following, is especially bullish, for instance, and we also find that news and popular stimulus are bullish, and that the public in general is also bullish, then we have a fair basis for logical " crossing " operations. We should, at the very minimum, follow such bullish inclination with extreme caution, if at all.

For there is no denying the continued truth of our previous study [1] on the psychology of professional crossing operations. Any stimulus which leads the majority of the public to act on a certain side of the market is most likely to be opposed by the insiders, and should therefore be considered with a maximum degree of skepticism.

Such a theory is not, in itself, a decisive argument against advisory services. It is merely a warning that if personal analysis suggests that one, or several, large agencies are advising the same thing, that the public is also in agreement with the same psychology, and that, therefore, the bulk of public trading will be in the direction of such advice, then the situation is dangerous on that particular policy, and may easily justify the adoption of an exactly opposite one. It is not often that such a situation occurs and it is not, therefore, a true argument against following the good advice which advisory services often give. It is simply an additional point to be remembered, for possible use in special circumstances, when, as and if the occasion should arise.

A Rule and Its Exception

The basis for such occasional danger, or usefulness, is an outgrowth of the one principle which should be well ingrained from frequent repetition: beware of following the crowd. Suspect any trend analysis which seems too widely

[1] See Chapter VIII, p. 200.

held in the public mind, and utilize the theory of crossing operations whenever the composite of professional advice and popular anticipation is overwhelmingly inclined on one side of the market only, to the practical exclusion of the other side.[1]

The writer is constrained here to mention, however, one rare but important qualification to such attitude. That is, when the services and reputable advisers have been consistently wrong in their forecasts for a tedious interval. In such case they are eventually likely to be correct — at just about the time that the public, and even perhaps the services themselves, have lost patience and faith in their proper analysis. The best major illustration of this situation was in 1929. Able forecasts had been bearish for over a year. They had been wrong for so long that no one heeded or respected their bearish warnings. In such circumstance the bearish side was logical, for it was still the "unpopular" view.

Degree of Accuracy in the Service Line

As regards the degree of accuracy of the high-grade counsel group, no general statement may be made, of course. Some have fairly good records, others have only mediocre ones. Practically all of them have "streaks" of being consistently correct for a considerable period of time, as well as those less welcome streaks when they appear to be almost 100 per cent wrong.

Naturally, none of them is infallible. This should be an easily understood thesis for the reader who has come this far, because he knows that no one is infallible in market forecasting. The corollary is not so much an argument for

[1] See Chapter VIII, p. 204.

compromise and conservatism in following such services as for the realization that no service — in fact no adviser — ever assumes the responsibilities for his own mistakes.

A counsel agency may make one error out of five forecasts, which is an exceedingly good record. But the "new subscriber" may just happen to accept the single piece of bad advice. Ordinarily it might be only a minor error of judgment. But for the client it may conceivably lead to disastrous loss and tragedy. But there is no recourse. The client, in true human fashion, may blame, curse and malign his advisory service to his heart's content, but that will not bring back his fortune or his market capital. So far as responsibility is concerned, the advisory service client is acting purely upon his own when he operates on an agency recommendation. For, if the advice goes wrong, the loss is his and not that of the agency.

Responsibility Remains with the Individual

The author has received plenty of letters which indicate a lack of this realization on the part of certain, admittedly inept, individuals. Their letters are always bitter, and naturally so. They often suggest even a lack of proper perspective and sanity. But that also is understandable when one reads of the crippling tragedy which they at least blame on their advisory service.

What they ask is redress. "This service told me to hang on, and I lost my entire savings of a lifetime. Why shouldn't this service make good on my loss?"

The intelligent reader knows that the entire responsibility, from a practical financial standpoint, is the client's and not the agency's. But the moral is that, because of this fact, the mere subscription to a good advisory service does not relieve the individual of risk, responsibility, or the necessity for his own native good sense and personal attention.

Selecting the Proper Service

Such consideration may also make timely a brief examination of the actual services which such agencies perform, in comparison with claims which, in some cases, run exceedingly close to plain misrepresentation.

If he subscribes to such a service at all, the operator should select it carefully. And no matter how highly the individual agency is recommended, he should be entirely familiar with its record before he begins to act on specific advice. In fact, it is both impossible and improper, in the author's opinion, to recommend a specific service to an individual, without his "trying it out" for a while before he risks financial capital on its advice.

Different services may suit different types of individual trading, and the author prefers to recommend trial subscriptions to a number of agencies before a permanent one is decided upon.

Many such advisory services have large statistical staffs and a goodly corps of analysts who decide on a composite forecast in assembled conference. There is nothing wrong with this type of forecasting — in fact, it has definite advantages. But the author's experience has led him to rate the service largely by the individual who heads it, or who is chiefly responsible for its recommendations.

This is self-apparent in the smaller services where perhaps one man is the entire personnel, but it is just as true and important in the case of larger agencies where analysis and forecast are divided between many individuals. In either case, the character and ability of the "chief" is an important criterion for the general valuation of the service itself.

Advertising Ethics

Our prior consideration of the degree of responsibility shared between the agency and the investor who takes the agency's advice makes timely a few words regarding the basic ethics in the general field of investment counsel. The author has already stated that he considers the general institution a valuable and a worthy one. But it has grown rapidly in recent years, and such growth has made certain not only a high degree of competition, but has added to the temptation for misrepresentation of what such services can do for the individual.

This is perhaps as much the fault of human frailty in potential subscribers as of the same frailty in counsel management. It seems to have been at least superficially proven that conservatism in service claims, no matter how much to be desired, does not bring in subscribers the way sensationalism does. The perfectly sound and worthy advisory service which advertises merely that it will "guide and aid" the investor does not stand so good a chance of winning subscribers as the less worthy competitor who shrieks that he "will double your money in 30 days."

As competition has increased, therefore, there has sprung up a regrettable tendency toward lurid and high-pressure claims for such advisory services which border upon pure misrepresentation. The result cannot but be disastrous, contributing directly to a general decline in prestige and public acceptance for the entire field if the tendency is continued.

Misleading Promotion Claims

One of the favorite " come-on " methods of recent years has been to publicize the news that " we recommended these ten stocks on January 1st and look at them now — 135 per cent profit in three months," and so on. The service does not go on to state that 20 other stocks were recommended at the same time, and with no such startling profits. It does not suggest that perhaps this particular campaign was the first successful one it has hit in many months. It does not add that at that particular time the general market advanced so rapidly that almost anybody could have made profits, nor does it suggest that the future may not be so easy.

Or the service may offer its " record " as showing consistent profits over a considerable period, having its brokerage statements checked and audited by certified public accountants. The record is probably correct, but no mention is made of other accounts which showed just as great a loss as this one did a profit. It is no difficult matter, of course, to operate two separate accounts, select fast-moving stocks and play for spectacular moves, but to do exactly the opposite in one account from the position assumed in the other. One of the two accounts will probably show a good gain, while the other shows an equal loss. The reader is entitled to his own fun in thinking out for himself which of the two accounts the " service " would select for auditing and advertisement.

As usual, there are both good and bad types of representation, just as there are good and bad types of advisory service. Therefore, if we are truly intent upon selecting one whose record and analysis we want to trust, we shall perhaps avoid at least the ones which offer flamboyant claims, misleading representation, and any great emphasis on "high-pressure" selling methods.

From Good Counsel to Bad

Thus far in our chapter, we have had in mind chiefly the legitimate type of advisory service, but it is perhaps needless to inform the reader that there is an entirely distinct field of illegitimate services. We have seen that there can be a semblance of unfair misrepresentation and operation even in the legitimate type of counsel, but it is a relatively harmless kind. The sharp practice consists rather in getting subscribers and their service fees than in giving deliberately false advice on market operation. The illegitimate advisory service, on the other hand, is set up for the specific purpose of misleading investors, of inducing them to put their money into worthless and fraudulent securities. The legitimate outfit makes at least a conscientious effort at profits for its subscribers, while the illegitimate service is dedicated to fraud from the very start.

Perhaps one of the chief dangers in such enterprise is the fact that the illegitimate service does not care much about the fees it may receive for giving advice. It makes its profit out of selling worthless stock. And so large are the profits in many of such fraudulent security selling schemes that the service itself can go to considerable expense in getting its subscribers and delivering its recommendations, suggesting to the unwary neophyte that here is a service which must be strong and prosperous. The advisory fees are low. If, indeed, there are any at all, they are merely to allay suspicion. There are grand and costly "brochures," handsome offices, dignified salesmen and a general air of confidence, ability and prosperity.

From Conscientious to Fraudulent Services

As a matter of fact, such illegitimate advisory services very often maintain a well-organized, highly-paid and capable staff of statisticians and analysts, giving perfectly good and sound advice on good and sound securities — all but one! The subscriber appreciates this sound advice on good stocks and perhaps makes money on it, gradually building up considerable confidence in the organization.

But after such confidence has been established for a while, that "one" stock which is *not* sound begins to be stressed more and more often. The client may be sure that the really capable analysts in the agency's employ either have had nothing to say about this pet recommendation, or else they simply tolerate the racket, know that the stock is worthless, but consider their salaries more important than their morals. Glowing reports and tantalizing recommendations multiply on this one stock. The theory — only too often successful — is that confidence has previously been built up, and that the unsuspecting "subscriber" will finally fall for at least a fair block of the worthless stock.

The "Sell and Switch" Racket

Quite similar in essence is another type of "fake stock racket" which has grown by leaps and bounds during the past couple of years. It is called the "sell and switch" method, building up the investor's confidence by sound advice on good stocks, usually starting with one he already owns and knows is good — and then later getting him to switch from a sound issue into the fraudulent security which the organization is distributing.

The "opening" on this racket is also new but now widespread. It usually consists of securing a list of stockholders in some widely-held and strong investment issue, listed on the New York Stock Exchange, and then circularizing this stockholders' list for suckers. Let us say that the investor owns some Standard Oil of New Jersey stock. He receives a printed circular in the mail, calling his attention to an "analysis" which the firm has made on Jersey. "What is wrong with your stock?" "Keep informed on this issue." "Some inside news for stockholders." Or some tantalizing "come-on" of similar import. "We shall be glad to send you this report free. Simply fill out the enclosed card, giving your name and address, without obligation."

The Sucker List

The temptation is strong, and no harm will be done at the start. But if the investor sends in his name and address for the report, he not only receives a fairly good and business-like "report" on Standard Oil of New Jersey, printed to simulate the similar reports of reputable statistical agencies, but he also begins to receive letters and 'phone calls from the fraudulent firm about his stock. By the simple act of sending in the return postcard he has automatically placed his name on the firm's "sucker list."

The organization continues to build up public confidence for a while, though the methods are always so typical of illegitimate firms that on occasion they almost inspire the author's sympathy. Either by letter or by telephone, the client will now be told either that Standard Oil of New Jersey is going up, and he should buy more, or that it is going down, and he should switch — not yet into the fake stock (that would be too sudden and suspicious) but into some other sound, standard security such as United States Steel, for instance.

Gaining the Investor's Confidence

Such early encounters, for building up confidence in the firm and its salesman, are often good for real market profit, since they are based upon the sound dictates of the firm's capable staff of legitimate analysts. The author makes it his business to be on as many of such "sucker lists" as possible. And he must admit, without much compunction, that he has followed such advice, when it corresponded with his own personal judgment, and has made money on it. In this stage of the game, of course, the fraudulent advisory service must be right, else it loses the interest and confidence of its suckers.

But there comes a day — usually after one or two trades have proven profitable — when the advice is to switch from a sound stock, not into another sound issue, but into the firm's fraudulent and worthless pet. It may be almost any type of stock, may even be listed on the New York Stock Exchange. But it is probably a low-priced one, and one that the client has heard little about, if anything, except from this particular firm.

Fraudulent Advice Follows Good Advice

At this stage of the game the service will "turn on the heat." There will be glowing stories and statistical reports on the pet issue. There will be telephone calls, telegrams, long-distance messages at considerable expense, perhaps even a personal call from some glib salesman. The forecast for "big profits" may even be made plausible by some advance in the stock.

But the constant advice will be to " Give it all you've got. This is the chance of a lifetime. You know how we've made money for you in the past. We want to see you make twice as much. And you must act immediately, before the stock goes up."

The firm may even offer to put up margin for the client, so that he can carry a big line. That makes the temptation to " plunge " all the stronger. And the firm will not lose anything, because all that it is after is the money that the client himself sends in.

Selling Worthless Stock

So long as the service can get more suckers to buy its stock than want to sell, the game continues. But eventually the point of saturation is reached. A few people begin to take profits. A few want their money back. They have been in long enough to begin thinking things over and are growing suspicious. Perhaps the authorities have finally gotten the scent.

Then comes the end. The " advisory service," or " security house," decamps inside of a few hours. The statistical staff, boiler-room laddies and star salesmen are either discharged or moved to another address where the firm, probably under a new name, starts the game all over again with a new stock and a new " service."

But the chances are that the " principal " can take a long vacation, if he desires. For he is likely to have cleaned up $100,000 or more inside of six months. The preparations were perhaps costly and tedious. But they were well worth it, if the firm has been able to sell only 50,000 shares of a worthless stock at the comparatively low and tempting price of but $4 a share.

Fraudulent Approaches Constantly Changing

These are only a few simple examples of how the illegitimate advisory service goes about its tragic work. The individual details and individual quirks in such fraudulent schemes are seemingly endless. The fake promoters are quick to change their methods when one approach becomes worn out or too well-known to the public. There have been the depreciated foreign exchange swindles, the bucket-shop racket, the foreign bond game, the worn-out mine story and countless others. The modern version appears to be the fraudulent "stock market advisory service" and its more recent refinement, the "sell and switch" racket.

There will be plenty of others in the future. But there is one sure way to avoid the pitfalls in such sucker games. That is to follow the slogan of the Better Business Bureau — "Before You Invest, Investigate." That is the only sure method, but we may also note some other suggestions.

General Characteristics Easy to Detect

Never deal in unknown issues. The reader may recall our previous advice [1] for trading in well-distributed and respected securities listed on the New York Stock Exchange. Even this rule is not air-tight, however, since various questionable counselors appear to have switched their operations into listed stocks in order to allay suspicion. Usually, however, the security is one which has not been heard about much, if at all.

Never deal with unknown houses. Constant circularization, repeated mailing of attractive literature, and even

---

[1] See Chapter X, p. 261.

eventual friendliness with a customer's man, do not, of course, constitute proper grounds for faith. In the matter of actual buying and selling of stock, perhaps the safest rule is to deal only with reputable *member* houses of the New York Stock Exchange, or with houses of similar unimpeachable reputation. Paid and legitimate advisory services are not usually so connected, of course, but the rule for well-known reputation still holds good.

Yet even this principle is not always iron-clad. An illegitimate swindler may sometimes buy the name of a well-known, old and honest firm, simply to gain public confidence. Thus all of the other tests must also be applied.

How to Spot Fake Stock Rackets

Another strong suggestion of fraudulent method, however, is the unauthorized or unexpected use of telephone and telegraph solicitation. Many questionable promoters use this method for their " high-pressure " tactics in closing the deal. It makes the client feel important to be so singled out, it emphasizes the salesman's argument for immediate action, and it evades the stricter, and more easily proven, legal consequences of " using the mails to defraud."

But perhaps the most important general warning of immediate danger is the " high-pressure " technique of the illegitimate service or broker. The urge for quick action is even more suggestive than mere promises of spectacular profit. We have already seen [1] that one's quickly-made decisions are always dangerous. That is one of the allies of the fraudulent stock promoter.

" This option is open only today. It expires at midnight. Let me put you down for 100 shares right now. The price

---

[1] See Chapter IX, p. 240.

is going up tomorrow." All such arguments for haste are danger signals of outright fraud. The unscrupulous salesman knows that if he gives the client time to think about the matter, time to seek legitimate counsel, time to let the imagination cool off and let common sense and logic have their innings, he will probably lose his sale. It is seldom that a truly good profit opportunity disappears in a few hours. And even if it did, the average investor will save more in the end if he learns never to make decisions hastily and without mature and calm judgment.

Some Simple Rules of Protection

The high-pressure methods are, of course, typical of the fraudulent promoter and are fairly well recognized, though not so well as to save the millions of dollars which stock swindlers collect every year. Let the "prospect" ask himself, on all such occasions, why he is thus being high-pressured into buying any security.

He may be certain that the less reputable the scheme the greater the necessity for sales pressure. And he may likewise be quite certain that if the stock is truly as good as the salesman represents it to be, the entire issue would have been gobbled up long since. It would have been taken by the truly astute bankers, brokers and insiders who know and seek out true profit opportunities, without forcing a promoter to pay salesmen high salaries to argue anyone into buying.

Summary on the Market Counsel Field

And thus we come back once more to the inescapable conclusion that all things, in security market operation at least, are relative. Nothing is perfect and nothing is worthy of total or complete trust. Our entire study has been an attempt to strike a composite compromise, through the consideration of rules, advice and theory, none of them infallible in themselves, but all of them useful in aiding our own approach to proper judgment and consistent profit.

We shall not be violating our course of individual analysis if we make full use of the unquestioned advantages which are offered by modern statistical and advisory services. We shall, in fact, be better able to draw those advantages into our own subjective investment pattern through our study of their general merits and shortcomings. We shall prepare ourselves to take the good, by the mere protective realization that there are also dangers and pitfalls involved in the general classification. But, having protected ourselves, through observation and study, against those pitfalls, we shall be in better position to profit from the unquestioned advantages which specialized counsel may offer in practical market policy.

CHAPTER XII

CONCLUSION

Summary and Review

At the very beginning of our introductory chapter we outlined the aim of our subsequent studies. And we may now, in our concluding review, survey that aim in the light of the many and various principles which we have considered in the intervening chapters.

The primary interest of any average individual in security market operation is, without need for argument, the profit motive. To the extreme idealist such an aim may seem unworthy. But we have noted the justification for profit on the basis of proper reward for study, concentration and effort.

And we have also established the actual duty of such application through the conception of personal " stewardship," on the part of every individual, with respect to the capital, the brains, the ability, the " talents " which nature or circumstance has given him.

The Basic Aims

Whether the individual considers his market operations a part-time venture, a full-time business or a plain hobby, his desire and aim, as well as his duty, is to make a profit from such activity. Anything worth doing at all is worth doing well, and this old adage applies just as much to security market activity as to any other form of endeavor.

And the security market, like any other business, is little more than a mirror of one's own attitude in this regard. If the individual considers it a game of chance, then he deserves to lose for playing it in that fashion. But if he considers it a serious activity, where he may be fairly repaid for conscientious study and effort, then the practical success which such an attitude logically brings is his just reward for this proper conception of his own activities.

If a man enters the field of selling groceries with the idea that it is an easy and simple line, requiring little work, practically no attention, and a minimum of preparation, he is almost certain to suffer loss in that business. And no one who knew his attitude would sympathize with him in his losses. It would "serve him right" for approaching the field with an improper attitude.

The successful groceryman is the one who realizes the seriousness of his business, who prepares for success, who gives maximum study, thought and attention to it. Yet that same man, having made a fortune through proper approach to his own business, will often literally throw much of that fortune away by sinking it in the stock market, expecting to get high return with no preparation, no study and a minimum of attention. Shall we blame the market for his losses, or shall we blame his own improper attitude?

Maximum of Gain

And so the theme of our entire approach to market success in this volume has been one of granting proper attention to the seriousness of such operation, to thought, to study, to careful consideration, to long-range planning and to all of the other aspects which will not only increase the probabilities of success from a practical standpoint, but will make such success morally justified as the proper reward for value given.

And yet, we have not insisted on " full-time " study of the stock market, in order to assure consistent profit. As a matter of fact, the author doubts whether such intensive attention would be advisable, even if it were practical, for the average operator. In this respect, the business of security operation differs from most other businesses. It *does* demand careful attention. But it demands less attention than most other lines, for proper success.

And therein lies one of its fundamental advantages. Once the proper mental attitude is attained, then it offers perhaps greater profit " per unit of attention " than any other business. This is, basically, because stock market success is so largely a matter of proper mental activity and so little a matter of physical activity. The man who runs a grocery store must give much physical time and attention in addition to his mental planning and thought. But the man who is operating on a moderate scale in the security market need devote practically no physical effort to this line of endeavor.

Minimum of Physical Labor

The penning of a short note to his broker or banker, the lifting of a telephone receiver — these are the approximate physical burdens of stock market operation. And they require a minimum of time and effort. But the great emphasis is upon thought, upon proper mental processes. And even these may not require more than an hour or two a day at the most. Proper judgment is all that is needed for average market success, as opposed to long physical time and attention in most other businesses. But the judgment must be efficient and able.

How then shall we cultivate this proper judgment which lies at the basis of the profit and success which we seek from our security business? A part of it is perhaps inborn, characteristic and almost subconscious. But by far the greater measure may be expressed in the terms which we have used so freely in the present volume — thought, study, logic and plain common sense.

It is on the fundamental principles which emanate from these considerations that our preceding study has been based. And our emphasis has been on such elements not merely because they are extremely important, but also because they provide perhaps the most valuable approach possible, in comparison with the time, study and preparation required. For true value received, in return for the time and energy invested, the utilization of such theories provides the greatest reward in practical profit of all other means of market approach.

" Hobby " of Market Operation vs. " Business "

This does not mean that we have covered the entire catalog of security technique, by any means. There have been enough suggestions in our previous chapters to convince the reader that many other fields are open to his further study. And there are plenty of other practical and valuable aids to market success which have not even been suggested in these pages.

But most of them are specialized, if not intricate. They require mathematical preparation, statistical analysis and the application of additional time and study. Many of them are exceedingly valuable, and may well be taken up by the individual who is preparing for a more specialized approach. But, in the main, they offer less practical advantage, in com-

parison with the time, preparation and energy required, than
do the principles of logic and common sense which we have
attacked in the current volume.

Hobby Can be a Thorough One

Nor need the reader feel that his education has been neglected by our less technical emphasis. The individual who
digests and conscientiously uses the principles here studied
may receive his full diploma to become a consistently successful market operator. The " average " reader, for whom
after all the volume has been written, may indeed find that
he is just as well off without delving into the more specialized fields of market science and study. His own individual
experience and the success of future operation must be the
eventual guide on such a point.

The author has long been convinced of the practical efficacy inherent in the pure and simple principles of logic and
common sense on which we have based our current approach. It has often been a marvel to him to see how many
operators fret and stew over highly intricate technique, when
a calm and quiet hour of communion with their own good
sense might show them the proper way to market profit.

Summary of Fundamentals

Is there anything very intricate, for instance, in our consideration of the fundamental approach toward proper investment policy on the longer-swing and fundamental basis
of business and economic cycles? Is it so difficult for the
long-swing investor to establish, with a reasonable degree of
accuracy, whether business is on the advance or the decline,
to decide whether industry and speculation are going to dan-

gerous extremes in one direction or another, and to await, with sensible patience, the development of such extreme cycles? Yet there is perhaps no more valuable or profitable factor to aid the judgment of the long-swing investor than just such a simple, logical and common-sense appraisal of current circumstances.

Or is there anything so intricate or difficult about our more technical manner of approach to profit for the short-swing operator? Admittedly, it is somewhat more specialized than the purely fundamental approach, but its general principles are not particularly intricate. And they are certainly valuable as an aid in our proper understanding and practical judgment.

Summary of Technical Factors

Part of this technical angle is the mere examination of past market performance through the medium of charts, and there can be no questioning the efficacy of seeing such past performance portrayed graphically and compactly before one's eyes. The man who is willing to give a little time and consideration merely to such a simple record, whether he applies the more intricate theories or not, is in infinitely better position to make sound judgments than the man who relies merely on his memory for a record of such performance, or than the man who ignores the past record completely.

And who can contradict the simplicity and plain logic in the principles of our general and practical approach to security operation? It is plain common sense to have one's entire plan of campaign mapped out, to weigh the chances of the unexpected and disappointing development as well as the anticipated and successful one. Yet this single, simple rule is almost regularly violated even by individuals who pride themselves on ability and experience. And such violation accounts for a multitude of losses and discouragements which could be avoided so consistently by its simple application.

Summary of General Considerations

Patience, conservatism, unhurried thought, logical anticipation of coming developments, the utilization of public psychology in crossing operations, independent thinking — all these are such simple and apparent virtues that we tend to ignore them, or at least to forget them at times. Yet here, in these basic principles of pure logic and common sense, we have some of the easiest and most successful factors in the resolution of composite judgment and consistently successful market policy.

Or, if we turn to the less positive, and more protective, elements of aid, we shall find our principles equally logical and equally valuable. Avoidance of plunging and over-trading, diversification of risk, the use of definite stop-loss protection, whether actual or mental, the avoidance of hasty judgment, the coupled-order formula — all these stand as simple and logical guardians, protecting us from crippling loss and tragic discouragement on those rare occasions when our more positive forecasts fail to work out as they had been expected to do.

All of them are principles that are likely to be overlooked as too simple and easy. Yet when they are properly cultivated, and when they have become characteristic, ingrained in our almost subconscious technique of market analysis, they shall provide additional and valuable bulwark for our consistent market success.

Co-ordinating .the Rules and Theories

For it is not out of place, as we near the end of our study, to suggest the necessity for just such a subconscious utilization of all our rules, formulae and principles — logical, technical, fundamental, practical or what not. It is not enough merely to memorize such principles, and then to attempt to apply each one separately to our specific problems. The individual who does merely that is still in the " learning " stage, and is not truly prepared for practical operation or consistent success. He will be too self-conscious, too intent upon recalling each individual theory, too involved in the details of many varying suggestions, to arrive at that calm and logical composite judgment which we are striving for.

He may be forced to *begin* in some such meticulous and methodical manner. But he will not be proficient in the art of proper operation until such time as he can apply the rules of logic without identifying them individually — even without thinking about them.

The Goal of " Subconscious Assimilation "

They must be so assimilated before they become truly and practically valuable. They must enter into his composite forecast almost subconsciously, without effort, without strain, without mental reference to the catalog to make sure that each rule has been checked off the list. This is the seasoning process, and it comes best and chiefly from experience.

It will come more naturally and more easily to the individual who is already of a logical mind, who has trained himself in the clear and unhurried " thinking out " of his every-day problems. But it is necessary for every successful operator. And to the average individual it is merely a combination of native common sense, a little time, thought and study, and a considerable amount of experience.

When the state of such proper assimilation is reached, the operator will find that he is moving slowly, but comfortably and surely, toward a certain line of thought and market judgment. He will not remember one certain rule and be swayed sharply and hurriedly in a single direction by the application of that single theory. He will find that his judgments are becoming trends or tendencies rather than sharp swings in either direction.

Tendency vs. Dogmatism

And when the time of such maturity arrives, he may take comfort, not only in development of this subconscious tendency toward proper market analysis, but in the valuable basis which it forms for the principle of compromise in practical operation.

It is very seldom that the mature and consistently successful operator rushes headlong from one side of the market to the other, especially in longer-term operation. He is much more apt to pursue our valuable principle of compromise, to lighten holdings when the " tendency " of his judgment turns less favorable, rather than to throw everything overboard, or to take on additional lines gradually when his feelings tend toward increasing confidence, rather than " buying the market " at one fell swoop.

If the individual attempts to " check " the market for definite forecast on every rule he has learned he will find the resulting forecasts not only contradictory, in many instances, but he will find himself in a maze of indecision and his judgment in a state of paralysis. Likewise, if he attempts to "act all at once" on his composite market analysis, he will probably find that he has stressed a certain factor too highly, that tomorrow he will stress another just as highly, and that he is literally jumping from one side of the market to another.

Composite Analysis as Second-Nature

The proper prescription, and the successful principle, is found in this simple theory of compromise. Just as his mature judgment is slow to change, so his practical market policy will be undergoing gradual and careful revision, on balance, rather than through a complete reversal.

So strong is this "tendency" of composite market judgment, that the author is often at a loss to explain exactly *why* he holds certain feelings toward the general market or toward a specific security. He might sit down and make a list of favorable and unfavorable factors. It might take hours, and it would probably result in a hundred items on one side of the ledger and almost an equal number on the other side. But it would not constitute the proof of true and efficient market analysis.

That is a "tendency," resulting from almost subconscious consideration of all of the listed factors, giving them each a certain weight and striking the final balance without conscious effort, perhaps without dogmatic conclusion on either side, but with merely this proper "tendency" toward one side or the other.

Often, the result would not be enthusiasm or complete disfavor. But it would be the formulation of a compromise policy, leaning today in the direction of today's tendency, but quite willing and ready to shift that tendency back in the opposite direction if tomorrow's developments should again turn the balance in such preceding channel.

Full Market Policies Seldom Advisable

As an example of this tendency toward ˙compromise in practical market policy, the author has long held that investment portfolios, for instance, should never be liquidated 100 per cent at the top of a bull market, no matter how bearish the indications. And conversely, that no investor should ever accumulate 100 per cent at the bottom of a bear market, no matter how bullish the indications.

Near the top of the long bull market which ended in 1929 the author, as market adviser for many individuals, had been recommending gradual liquidation of long investment holdings for well over a year, but only on a scale up. And when the crash came he was quite content that most of such clients still retained from 10 to 20 per cent of their capital in long holdings. Why? Because no one could be absolutely certain that the market would not go still higher before the debacle. It was *unlikely* that stocks would go much higher. That was taken care of by 80 to 90 per cent liquidation. But it was at least possible. And *that* was taken care of by the compromise policy of retaining 10 to 20 per cent in long commitments.

Gradual Accumulation

Likewise, near the end of the major bear market which ended in 1932, the author had long been recommending gradual purchase of investment securities, but only on a scale down. And when the turn finally came he was equally content that most of his "followers" still had 10 to 20 per cent of their total market capital in cash. Again, why?

Simply because no one knew for an absolute certainty that the market would not go still lower before the final upward turn.

Once again, it was highly unlikely that it would go much lower, but that was taken care of by 80 to 90 per cent gradual accumulation of securities on a scale down, and therefore at a fairly low average level. But the slight chance that there would be further weakness made it advisable, from a psychological as well as a practical standpoint, to have a moderate amount of cash reserve left to guard against such an eventuality.

A Practical Illustration

So important is this principle of compromise that perhaps one final example may be justified for our certain understanding of its practical application. If we turn back once more to Plate VII, on page 163, we may follow just such a compromise tendency in a practical, but hypothetical, investment policy. Let us assume, for simpler illustration, that this market average chart represents a single stock, or that we are able to trade in the " average."

Let us also assume that our total market capital would support purchase of 100 shares at 150, or a total capital of $15,000. At Point D the market looked ready for at least intermediate recovery. And we must remember that so far as length of decline and many other factors were concerned, it was at least possible for the bear market to end and give way to a new bull market at practically any time.

Do we turn suddenly bullish and rush in to buy our 100 shares at Point D? We do not. Our composite investment judgment does not work that way. It does not switch from bearish to bullish overnight. But the " tendency " of such judgment swings toward the constructive side. Following this tendency, and our principle of compromise, we shall buy, not 100, but, perhaps, 10 shares, at 137½, around Point D. Granting the somewhat radical theory, however, that we might have turned still more favorable at Point E, we might take on another 10 shares at 142½, giving us 20 shares at an average price of 140.

Scale Accumulation Campaign

At Point F, the market forced us (even if other factors did not) to turn less favorable, and we sold out 10 shares at 135. We might well have sold all 20, but we are going to be perfectly fair to our long-term principle of compromise and gradual accumulation on a scale down, because the further down stocks went the nearer came the eventual upward turn which we knew must develop some day. So we decided to retain 10 of the 20 shares.

There was good justification for taking on more at around Point K, or even at Point J, but we shall assume that we waited until Point L was reached, when we bought another 10 shares at 125. Merely to consider the worst possible judgment, instead of the best, let us say that we turned still more favorable and took on another 10 shares at Point N, around 140. This last purchase, however, should have been sold out at the same price, around Point Q. And following Point S another 10 shares should have gone overboard, at 130.

At around Point T, 10 shares might have been bought back again, at 125. But they would have been resold at Point U, around 120. At Point Y, things looked so bad that the investor would have been quite justified in tossing overboard the remaining 10 shares of his commitment, also at around 120.

Results of a Compromise Policy

Let us see the results of our compromise policy. We bought five lots of 10 shares each at an average price of 134. We sold five lots of 10 shares each at an average price of 129. Our average loss was 5 points on 50 shares, or a total loss of $225 plus commissions, or approximately two per cent of our total capital. As a matter of fact, the experienced operator might easily have made an actual profit out of this compromise campaign, or at least have broken even.

We have assumed only fair judgment, however, for our illustration. And even on such a basis the loss was exceedingly small when compared with what the individual might have suffered if he had "gone the limit" of his market capital every time his judgment had changed toward the market.

The Advantages Over a "Plunging" Policy

On the compromise basis the loss was a negligible one. On the "plunging" basis of dogmatic judgment and full shifting of commitments, the loss might easily have been a serious one, to say nothing of increased commission charges. We have selected as our example this specific chart because it is an easy one for reference and because it serves our purpose of practical illustration. Needless to say, it was not selected to show a profitable campaign on the compromise principle.

If that had been our aim we should have selected the Summer of 1932, showing the final turn from bear market into bull market, or some other bull-trend example where early profits would have been definite and substantial.

Playing for the Final Turn

The point of our current illustration is simply that the individual was playing for the eventual turn from bear to bull market, which he knew must come some day. He was protecting himself against further decline, but was also preparing to take advantage of the turn, if this was it.

But he was also operating on the basis of compromise. And the negligible loss which he suffered because this was *not* the final turn was a small fee for the chances of profit which he assumed. He could have repeated such action, with similar loss, again and again as the market pursued its long downward course from 1929 to 1932. And those losses would have been much more than made up in the first upward push of the new bull market when it finally did materialize in the early Summer of 1932.

Catching the Bottom in 1932

As each bottom moved lower, reaching nearer and nearer to the extremes of possible decline, he would have been more and more justified in the compromise policy of gradually buying more than he sold, of slowly building up his long portfolio and increasing his percentage accumulation, always on a scale down and thus always reducing the average price of his entire purchase line.

He should not have been entirely accumulated in the early Summer of 1932, but he might well have been 75 per cent accumulated just before the final turn and 85 or 90 per cent accumulated just after it developed. He would not have had all of his capital invested, but he would have had sufficient to keep him happy for some time to come. And meanwhile, if the turn had *not* materialized at that point and at that time, he would still have had the psychological, as well as practical, satisfaction of retaining some moderate reserves against even this small possibility of further weakness.

Feeling the Market

Thus we may co-ordinate all of the many theories and principles which we have studied in the current volume, gathering together in our subconscious mind the technical factors, the fundamentals, the logical formulae and the practical rules of common-sense operation, until they become our second nature, leading us without conscious effort into proper composite judgment and toward gradual shifting of our longer-term market policies through the habit of compromise.

The mere "feeling of the market," which accompanies the subconscious tendency toward compromise of practical balance, will be the operator's apprisal that he has emerged from the state of study into that of experience.

Yet even such feeling is not to be wholly trusted in a practical way, for it would not disclose a sufficiently definite or concrete knowledge of operation to justify immediate risk of capital. The only true test of one's assimilation and graduation is the critical test of practical market experience in the present, and not in working out hypothetical problems of the past. The reader must actually buy and sell. He must give orders and make current decisions, before he has a final test of his ability.

For the average reader who has already had experience in active operation, there need be no great danger in submitting himself to the practical test through his own continued market activity, with cold cash, provided of course that he maintains proper principles of conservatism and protection during the process.

Paper Trading

For the individual who is not currently an active trader, however, the author would strongly recommend " taking his examination " without actual financial risk. This may simply and easily be accomplished through the medium of paper trading.[1] No capital is needed. No account is opened with the broker. The student simply keeps a book with his orders and their results, entering them just as he would if he were actually trading with his broker, but without risking the capital which would be required in real market operation.

He may enter his orders at any time and give them with whatever limits and instructions he decides upon, using stop-loss levels, and all of the other principles we have studied. The crux of the whole system in paper trading, of course, is absolute honesty with oneself. If a buying order is entered at 100, and the price reacts only to 100⅛ and then soars upward, the temptation to consider the stock bought must be conscientiously avoided. Any " cheating " will be merely at the expense of the individual, and will be misleading as well as unfair.

Needless to say, the student is not justified in graduating himself from paper trading to actual cash operation until his paper trades have shown a consistent profit balance for some time. The minimum interval for testing ability on paper should be not less than a month for the average individual.

[1] See " Stock Market Theory and Practice," p. 545.

Approaching the Conclusion

In approaching our conclusion, let it be said once more that we have not attempted to cover the entire field of market technique in the current volume. What we have done is to give proper consideration to the most important and basic aspects of the broad subject, laying the foundation for study, progress and continued experience in the future, and attempting to draw the greatest gain from the most simple principles, through emphasis upon the value of individual thought, careful analysis, common sense and logic in our general market approach.

Throughout our entire study we have directed our main attention to stocks, and have drawn our chief examples from this more speculative type of security medium. We have done so largely from a practical standpoint, and because this group is quite justifiedly of greater interest and greater profit to the average individual.

Stock Rules Applied to Other Markets

But there has been no intention of ruling out the other various classes of security. In a broad sense, most of the rules and theories which we have considered may be applied just as easily and just as successfully to preferred stocks, bonds and other classifications as to common stocks.

As a matter of fact, such rules may also be applied to almost any free and open market for organized trading. And such application includes wheat, corn, oats, cotton and the many other commodity markets. Naturally, fundamental considerations such as balance sheets, dividends, earnings, and so on, cannot thus be applied. But the factors such as charts, technical considerations, campaign plans, common sense, logic, psychology, crossing principles, stop-loss protection formulae, etc., which have been our main considerations, are all extremely valuable in commodity market operation.

Trading in Commodities

A final word is perhaps not out of place, on the comparative profit possibilities for speculative operation in stock and commodity markets. As a result of recent legislation providing strict regulation for stock exchanges, many individuals appear to have deserted, at least temporarily, large-scale operations in the stock market, and to have shifted their interest to the commodity markets.

During the Summer of 1934 there was no questioning such a shift from stock market to commodity market interest. The possibility of permanence lay chiefly in less stringent regulation of commodity trading than stock trading. Such a theory, however, does not appear logical. Government regulation simply attacked the stock exchanges first and there is no sound basis for anticipating that artificial manipulation will be condoned in one market and condemned in another.

Growing Possibilities in Commodity Operation

The temporary factor appears the more valid, therefore. Reduced production in the United States, previously subnormal price levels, inflation psychology and public interest, all combined to make bullish demonstrations in the commodity markets easier than in the stock market. The latter had just been "stringently regulated." Corporation profits were being held back by Summer business recessions, increased costs and lower profit margins under the Government socialization campaigns. The stage was better set for commodity interest than stock interest. But there was by no means any guarantee that such comparative situation would be anything more than temporary.

Results of Securities Exchange Act of 1934

Since enactment of the Securities Exchange Act of 1934, the author has been impressed by the rather pessimistic and terrifying ideas which many individuals appear to hold regarding the future for security operation. He considers such dismal forebodings almost totally groundless.

The Securities Exchange Act of 1934 is admittedly drastic in certain directions. It imposes radical restrictions, and it has definite dangers of administration. But it appears highly improbable that the effects will be as serious as the public has been led to anticipate.

In previous chapters we have noted briefly some of the logical bases for such impression. While they may be moderately curtailed, the author is thoroughly convinced that future activity, price swings and profit possibilities will undergo no very drastic changes under the new law. Volume of trading may well be reduced, but narrowing of price swings appears by no means certain. And the latter factor, of course, is more directly connected with possibilities for profit.

Effects on Future Trading

As a matter of fact, there seems fair ground for anticipating even wider price swings in the future than in the past, at least in relation to market activity. The new legislation, as it tends to discourage professional manipulative devices used in the past, tends also to reduce the breadth and liquidity of the market. Pools, professionals, floor-traders, and powerful individual traders are not so likely to "cushion" the shocks of public impetus in the future as in the past. The result is likely to be more sudden moves, and wider swings, on smaller volume of trading.

Even as early as the Summer of 1934 there was decided suggestion that this theorem was proving valid. Toward the close of July, following a period of lethargic price movement on small volume, liquidation which would hardly have been apparent in a more active and broader market, sent prices precipitously lower in only a few days. The possibilities for profit and loss, for sharp and wide swings, as well as for "new types" of professional manipulation on such a basis should by no means be overlooked under the "new deal" for security markets.

Old Rules Still Apply

Another credo of the "post regulation" era appears to be that market trading under the new law will be so radically changed that many of the old rules and solid theories of trading must be completely deserted, or at least thoroughly revised. Such a thesis is just as unsound as the one we have discussed above, and largely for similar reasons. As we have previously noted,[1] the theories and rules which we have studied in this current volume are basic and valid for a regulated, as well as an unregulated, market, so long as any market is allowed at all.

Especially has the author received many inquiries regarding the validity of "technical" theory under the new law. Such questionings are understandable but groundless.

---

[1] See Chapter VII, p. 175.

Technical authorities have, in the past, been guilty of perhaps too great emphasis on the efficacy of charts in detecting pool manipulation. The average individual thus calculates that, with "pool manipulation barred by law," one of the important assets of technical theory is destroyed.

Technical Analysis Remains Basic

We have already noted two bases for thorough disqualification of any such fear. In the first place, charts are much more useful in detecting basic trends and the "judgment of the market place" than in detecting pool manipulation.[1] We can leave such considerations entirely outside of the picture, for just so long as the market moves at all, in any free and open trading, so long will technical analysis weigh and interpret the composite stimulus for future movement, whether such movement is to be based upon professional activity, pool manipulation, plain public impetus, or what not.

In the second place, we have also noted that mere legislation against manipulative practices is no guarantee that they will entirely disappear.[2] They may take on new forms, and may even lose some of their former effectiveness. But so long as human nature itself remains impervious to the dictates of legislation, it seems at least worthy of consideration that methods may be devised to "get around" the word of the law.

In any case, the author is quite certain in his own mind that the rules of technical analysis, as well as the entire catalog of theory considered in our current volume, will be just as valid, just as useful and just as profitable in future operation under the new laws of regulation as in the past.

[1] See Chapter VI, p. 129.   [2] See Chapter VII, p. 174.

Legislation vs. Human Nature

The reader may thus take comfort in the sure knowledge that "the old rules" of logic and common sense do not change overnight. The world moves on. "The old order changeth, yielding place to new." But the "new" is still built upon basic principles of economic law and human nature, and will eventually be found not quite so new after all.

Our aim has been to draw profit from these underlying principles of immutable truth, through simple but seldom-used methods of thought and logic. The mastery of such efficient thinking should not only set us apart from the "public," but should see us well on our way to consistent success and practical profit.

Valedictory

Let us remember that no operator is infallible, that no rule or formula or theory is certain. Let us realize, nevertheless, that our true goal is not the quick and easy profit, but rather the slow balance of consistent success that comes from efficient handling of any business or hobby. Let us remember that the stock market is no respecter of persons, that such success is not only possible but logical for any individual who is willing to use time, thought and natural wisdom in preparing himself for a just reward.

Let us remember, finally, that the security markets are not idealistic wishing lamps out of the Arabian Nights. They are valuable institutions of service and profit, but they can also be mazes of danger and tragedy. The measure of what we shall receive from our market operations is the exact measure of our attitude toward them. The man who looks for "easy profits" will be disappointed eventually, if not immediately. But the man who is willing to play fair with the laws of nature as well as with the markets themselves, who is willing to invest his own time, energy and mentality, automatically places himself in a position not only to reap his profit but to deserve it.

Such an individual, and such a one alone, will justify not only the inherent morality of his market interest but will justify also the success which such a legitimate interest can bring. And, what is perhaps most important of all, he will be broadening his own life mentally as well as financially, through the progressive satisfaction which emanates from the mastery of so rich and important an aspect of modern life and business.

APPENDIX

Quantitative Comparison of Business and Stock Index Movements.
Monthly, 1915–1924 (See Plate II on p. 55 and text on
p. 53 and following)

		Bus. Index	Stock Index	Chg. From Prev. Month Bus.	Stock	Cum. Change Bus.	Stock
1915	Jan.	− 12	62	+ 2	+ 2	+ 2	+ 2
	Feb.	− 9	60	+ 3	− 2	+ 5	0
	Mar.	− 8	65	+ 1	+ 5	+ 6	+ 5
	Apr.	− 6	73	+ 2	+ 8	+ 8	+ 13
	May	− 5	68	+ 1	− 5	+ 9	+ 8
	June	− 1	71	+ 4	+ 3	+ 13	+ 11
	July	0	73	+ 1	+ 2	+ 14	+ 13
	Aug.	+ 1	77	+ 1	+ 4	+ 15	+ 17
	Sept.	+ 5	85	+ 4	+ 8	+ 19	+ 25
	Oct.	+ 7	93	+ 2	+ 8	+ 21	+ 33
	Nov.	+ 10	91	+ 3	− 2	+ 24	+ 31
	Dec.	+ 13	92	+ 3	+ 1	+ 27	+ 32
1916	Jan.	+ 12	85	− 1	− 7	+ 26	+ 25
	Feb.	+ 14	84	+ 2	− 1	+ 28	+ 24
	Mar.	+ 14	87	0	+ 3	+ 28	+ 27
	Apr.	+ 13	84	− 1	− 3	+ 27	+ 24
	May	+ 14	87	+ 1	+ 3	+ 28	+ 27
	June	+ 14	86	0	− 1	+ 28	+ 26
	July	+ 11	85	− 3	− 1	+ 25	+ 25
	Aug.	+ 13	87	+ 2	+ 2	+ 27	+ 27
	Sept.	+ 14	95	+ 1	+ 8	+ 28	+ 35
	Oct.	+ 16	97	+ 2	+ 2	+ 30	+ 37
	Nov.	+ 16	96	0	− 1	+ 30	+ 36
	Dec.	+ 14	88	− 2	− 8	+ 28	+ 28
1917	Jan.	+ 14	84	0	− 4	+ 28	+ 24
	Feb.	+ 13	81	− 1	− 3	+ 27	+ 21
	Mar.	+ 14	83	+ 1	+ 2	+ 28	+ 23
	Apr.	+ 13	80	− 1	− 3	+ 27	+ 20

| | | Bus. Index | Stock Index | Chg. From Prev. Month | | Cum. Change | |
				Bus.	Stock	Bus.	Stock
	May	+ 14	81	+ 1	+ 1	+ 28	+ 21
	June	+ 13	82	− 1	+ 1	+ 27	+ 22
	July	+ 12	80	− 1	− 2	+ 26	+ 20
	Aug.	+ 13	74	+ 1	− 6	+ 27	+ 14
	Sept.	+ 9	73	− 4	− 1	+ 23	+ 13
	Oct.	+ 11	66	+ 2	− 7	+ 25	+ 6
	Nov.	+ 11	63	0	− 3	+ 25	+ 3
	Dec.	+ 6	64	− 5	+ 1	+ 20	+ 4
1918	Jan.	+ 2	69	− 4	+ 5	+ 16	+ 9
	Feb.	+ 3	70	+ 1	+ 1	+ 17	+ 10
	Mar.	+ 7	68	+ 4	− 2	+ 21	+ 8
	Apr.	+ 8	67	+ 1	− 1	+ 22	+ 7
	May	+ 9	70	+ 1	+ 3	+ 23	+ 10
	June	+ 7	72	− 2	+ 2	+ 21	+ 12
	July	+ 9	71	+ 2	− 1	+ 23	+ 11
	Aug.	+ 11	72	+ 2	+ 1	+ 25	+ 12
	Sept.	+ 9	72	− 2	0	+ 23	+ 12
	Oct.	+ 9	74	0	+ 2	+ 23	+ 14
	Nov.	+ 6	73	− 3	− 1	+ 20	+ 13
	Dec.	+ 6	72	0	− 1	+ 20	+ 12
1919	Jan.	0	70	− 6	− 2	+ 14	+ 10
	Feb.	− 4	74	− 4	+ 4	+ 10	+ 14
	Mar.	− 8	73	− 4	− 1	+ 6	+ 13
	Apr.	− 5	78	+ 3	+ 5	+ 9	+ 18
	May	− 6	86	− 1	+ 8	+ 8	+ 26
	June	0	87	+ 6	+ 1	+ 14	+ 27
	July	+ 4	90	+ 4	+ 3	+ 18	+ 30
	Aug.	+ 7	86	+ 3	− 4	+ 21	+ 26
	Sept.	+ 4	93	− 3	+ 7	+ 18	+ 33
	Oct.	+ 2	98	− 2	+ 5	+ 16	+ 38
	Nov.	+ 1	85	− 1	− 13	+ 15	+ 25
	Dec.	+ 2	90	+ 1	+ 5	+ 16	+ 30
1920	Jan.	+ 12	86	+ 10	− 4	+ 26	+ 26
	Feb.	+ 12	80	0	− 6	+ 26	+ 20
	Mar.	+ 9	81	− 3	+ 1	+ 23	+ 21
	Apr.	+ 3	83	− 6	+ 2	+ 17	+ 23
	May	+ 5	83	+ 2	0	+ 19	+ 23
	June	+ 6	82	+ 1	− 1	+ 20	+ 21
	July	+ 4	78	− 2	− 4	+ 18	+ 18

		Bus. Index	Stock Index	Chg. From Prev. Month		Cum. Change	
				Bus.	Stock	Bus.	Stock
	Aug.	+ 4	79	0	+ 1	+ 18	+ 19
	Sept.	0	80	− 4	+ 1	+ 14	+ 20
	Oct.	− 4	81	− 4	+ 1	+ 10	+ 21
	Nov.	− 12	70	− 8	− 11	+ 2	+ 10
	Dec.	− 17	66	− 5	− 4	− 3	+ 6
1921	Jan.	− 23	70	− 6	+ 4	− 9	+ 10
	Feb.	− 24	69	− 1	− 1	− 10	+ 9
	Mar.	− 27	68	− 3	− 1	− 13	+ 8
	Apr.	− 27	70	0	+ 2	− 13	+ 10
	May	− 25	68	+ 2	− 2	− 11	+ 8
	June	− 26	63	− 1	− 5	− 12	+ 3
	July	− 27	64	− 1	+ 1	− 13	+ 4
	Aug.	− 24	62	+ 3	− 2	− 10	+ 2
	Sept.	− 23	68	+ 1	+ 6	− 9	+ 8
	Oct.	− 20	66	+ 3	− 2	− 6	+ 6
	Nov.	− 20	68	0	+ 2	− 6	+ 8
	Dec.	− 22	69	− 2	+ 1	− 8	+ 9
1922	Jan.	− 19	69	+ 3	0	− 5	+ 9
	Feb.	− 15	72	+ 4	+ 3	− 1	+ 12
	Mar.	− 11	75	+ 4	+ 3	+ 3	+ 15
	Apr.	− 15	79	− 4	+ 4	− 1	+ 19
	May	− 11	81	+ 4	+ 2	+ 3	+ 21
	June	− 6	79	+ 5	− 2	+ 8	+ 19
	July	− 7	83	− 1	+ 4	+ 7	+ 23
	Aug.	− 8	88	− 1	+ 5	+ 6	+ 28
	Sept.	− 4	86	+ 4	− 2	+ 10	+ 26
	Oct.	+ 2	87	+ 6	+ 1	+ 16	+ 27
	Nov.	+ 6	83	+ 4	− 4	+ 20	+ 23
	Dec.	+ 9	85	+ 3	+ 2	+ 23	+ 25
1923	Jan.	+ 7	87	− 2	+ 2	+ 21	+ 27
	Feb.	+ 8	92	+ 1	+ 5	+ 22	+ 32
	Mar.	+ 11	90	+ 3	− 2	+ 25	+ 30
	Apr.	+ 14	85	+ 3	− 5	+ 28	+ 25
	May	+ 14	87	0	+ 2	+ 28	+ 27
	June	+ 14	78	0	− 9	+ 28	+ 18
	July	+ 11	77	− 3	− 1	+ 25	+ 17
	Aug.	+ 10	83	− 1	+ 6	+ 24	+ 23
	Sept.	+ 8	79	− 2	− 4	+ 22	+ 19
	Oct.	+ 5	80	− 3	+ 1	+ 19	+ 20

		Bus. Index	Stock Index	Chg. From Prev. Month		Cum. Change	
				Bus.	Stock	Bus.	Stock
	Nov.	+ 4	83	− 1	+ 3	+ 18	+ 23
	Dec.	+ 3	85	− 1	+ 2	+ 17	+ 25
1924	Jan.	+ 5	89	+ 2	+ 4	+ 19	+ 29
	Feb.	+ 7	87	+ 2	− 2	+ 21	+ 27
	Mar.	+ 5	84	− 2	− 3	+ 19	+ 24
	Apr.	− 1	84	− 6	0	+ 13	+ 24
	May	− 7	85	− 6	+ 1	+ 7	+ 25
	June	− 12	90	− 5	+ 5	+ 2	+ 30
	July	− 13	94	− 1	+ 4	+ 1	+ 34
	Aug.	− 8	96	+ 5	+ 2	+ 6	+ 36
	Sept.	− 3	95	+ 5	− 1	+ 11	+ 35
	Oct.	− 2	95	+ 1	0	+ 12	+ 35
	Nov.	0	102	+ 2	+ 7	+ 14	+ 42
	Dec.	+ 4	108	+ 4	+ 6	+ 18	+ 48

INDEX

Advisory services (*see* Market
  Counsel)
Alaska Juneau, 121
American Can, 229–233, 231
  speculative campaign in, 232
American Commercial Alcohol
  effect of repeal on stock of, 114
American Radiator, 122
Analysis
  (*see also* Market Analysis)
  avoid hurried, 240
  fundamental, 103
    long-term, application to, 103
    short-term, application to, 103
  long-term, 161
  "*pattern*" theory of, 142
  "*second nature*" attitude toward,
    313
  short-term, 105
  technical, 128, 168, 169
    basic logic of, 158
    remains same under Securities
      Act, 325
    volume of trading in, 148
Annalist averages, 191, 193
Atchison, Topeka & Santa Fe
  movement of common stock of, 89–
    96
Atlas Tack, 121
Averaging operations, 264, 274
  combined with diversification, 274
  illustration of, 267, 269
  right and wrong methods of, 272
Ayres, Col. Leonard P.
  long-range study of business ac-
    tivity by, 54, 55

Better Business Bureau, 300
"*Blast furnaces*"
  outmoded rule of, 48
Bonds
  diversified with stocks, 255
Booms
  1927–29, 5

1932, generated by advance in security prices, 53
Brokers' loans
  formulae on, 61
  ratio of, 62
Brooklyn-Manhattan Transit, 120
Business cycle
  automatic theories of, 48
    difficulties of, 49
  effect of regulation of security
    trading on, 174
  logical basis for, 31, 32, 50
  stages of the, 37, 39, 40
Business index, 50
  statistics not immediately avail-
    able on, 57
  study in comparative history of, 54
Business profits
  relationship between security prof-
    its and, 30
Buying securities, 65, 239
  avoid plunging in, 238
  based on business activity, 51
  course to follow in, 238
  for long pull, 65
  influence of fundamental factors
    on, 103
  influence of technical factors on,
    128
  on good news, 180
  when prices are at extreme low,
    59

Capital
  diversification of, 247
Capital Rotation
  advantages in, 86
Cash
  hoarding of, 253
  part of, in diversification policy,
    253
Charts
  application of trend lines to, 144,
    165

comparison of different types, 151–158

daily average, 162

for study of technical factors, 133

minor-swing or geometric, 150

advantages and disadvantages of, 154–155

point and figure, 149

advantages and disadvantages of, 154–156

vertical-line, 149

construction superior in, 154

Chrysler, 120

Commission rates, 251

Commitments

(see also Buying securities)

coupled theory, applied to, 228–233

incorrect, 210, 221

loss limitation to precede, 22, 23

management of, 19

profitable, 213

proposed, 216

protection of, 226, 227

scaling down, 218

speculative percentage, gain or loss, 260

Commodities, trading in, 322, 323

Compromise Principle, 96, 215, 254, 314

Continental Can, 121

Coupled Formula, 227

success of, 233

" Crossing " operations, 181, 190, 192, 289

activity of, 182

advisory services and, 288

example of, 197, 198

fundamental indications, 203

necessary for market profit, 184

not affected by government regulation, 196

psychology connected with, 195

technical indications of, 202

two types of, 191

Cycles

actual operation, 58

business and security, compared, 53

effect of " planned economy " on, 34

movement of, 33

profits from observing, 58

prospective, 69

psychological, 40

tend to disparity, 68

Cyclical Interest Rate Formulae, 60

Cyclical Theory, 30, 31, 38, 49, 59, 65, 67

aids short-swing analysis, 92

business indexes in relation to, 60

Democratic National Convention, 113, 116

De Villiers, Victor, 149

Discretionary accounts, 284

Diversification

(see also Risk)

bonds compared with stocks, 255

combined with averaging, 274

compromise in, 254

example in, 250

illustration of, 256, 257

logic of, 246

types of securities for, listed or unlisted, 261

Dollar stabilization

helped by gold dollar devaluation act, 204

Dow, Charles H., 136

Dow, Jones & Company, 136

averages, 21, 32, 43, 137

Dow Theory, 136, 204

illustrations of, 137

logic of, 137, 156

applied to long-term trends, 139

valuation of principles, 142

Earning power

value reduced by fundamentals affecting, 110

Eastman Kodak, 122

Factors, speculative

comparison between, 124

" crossing " operations and, 181, 202, 203

fundamental, 100–123, 308

anticipation of, 111

valuable to long-swing investor, 103

technical, 101, 102, 124–148, 309

approach important, 132
more useful for short-swing
   trader, 103
not infallible, 131
study of, 127, 130, 132
value of, 124
Failure
blame for, 4
reasons for, 1–5, 9
"False investors," 5
Financial Services (see Market
   Counsel)
Flattening Trend Reversal, 145, 158
Forbes Magazine, 250 ff, 256 ff
Forecasting (see Market Forecasting)
Formulae
brokers' loans, based on, 61
coupled system, 227
cyclical interest rate, 60
diversification applied to, 256
minor, 62
popular psychology based on,
   64
price-earnings ratio, 61
volume of trading, 63
"Frozen" assets, 261
Fundamental Forecasting, 111
Fundamental statistics
disadvantages of, 107–109
reliance placed on, 107

Gains cancelled out by losses, 185
General Motors, 120
Geometric charts, 150
Gold dollar devaluation act, 204
Government legislation
survival of manipulation under,
   126
Government regulation, 34–35, 219
crossing operations not affected
   by, 196
dangers of, 174
may eliminate stop-loss orders,
   234

Hamilton, William Peter, 136
Head and Shoulders formation, 143,
   146, 162
Hiram-Walker
effect of repeal on stock of, 114

Indexes
business, 50, 206
comparative study in, 54
stock market, 51, 53
"Insiders," 172, 180, 181, 186–198,
   204, 281
Interborough, 120
Interest rates
long-term operations and, 60
Intermediate trading
(see also Investments — short-
   swing)
applying rules to, 96
development of price movement,
   89–96
technical approach more important to, 132
Intra-Day Moves, 151
Investing
(see also Trading)
business cycle study aid to, 30
study of successful, 29
Investment Trust
in managing accounts, 285
useful for types of individuals, 286
Investments
comparisons between short- and
   long-term moves, 89, 99
diversification of, 244, 279
groups of, 256
long-swing
   advantages in, 45
   business index, importance of,
      in, 49
   buying in, 65
   comparison between short-swing
      and, 76, 77
   conflicting vs. unanimous indi-
      cations in, 66
   difficulties in, 44, 45, 83
   formulation of, policies, 67
   gauging the market in, 46
   historical evidence on, 59
   importance of close observation
      of price movements in, 47, 48
   lag in business activity on, 50
   lag in formulae on, 49
   policy in, 12
   "portfolios," when to liquidate,
      314
   rules for success in, 68

safest method in, 42
security price forecast of business in, 50
selling, 65
use of automatic formulae in, 59
volume of trading valuable evidence of, 64
long-term principle in, 59
marketability of, 262
minor-swing, 72
short-swing
(see also Intermediate trading)
close protection of, 82
comparison of, and long-swing, 76, 77
examples of intermediate movements in, 73
flattening trend reversal aid to, 146
greater risk in, 77
more natural, 82
profit advantages in, 74, 76, 85
rotation of security operation in, 86
technique of, 88
total travel vs. net travel in, 75
use of fundamental factors in, 109–112
Investors
(see also Operators and Traders)
accounts of, handled by services, 284
advantage of cyclical theory to, 38
analyzed loss of, 14
avoid sucker games, 300
avoidance of dogmatic extremes, 97
classes of, 258
combination of short- and long-swing trading best for successful, 78
confusing short- and long-term trades by, 79
cyclical aspect, 57
dangers and advantages of advisory services to, 283, 287
difficult to ingrain rules in average, 26
effect of advisory services forecast to, 290, 291

following through a decision for, 80, 81
independent approach for, 281
influence of advertising by services on, 293
investment trusts useful to certain, 286
long-swing, 43, 59
loss limitation for, 20
reasons for "hanging on" to stock by, 266
recognition of signals by, 97
services selected with care by, 292
should know all types of trading, 78, 79, 84
study of cycles helpful to, 31, 32
useful theories for, 64
value of diversification to, 251

Line charts (see Charts)
Logic
objective, 134, 166, 167
on major swings, 159
of psychological approach, 199
of diversification, 246
subjective, 134, 167
Long swing (see Investments — long-swing)
Long-term success, 27, 29
vs. perfection, 166
Long-term trends
application of Dow Theory to, 139
Losses
"averaging down" common basis for, 263
blame for, 17
cancel out with gains, 185
cutting short, 160, 167
growth of, 21
limitation of, 20, 22, 25, 220, 243
plan for, 23, 24, 25
rules for avoiding, 19
theoretical, 184

Major swings (see Investments — long-swing)
Major trends
history of, 166
Manipulation, 125, 173, 174

Margin call, 279
Margin trading, 275
  (*see also* Trading)
  avoid over-trading in, 279
  dangers of, 276
  use of stop principle in, 278
Market (*see* Stock Market)
Market Analysis
  (*see also* Analysis)
  fundamental approach to, 100, 103, 105
  important to study each day, 241
  psychological aspect in, 178, 310
  technical approach to, 101, 103, 105
Market Counsel, 281–303
  advertising policies, 293, 294
  by subscription, 283
  classifications in, 283
  forecasts of, 290
  illegitimate, 295
    methods constantly changing, 300
    operations of, 296–299
    types of, 300
  misrepresentation by, 294, 295
  special accounts handled by, 284–286
Market Forecasting, 170
  by advisory services, 290
  logic of psychological approach in, 199
  psychology applied to, 179
Money market, 60

National Distillers Products, 114–116, 196
  effect of repeal on stock of, 114
New era
  characteristics of, 5
  swings affected by collapse of, 35, 36
New York Curb Exchange, 263
New York Stock Exchange, 263, 297, 298, 300
  Bank Holiday closing of, 139
  compilation of brokers' loans by, 62
New York Times averages, 54, 55, 191, 193, 194, 273

Newspaper propaganda, avoidance of, 200
NRA Codes, 195

Operations (*see* Stock Market Operations)
Operators
  (*see also* Investors *and* Traders)
  analytical considerations for, 201
  approach to technical trading for, 167, 175
  avoid hurried decisions, 240, 302
  blame losses on economic change, 18
  cancelling orders when advisable, 243
  " *chart-bug,*" 170, 171
  compromise theory for, 217
  cutting losses short by, 160
  danger of " *holding on*" by, 222
  disadvantages of stop order to, 223
  diversification of investments by, 244–280
  experienced, 12
  flattening trend reversal aid to, 146
  importance of stop orders to, 218
  influence of psychological forces on, 83
  not dependent upon single method, 130
  rules for, 14–19, 26
  successful, 188
  sudden strength in market and, 236
  technical science valuable aid to, 175
  types of, 126
  value of charts to, 149
  value of stop order to, 221
  value of technical theory to, 135
Orders — cancellation of, 242, 243
Organized security markets restricted by law, 174
Over-enthusiasm, dangers of, 13

Paper loss, 222, 279
Paramount Famous-Lasky Corporation, 196, 197, 198
Paramount Publix Corporation, 267
" *Pattern* " theory, 142

Planned economy, effect of, on cycles, 34
Plunging, 214, 246
Point and figure charts, 149
Pool operations regulation of, 175
Popular psychology formulae, 64
Price-earnings ratio formula, 61
Price movement, 47, 48, 69, 72, 127–129, 139, 150, 167, 179
Prices, security
affected by panic conditions, 40
business influences on, 52
relation to brokers loans, 61
turning points in trend of, move counter to reason, 201
Price swings
affected by collapse of " new era," 35, 36
economic, 18
Property ownership, 100
Protective technique, 210
Psychology
applied to market operations, 177
connected with crossing operations, 195
definition of, 178
generated naturally and artificially, 194
practical application of, 199
public, 180, 192
usefulness of, in market operation, 181, 207
Public opinion
psychological effect of, 33–35

Rackets
fake stock, 296, 301
Republicans, 114
Rhea, Robert, 136
Risk
(see also Diversification)
concentration of, 248
constantly changing policy of, 259
diversification of, 12–13, 244–280
greater in short-swing than long-swing securities, 77
limiting, 220
marginal trading and, 275
reduction of, 25

Roosevelt, Franklin D., 116
Rules (see Speculation — rules of)

Schenley Distillers
effect of repeal on stock of, 114
Securities
dependent on interest rates, 60
diversification of, 247
formulae for purchase and sale of, 60
listed vs. unlisted, 261
long-term purchase and sale of, 60
movements, 42, 174
profits
relationship between business profits and, 30
Securities Exchange Act, 192
effects of, on future trading, 324
psychological effect of, 192
results of, 323
technical analysis and, 325
Security cycle
(see also Cycles)
effect of regulation of security trading on, 174
logical basis for, 31, 32, 50
stages of the, 37, 39, 40
Security market regulation bill
announcement of, 205
" Sell and Switch " racket, 296
Selling the market
on bad news, 180
when public interest is high, 65
Servel, 121
Short selling, 223
Short swings (see Investments — short-swing)
Speculation, 5
regulation of operations, 175
rules of
accumulation, period of, 314, 315
illustration of, 315, 316
coordination of, 311
dangers overcome by simple and basic, 169
difficulty of automatic, 49
disregard of tips in, 15
diversification applied to, 13
" dogmatism," evils of, 312
elements of chance and, 248

for avoiding pitfalls in, 300
general, 9–12
hasty decisions in, 14, 209, 310
over-confidence on, 169, 209
over-enthusiasm about, 13, 310
short-term, 85
    principles of, 88
simple but important, 26, 302
simplicity and logic of, 138
stop-loss, 234
subconscious assimilation of, 311, 312
scale accumulation in, 316
unlisted issues and, 262
Speculative stocks
    examples of diversification in, 250
Standard Oil of New Jersey, 297
Statistics
    fundamental, 107–109
    complete, 107
" *Stock bundles,*" 251
Stock charts (*see* Charts)
Stock Exchange (*see* New York Stock Exchange)
Stock market
    advantages in active, 261
    changes in sentiment in, 179
    course on " *Technical Analysis and Market Profits,*" 132, 164 ff.
    daily activity of, 242
    dangers of sudden strength in, 237
    diversification in depression on, 249
    influence of public opinion on, 33
    logical reasoning in, 206
    movements studied, 28
    public criticism of, 5–6
    seldom does the obvious, 199, 200
    success in, 6, 8, 19–20, 27
    summer declines of 1934 in, 205
    sweeping trends of movement in, 201
    usefulness of, 7
Stock market index, 51
    figures immediately available for, 57
    study in comparative history of, 54
Stock market operations
    aims of, 304

approach to, 3, 4, 6, 8–10, 104, 210, 305
averaging, 263–274
avoid hasty decisions in, 14, 209, 310
avoid over-enthusiasm in, 13, 310
buyers vs. sellers in, 183
consistent profit in, 12
coupled theory in, 228
cultivate independent thinking in, 16
diversification of capital in, 13
false and illogical attitude toward, 4, 5
gains and losses of, 182, 185
justification of, 7
lack of knowledge for, 2
long-swing, 42–71
marginal, 275
pitfalls of, 303
practical, 9, 19
professionals in, 185, 190
profit motive and, 1
psychology applied to, 177
rules of, 26
short-swing, 72–98
stop orders and, 218–227, 234
successful, general rules for, 9
technical advantages in, 167
technical approach to, 168
temporarily affected by Securities Act, 192
Stock market success
    proper judgment for, 306
Stock Market Theory & Practice, 14 ff., 60 ff., 69 ff., 106 ff., 132, 223 ff., 227 ff.
Stocks
    Alaska Juneau, 121
    American Can, 229–233
    American Commercial Alcohol, 114
    American Radiator, 122
    Atchison, Topeka & Santa Fe, 89–96
    Atlas Tack, 121
    bonds diversified with, 255
    Brooklyn-Manhattan Transit, 120
    buying and selling, by crossing operations, 181
    buying, at extreme low, 59

Chrysler, 120
Continental Can, 121
Eastman Kodak, 122
fake rackets in, 296, 301
General Motors, 120
gold
affected by the U. S. abandoning gold standard, 121
benefit through business, depression, 121
Hiram-Walker, 114
Interborough, 120
liquidation of, 239
motor, 117–119
National Distillers Products, 114–116, 196
Paramount Famous-Lasky, 196
Paramount Publix Corporation, 267
sales of worthless, 299
Schenley Distillers, 114
Standard Oil of New Jersey, 297
United States Industrial Alcohol, 114
United States Steel, 298
Western Union, 139
Stop-loss principle
disadvantages of, 223
importance of, 218, 234
use of, in marginal trading, 278
Stop orders, 218, 227, 234
brokers will not accept all types of, 219
examples of, 225
important points in, 235
" Suckers," 183
" Sucker list," 297
Supervisory accounts, 285

" **T**echnical Analysis and Market Profits," 132
Technical science, 171, 178, 179
patterns in, 143
Technical theory, 168, 172
Theories
exploitation of untried, 172
Traders
(*see also* Investors *and* Operators)
conservative, 213, 215

plunger type of, 214
professional, 185–195
usually successful, 281
vs. public, 187
Trading
(*see also* Investing)
" *catching the bottom*," 318
commodity, 322
common sense in, 209–243
compromise policy in, results of, 317
conservatism in, 12, 209
distinguishing between reaction and reversal in, 164
hypothetical, 319
on margin, 275
over-confidence in, 12, 209
" *paper*," 320
personal market, 10
rules of, 26, 29
sane judgment in, 13, 14
scale, 96
short-swing, profits from, 85
stop principle in short, 223
technical, 168
Transactions
theoretical, 184
Trend lines
application of, 144, 165

United States
abandoned gold standard, 121
United States Industrial Alcohol
effect of repeal on stock of, 114
United States Steel, 298

Vertical-line charts (*see* Charts)
Villiers, Victor de (*see De Villiers*)
Volume of trading formulae, 63

Wall Street
adage of, 215
opinion of, 204
speculative advice and, 10, 11
Wall Street Journal, 136
Western Union, 139–148, 153
" *Whip-sawing* "
future danger of, 173
Wyckoff, Richard D., 149

TRADING RESOURCES

Hit and Run Trading: *The Short-Term Stock Traders' Bible - Updated*

by Jeff Cooper

Discover winning methods for daytrading and swing trading from the man who wrote the bible on short-term trading. Jammed packed with a full arsenal of new tools and strategies to help short-term traders compete and survive in this fast-paced, volatile arena.

$100.00 Item #BC103-3156887

Swing Trading Simplified

by Larry D. Spears

Learn the basics - or refine your skills - with this fast-reading swing trading primer. With a foreword by the popular "MrSwing.com" - this new guide from Larry Spears makes the powerful swing trading concepts more accessible and easier to implement than ever. Find out how to implement your own profitable program without being glued to your monitor. Simply pick your position, enter a close, and a protective stop, and go back to your day - it's that easy! Add or restore vitality to any investment program - using the simplified techniques found in *Swing Trading Simplified*.

$29.95 Item #BC103-1674501

**To order any book listed
Call 1-800-272-2855 ext. BC103**

Technical Analysis Simplified

by Clif Droke

Here's a concise, easy-reading manual for learning and implementing this invaluable investment tool. The author, a well-known technician and editor of several technical analysis newsletters, distills the most essential elements of technical analysis into a brief, easy-to-read volume.

$29.95 Item #BC103-11087

12 Simple Technical Indicators That Really Work - *DVD*

by Mark Larson

Discover how the right technical indicators will help you get in and out of the markets - with profits in tow. Join market educator Mark Larson, author of *Technical Charting for Profits*, as he shares his 12 favorite indicators and details how he picked them, how he tested them, and how they work together to give traders the kind of success he's enjoyed for nearly a decade. Learn why certain indicators work during certain markets, 2 indicators with a 90% accuracy record, choosing the most effective moving averages, and more. With Mark's thorough new workshop, and online support manual, you'll soon see why "Your profits are within your chart." Comes with Online Support Manual.

$99.00 Item #BC103-3384832

▲ ▲ ▲ ▲ ▲ ▲

**To order any book listed
Call 1-800-272-2855 ext. BC103**

New Frontiers in Fibonacci Trading: *Charting Techniques, Strategies & Simple Applications*

by Michael Jardine

Traders caught at the crossroads of traditional, proven, trading techniques - and new online tools and methods - have struggled to find a way of blending the two together into a unified trading system. Now, the marriage of the methods is complete, and brought into sharp focus in *New Frontiers in Fibonacci Trading*. This groundbreaking new work combines the foundations of Fibonacci trading with classic charting techniques, modern applications, and cutting edge online analysis tools.

$59.95 Item #BC103-1739885

Charting Made Easy

by John J. Murphy

Renowned market technician John Murphy presents basic principals of technical analysis in easy-to-understand term. He covers...

- All types of chart analysis
- "Need to know" concepts, including trendlines, moving averages, price gaps, reversal patterns, volume & open interest spreads, and more!
- Price forecasting and market timing applications
- A full resource guide of technical analysis aide
- How to use the industry's top tools to obtain a better understanding of what charts can do-and how they can help you grab your portion of today's trading profits.

$19.95 Item #BC103-11353

Moving Averages Simplified

by Clif Droke

Successful traders know that using Moving Averages can result in more profitable trades -if applied properly. But, what are Moving Averages? When -and how- should they be used? Now, noted trader Clif Droke takes the mystery out of Moving Averages by explaining them in detail, describing how they can be employed to zero in on buy/sell signals that result in more profitable trades- more often.

$29.95 Item #BC103-12169

Targeting Profitable Entry & Exit Points - *DVD*

by Alan Farley

Learn what tools "Master Swing Trader" Alan Farley uses to enter and exit trades and how he maximizes his profits this way. You will be on track to master the skills necessary to know when to get in, when to get out and when to stand aside. Included in this tape are:

- his powerful swing management tools
- how to use a failure target and implement price sensitive execution
- how to adjust your methods to changing market conditions

Farley shows you how to combine Bollinger bands, fibonacci and candlesticks to isolate trades with favorable risk/reward profiles and more.

$64.95 Item #BC103-3384831

**To order any book listed
Call 1-800-272-2855 ext. BC103**

Free 2 Week Trial Offer for U.S. Residents From Investor's Business Daily:

INVESTOR'S BUSINESS DAILY will provide you with the facts, figures, and objective news analysis you need to succeed.

Investor's Business Daily is formatted for a quick and concise read to help you make informed and profitable decisions.

To take advantage of this free 2 week trial offer, e-mail us at customerservice@traderslibrary.com or visit our website at www.traderslibrary.com where you find other free offers as well.

You can also reach us by calling 1-800-272-2855 or fax us at 410-964-0027.